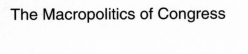

The Macropolitics of Congress

The Macropolitics of Congress

Edited by

E. Scott Adler *and* **John S. Lapinski**

PRINCETON UNIVERSITY PRESS·PRINCETON AND OXFORD

Copyright © 2006 by Princeton University Press
Published by Princeton University Press, 41 William Street,
Princeton, New Jersey 08540
In the United Kingdom: Princeton University Press,
3 Market Place, Woodstock, Oxfordshire OX20 1SY

Library of Congress Cataloging-in-Publication Data

The macropolitics of Congress / edited by E. Scott Adler and John S. Lapinski.
p.   cm.
Includes bibliographical references and index.
ISBN-13: 978-0-691-12149-9 (cloth : alk. paper)
ISBN-10: 0-691-12149-4 (cloth : alk. paper)
ISBN-13: 978-0-691-12159-8 (pbk. : alk. paper)
ISBN-10: 0-691-12159-1 (pbk. : alk. paper)
1. United States. Congress.   2. United States—Politics and government.
I. Adler, E. Scott.   II. Lapinski, John S., 1967–

JK1021.M33 2006
328.73—dc22   2005044504

British Library Cataloging-in-Publication Data is available

This book has been composed in Times Roman

Printed on acid-free paper. ∞

pup.princeton.edu

Printed in the United States of America

1   2   3   4   5   6   7   8   9   10

To Lucille Adler, and the memory of Sheldon Adler

E.S.A.

To the memory of Annabel Lapinski

J.S.L.

Contents

Part IV: Macropolitics and Public Policy

Part V: Understanding the Macropolitics of Congress

Contributors

E. Scott Adler is Associate Professor of Political Science at the University of Colorado at Boulder. His current research uses theoretical models of legislative organization to examine congressional committee powers and agenda setting. Other projects include a study of the macropolitics of Congress (long-range trends in the production of legislation). He has published articles in the *American Journal of Political Science, Legislative Studies Quarterly*, and *Urban Affairs Review*. His book, *Why Congressional Reforms: Fail: Reelection and the House Committee System* (University of Chicago Press), won the Alan Rosenthal Prize.

David Brady is Senior Fellow and Associate Director for Research at the Hoover Institution at Stanford University. He is also the Bowen H. and Janice Arthur McCoy Professor of Political Science and Ethics in the Stanford Graduate School of Business and Professor of Political Science in the School of Humanities and Sciences at the university. His current research focuses on the political history of the U.S. Congress, the history of U.S. election results, and public policy processes in general. Professor Brady is author of *Congressional Voting in a Partisan Era* and *Critical Elections and Congressional Policy Making* and has coedited *Change and Continuity in House Elections* and coauthored *Revolving Gridlock: Politics and Policy from Carter to Clinton*. Among other journals his work has appeared in the *American Political Science Review*, the *Journal of Law, Economics, and Organizations*, and *Journal of Comparative Political Studies*.

Charles M. Cameron is Professor of Politics and International Affairs at Princeton University. He specializes in American politics with research and teaching interests in applied formal theory and political institutions. Professor Cameron has been a Research Fellow at the Brookings Institution, a National Fellow at the Hoover Institution, and a recipient of multiple grants from the National Science Foundation. He is the author of *Veto Bargaining: Presidents and the Politics of Negative Power*, which won the Richard Fenno Jr. Book Prize awarded for the best book on legislative studies. His work has appeared in the *American Political Science Review*, the *American Journal of Political Science*, and the *Journal of Politics*, as well as scholarly journals in economics and law.

Brandice Canes-Wrone is Associate Professor of Political Science at Princeton University. Her research interests center on American political institutions, particularly the presidency, legislative politics, and public bureaucracy. She has published in the *American Political Science Review*, the *American Journal of Political Science*, and the *Journal of Politics*, among other journals. Her book, *Who Leads Whom? Presidents, Policy, and the Mass Public*, is forthcoming from the University of Chicago Press. She has taught at the Massachusetts Institute of Technology, the California Institute of Technology, and Northwestern University, and is an invited fellow at the Center for Advanced Study in the Behavioral Sciences at Stanford University.

Robert S. Erikson is Professor of Political Science at Columbia University and formerly the Dr. Kenneth L. Lay Professor of Political Science at the University of Houston. He has written numerous journal articles on American politics and elections, and has coauthored *American Public Opinion*, *Statehouse Democracy*, and *The Macro Polity*. He is the former president of the Southwest Political Science Association, and former editor of the *American Journal of Political Science*. His research interests include American political behavior, elections, methodology, and statistics.

Grace R. Freedman currently works at Thinkmap, Inc., a privately held software firm that specializes in visualizing complex information. She has a Ph.D. in political science from Columbia University and has research interests in several policy areas (telecommunications and Internet policy, regulatory policy, and health system and public health policy), in addition to her interest in longitudinal studies of congressional legislative behavior.

Valerie Heitshusen is a Senior Fellow at the Government Affairs Institute at Georgetown University. She has published journal articles on the nature of the House committee system, interest group lobbying and participation in the committee hearing process, and the allocation of federal aid money across congressional districts. She has also conducted research on legislative representation in the parliaments of the United Kingdom (where she served as an intern), Canada, Ireland, Australia, and New Zealand.

John D. Huber is Professor of Political Science at Columbia University. His research focuses on the comparative study of democratic processes. He is the author of *Rationalizing Parliament: Legislative Institutions and Party Politics in France* and (with Charles R. Shipan) *Deliberate Discretion? Institutional Foundations of Bureaucratic Autonomy*.

Ira Katznelson is Ruggles Professor of Political Science and History at Columbia University. His most recent books are *When Affirmative Action Was White* (W. W. Norton, 2005) and *Desolation and Enlightenment: Political*

Knowledge after Total War, Totalitarianism, and the Holocaust (Columbia University Press, 2003). With Helen Milner, he edited *Political Science: The State of the Discipline, Centennial Edition* (W. W. Norton, for the American Political Science Association, 2002). A former President of the Politics and History Section of the American Political Science Association and President of the Social Science History Association, he is President of the American Political Science Association for 2005–6.

Keith Krehbiel is Edward B. Rust Professor of Political Science at the Stanford Graduate School of Business. He is a scholar of American politics who specializes in the U.S. Congress and its strategic interactions with the president. His research interests also include legislatures, political parties, and U.S. political institutions. His publications have appeared in *Legislative Studies Quarterly,* the *American Journal of Political Science*, and the *Journal of Law, Economics, and Organization.*

John S. Lapinski is Assistant Professor of Political Science at Yale University. He is a resident fellow in the Institute for Social and Policy Studies. His research concerns Congress, political parties, elections, history, public opinion, and quantitative methods. His publications have appeared in the *American Journal of Political Science*, the *Journal of Politics, Public Opinion Quarterly*, and the *British Journal of Political Science.*

David Leblang is Associate Professor of Political Science at the University of Colorado at Boulder. His current research examines the relationship between political information and volatility in international financial markets. Some of his work has been published in the *American Journal of Political Science*, the *British Journal of Political Science, International Organization*, and *International Studies Quarterly.*

Michael B. MacKuen is Burton Craige Professor of Political Science at the University of North Carolina at Chapel Hill. His coauthored works include *The Macro Polity, Affective Intelligence and Political Judgment*, and *More Than News: Two Studies of Media Power.* He has published articles in the *American Political Science Review*, the *Journal of Politics*, and the *American Journal of Political Science.*

David R. Mayhew is Sterling Professor of Political Science at Yale University, where he has taught since 1968. He is the author of *Party Loyalty among Congressmen, Congress: The Electoral Connection*, "The Case of the Vanishing Marginals," *Placing Parties in American Politics, Divided We Govern, America's Congress*, and *Electoral Realignments: A Critique of an American Genre.* His current work includes "Wars and American Politics" and "Events as Causes: The Case of American Politics."

Nolan McCarty is Professor of Politics and Public Affairs at Princeton University. His areas of interest include U.S. politics, democratic political institutions, and political game theory. Recent publications include *The Realignment of National Politics and the Income Distribution* (with Keith Poole and Howard Rosenthal), "Bureaucratic Capacity, Delegation, and Political Reform" (with John D. Huber) in the *American Political Science Review*, "The Appointments Dilemma" in the *American Journal of Political Science*, "Political Resource Allocation: The Benefits and Costs of Voter Initiatives" (with John G. Matsusaka) in the *Journal of Law, Economics, and Organization*, "The Hunt for Party Discipline" (with Keith Poole and Howard Rosenthal) in the *American Political Science Review*, "Cabinet Decision Rules and Political Uncertainty in Parliamentary Bargaining" (with John Huber) in the *American Political Science Review*, and "The Politics of Blame: Bargaining before an Audience" (with Timothy Groseclose) in the *American Journal of Political Science*. He has been a fellow at the Center for Advanced Study in the Behavioral Sciences and the Robert Eckles Swain National Fellow at the Hoover Institution.

Charles R. Shipan is Professor of Political Science at the University of Iowa. Professor Shipan has followed the political careers of several candidates in his studies of congressional policies and congressional/executive relations. He has authored *Designing Judicial Review: Interest Groups, Congress, and Communications Policy* and coauthored, with John D. Huber, *Deliberate Discretion? Institutional Foundations of Bureaucratic Autonomy*. His research has appeared in *Legislative Studies Quarterly*, the *American Journal of Political Science*, and the *Journal of Theoretical Politics*, among other publications.

James A. Stimson is Raymond Dawson Professor of Political Science at the University of North Carolina at Chapel Hill. The focus of his current work is macrotheory and research on American politics, with particular emphasis on connecting mass behavior to governance in Washington and on the role of economics in political life. Former editor of *Political Analysis*, he has served on the editorial boards of the *American Journal of Political Science*, the *Journal of Politics*, *Political Methodology*, *Public Opinion Quarterly*, and *American Politics Quarterly* and authored articles in all the major journals of political science. He has authored or coauthored the following: *Yeas and Nays: Normal Decision-Making in the U.S. House of Representatives*, *Issue Evolution: Race and the Transformation of American Politics*, *Public Opinion in America: Moods, Cycles, and Swings*, and *The Macro Polity*. His most recent book, *Tides of Consent*, is an extension of opinion dynamics work written for a general audience.

Garry Young is Assistant Professor of Political Science at George Washington University in Washington, D.C. Most of his research and teaching focuses on U.S. political institutions, such as Congress and the presidency. His work has appeared in a variety of academic forums including the *British Journal of Political Science, Congress Reconsidered, International Interactions, Journal of Conflict Resolution,* the *Journal of Theoretical Politics, Legislative Studies Quarterly, Political Research Quarterly,* and *Politics and Policy.*

Acknowledgments

This book, like others before it, grew out of a conference, this one held in Boulder, Colorado, in June 2001. The volume relied upon the help of many individuals. We owe special thanks to the Provost Fund at Yale University, the Dean's Fund and Department of Political Science at the University of Colorado, Boulder, and the Dirksen Congressional Center, for providing the necessary resources. In particular, Frank Mackaman, the Executive Director of the Dirksen Center, was especially supportive. In addition to the contributing authors, we are especially grateful for the individuals who served as discussants and roundtable participants. Their hard work provided comments that led to revisions in each chapter, making them much stronger. This group of discussants deserves recognition. They include David Brady, Kelly Chang, Alan Gerber, David R. Mayhew, Rose Razaghian, Eric Schickler, and Greg Wawro.

The Macropolitics of Congress

Introduction

Defining the Macropolitics of Congress

John S. Lapinski and E. Scott Adler

In June 2001, the Republican Party was surprised to learn that Senator James Jeffords (Vt.) was leaving the party, resulting in a swing of control of the Senate to the Democrats and transforming a unified Republican government into one with divided control of Congress. This was the first time that such a switch occurred *during* a congressional session and offered scholars the rare opportunity to study its effect in legislative midstream. The event consumed the national media for days and provided political scientists with an exceptional opportunity to test an important and perplexing theoretical question— what effect does the switch between unified and divided government have on policy outputs?

Fortuitously, the Jeffords switch happened simultaneously with a conference on macro-level research on Congress that was considering, among other issues, the long-range effects of unified and divided government.[1] As most conference participants were students of Congress, our initial collective inclination might have been to think of this event in terms of related micro-oriented work.[2] Questions that could arise would include, how would the Jeffords switch alter congressional committee portfolios? How would Jeffords's act of dropping Republican affiliation affect his own voting? How would this change impact the overall work and agenda of Senate committees? In short, questions and subsequent analyses would center on the ways this switch might influence micro-level behavior.

The conference, however, was not about the microbehavior of lawmakers— at least not directly. Instead its theme was "the macropolitics of Congress," focusing specifically on the macro-level *outcomes* produced by Congress, oftentimes in conjunction with the president and the courts. This distinction influenced the questions conferees focused on with regard to the Jeffords switch. Our discussion concentrated on how this event would affect aggregate policy outputs. Would it change the agenda or content of policymaking in the 107th Congress? Specifically, how could the switch of one member be "outcome consequential" in a supermajoritarian institution that technically requires, by its own rules, 60 senators to transform policy ideas into public statutes? These types of questions, among many others, were asked and discussed by conference attendees. Of course, no one suspected at the time that the tragic events of September 11 would introduce a huge shock to normal politics, removing the partisan divisions that emerged that summer and eviscerating almost any possibility to analyze in a meaningful way this transformation from unified to divided government. The bipartisanship that followed the terrorist attacks was short lived. Extreme partisanship and unified control of government returned with the midterm election of 2002.

Political scientists, sociologists, economists, (some) historians and journalists alike are very much interested in how control of government institutions (e.g., divided government) impacts policymaking. It almost goes without saying that for many political scientists the motivation for studying politics is to understand how governments perform under differing political conditions. This is perhaps why the debate over divided government has had such a long life, as it is considered by many to be perhaps the most important factor in explaining policy gridlock, which is a key indicator of system performance. Understanding the causes (Fiorina 1992; Jacobson 1990) as well as the consequences of divided government (Mayhew 1991; Binder 1999, 2003; Coleman 1999; Edwards, Barrett, and Peake 1997; Howell et al. 2000) is therefore a topic that political scientists have deemed worthy of study.[3]

If the debate over divided government is placed in a larger context, it leads to consideration of how our political institutions, specifically the separation-of-powers system, operate. This timeless debate about institutional design and the performance of our political system has existed since the Founding. It was of vital concern to early political scientists, gaining prominence in Woodrow Wilson's tour de force, *Congressional Government* (1885). His book painstakingly argued that the institutional arrangements of the U.S. separation of powers were pathologically flawed.[4] Like Wilson, other early scholars of American political institutions, such as Henry Jones Ford (1898), were profoundly concerned with the macro-level performance of our political system. Interestingly enough, these concerns emerged at a time when the federal government was much less active than today's government. It is ironic that as government growth exploded in the period after World War II (Higgs 1987), this line of study nearly ceased to exist. This silence is particularly noticeable in recent work within the subfield of congressional studies, which collectively has given surprisingly little attention to long-range perspectives on the policymaking process. To the contrary, the vast majority of contemporary congressional research explores individual-level behavior of members of Congress (MCs).

The trend toward studying micro-level behavior at the expense of consideration of system performance began its reversal with the publication of David Mayhew's examination, in *Divided We Govern*, of policy change under unified and divided government over the last half-century. His seminal study led to a surge in research examining policy performance in American politics, particularly the performance of Congress. Despite the debates about the causes and consequences of divided government generated by Mayhew's study, there is still little synthesis between studies of legislative production and the theories put forward in the macro-oriented political science literature. Consequently, we felt the need to improve the conversation among scholars working on related topics (i.e., those who study macro policymaking but focus on different inputs that drive policymaking such as institutional change and public opinion) that had previously not been connected in any systematic way. This book is an attempt to facilitate that conversation.

MAKING MACROPOLICY—THE ROLE OF CONGRESS

Congress undeniably plays a special role in forging macropolitical outcomes in the United States. In fact, Congress's privileged position in lawmaking is what distinguishes it from other national legislatures (Katznelson and Lapinski 2004). When we think of politics and policymaking in the United States, such as "foreign policymaking" or "health policymaking," we cannot escape the conclusion that Congress plays an integral role in manufacturing relevant outputs. This is not to say that other institutional players in our separation-of-powers system are not important.[5] Who would argue that George W. Bush's administration has not played a guiding role in setting the policy agenda in post–September 11 America? But we must also remember that President Bush had much less success controlling the policy agenda in the first part of his administration, primarily because Congress did not agree with many of his proposals and had its own agenda.[6] In fact, he did not sign his first major piece of legislation into law—the $1.35 trillion tax cut—until well past his first one hundred days in office. Legislation covering education reform, prescription drugs, and campaign finance reform, among others, had to wait until a new-found bipartisanship sprang from the September 11 tragedy. More recently, many Bush administration proposals in 2003 and 2004 outside the realm of security and defense policy languished in Congress with little or no legislative action (Babbington 2004).

Accordingly, many observers see Congress as the institution where the collective choice of the nation is forged into outcomes. Some have argued that studying Congress is key to understanding how policy inputs map into policy outputs. This means, in brief, that Congress can be seen as the critical link to understanding how the factors that shape the way government operates as a whole (its partisan configuration, the working relationship between branches, etc.) result in aggregate policy outputs. In addition, how do changes in those factors affect changes in overall policy? Two central questions motivate our attempt to better explain this relationship. The first is what macro-outputs are. In other words, what are the dependent variables and what makes them "macro?" The second question asks what mechanisms govern the processes that produce different macro outputs. Thus we attempt to determine the role and the weight accorded to Congress in producing outputs along with other policymaking bodies.

Interestingly enough, the focus of congressional scholars for decades has been on the actions and behavior of lawmakers and the structure of the institution, with little attention paid to what is removed from the forge. This is what we refer to as macro-outputs. We distinctly see the roots of this tradition in the work of Richard Fenno and David Mayhew. Consider chapter 1 of Fenno's second book, *Congressmen in Committees* (1973), which begins, "A member of the House is a congressman first and a committee member second," after which he examines the individual behavior of MCs inside the committee system. Building on earlier work, Fenno's next pathbreaking study, *Home Style: House Members in Their Districts* (1978), expands on the exploration of the behavior of members of Congress by probing representative-constituency linkages. In his hallmark work *Congress: The Electoral Connection* (1974), Mayhew explores the policymaking activities of lawmakers as they relate to their own reelection strategies.[7] The focus in this work is on understanding the behavior of individual MCs. While understanding individual behavior certainly provides insights into macro-level phenomena, elaborating on those insights is simply not the primary purpose of this earlier work.

While the successes in studying congressional organization and legislative behavior have been many, they are only a part of a larger understanding of our democratic institutions and governance. One way to appreciate the remaining void is to look at congressional research from the point of view of the structure-conduct-performance paradigm that has long been part of the industrial organization subfield in economics. This work provides an interesting example of how one might bridge micro-oriented work with macro-level outputs. Roger Myerson (1995), in his review essay "Analysis of Democratic Institutions: Structure, Conduct, and Performance,"[8] argues that we must fully identify and understand the organization of democratic political systems and the actions of policy actors so that it is possible to appreciate the linkage of structure and conduct to performance. Industrial organization scholars built microfoundations for their subfield through careful inductive work, using industry-specific qualitative case studies followed by empirical analyses. Later, these scholars turned to the study of macro-level performance focusing primarily on efficiency and profits.

In contrast, the literature on Congress has yet to truly connect micro-oriented work to macro-level phenomena. The recent attention given to studying how members of Congress behave is akin to studying how firms act given a certain set of rules governing market structure. The theories explaining why and how individual members of Congress behave have been a real success story, and this success at the micro level makes it possible to expand our horizons and begin to fully explore the consequences for political outcomes. Furthermore, we believe that the study of macropolitics can simply be thought of as the next logical step for the field of congressional scholarship. Our micro theories that explain member behavior, combined with micro-oriented understanding of internal structure (e.g., the committee system, and organizational rules), provide us with the building blocks for a macro theory of policy performance. Nonetheless, the long-range implications of our micro insights have not been properly explored. It is at this aggregate level where performance must be measured.

The work found in this volume tries to link the microfoundations that already exist in current literature more directly to macro-oriented policymaking and congressional operations. We do this to increase our understanding of how Congress performs over time and in relation to other political actors. Questions central to this concept of the "macropolitics of Congress" include these: Does Congress as a representative body broadly reflect public desires? What are the aggregate implications of Congress as ombudsman for the way people relate to their government? How does Congress manage the administrative state, including its role in the creation of agencies as well the Senate's special role in filling such agencies (or leaving them empty) with its advise and consent power over nominations? To properly synthesize what is a diverse body of work, it is first necessary to define the key term—macropolitics. It is to this complicated task that we turn next.

TOWARD A DEFINITION OF MACROPOLITICS

Defining what we mean by macropolitics is necessary to further advance this new genre of work. The long tradition of a micro-oriented focus in congressional scholarship means that our first obstacle is coming up with a definition sufficiently narrow to give the field meaning and boundaries, but not so narrow that large areas of congressional research will easily fall between the micro and macro approaches. This is made all the more difficult by the tremendous heterogeneity in the study of macropolitics, as demonstrated in the chapters that follow. Each tries to explain policymaking; however, different emphases are placed on such influences as public opinion, mood, preferences, elections, divided and unified government, committee chairs, bureaucratic agencies, and political parties. To construct a cohesive yet parsimonious definition of macropolitics, we return to the two questions laid out in the previous section: What are macro-outputs, and what mechanisms govern the processes that produce macro-outputs? As alluded to above, studying macropolitics is about developing and testing theories that explain how collective choice maps into policy outputs across time. To understand this mapping process, we first turn our attention to the policy outputs that serve as the dependent variable for macropolitics. Policy outputs, or "system performance," comprise aggregate views of legislation, impeachment, and ombudsman activities, advice and consent in shaping the executive branch of government, or approval of matters concerning foreign affairs. What differentiates these outputs from past work on Congress is that we are looking at "outcomes" and, for the most part, think of these in their aggregate form (e.g., the proportion of a party's platform adopted into law instead of individual enactments passed from a platform considered in isolation).

For an example, consider Cain, Ferejohn, and Fiorina's seminal book *The Personal Vote: Constituency Service and Electoral Independence* (1987). They show how constituency service enhances lawmakers' reelection prospects. Though their focus is on the behavior of individual members of Congress, they speculate about the system-level or macro-level consequences of these activities. An important implication of increased constituency service is that it insulates members' electoral fortunes from the fate of the party. This leads to the macro implication that parties' legislative programs might lose cohesiveness and perhaps are less likely to pass. Thinking about these ombudsman activities at the macro level, we might analyze party programs across time and determine whether the success or failure of party platforms and legislative agendas can be explained by changes in constituency service. This illustration demonstrates that a boundary between a micro and macro approach is that the macro perspective looks at the outcomes that are produced out of collective choice. In other words, the emphasis is on the products that flow out of our political institutions.

Creating a list of topics or categories that might be reasonably considered part of the macropolitics genre takes us a step closer to defining what macro-outputs are, but is clearly not sufficient. We need to go further and explore *how* macropolitics is studied. How does analyzing macropolitics differ from micro-level analysis? As should be clear from the preceding paragraph, studying macropolitics makes *outputs* the important dependent variable. This contrasts with studies of policy inputs that use congressional structure or the actions of individual lawmakers as left-hand-side variables. Thus, macropolitics literature is far less interested in discovering the factors that impact such common subjects of research as roll call votes, committee tenure rates, measures of careerism, or the determinants of institutionalism. This is not to say that these factors are not important for output production. They most certainly are. For instance, a macro approach is not necessarily interested in understanding the mechanisms that lead to the disappearance of competitive (marginal) legislative districts. However, those differences in district competitiveness might be quite important from a macropolitics perspective in shifting the location of median preferences in Congress and thereby affecting the complexion of policy.

We certainly are not the first to observe the need for studies of macropolitical performance. Joseph Cooper and David Brady's underappreciated review essay published over two decades ago in the *American Political Science*

Review (1981) offers perhaps the clearest vision of the utility in focusing attention on congressional organization as an *independent variable*. They argue that this is necessary in order to better understand and pinpoint the impact of institutional changes on the policymaking process. More research, Cooper and Brady contend, is required to evaluate how long-range trends in congressional development and relations with other political actors influence the output side of the political system.[9] In effect, congressional scholars need to refocus a portion of their attention away from the institutional and behavioral trees that so often occupy us and toward the governing forest.

This leads to a second component critical to defining the boundaries of a macropolitics approach—understanding what is meant by system performance. This concept is central to the viewpoint of congressional structure serving as an independent variable. In effect, the long-term performance of the governing system in general, and Congress in particular, is what we are trying to understand and predict. This is very much related to the questions of both what macro-outputs are and how to study macropolitics. The choices made in defining and conceptualizing system performance are not to be taken lightly. If we decide that system performance is best captured through the implementation of public statutes at the aggregate level, we will likely find that the mechanisms that govern this process differ considerably from those involved in passing legislation. In the former, we might draw on an extensive literature that deals with principal-agent problems between Congress and the bureaucracy (Epstein and O'Halloran 1999), while in the latter we might look at literature that examines the relationship between Congress and the executive branch (Cameron 2000). Cooper and Brady touch on this specific aspect of congressional studies as it relates to macropolitics. While noting the difficulties in analyzing institutional operations, they conceptualize congressional performance in two ways. The first conceives of performance in output or productivity categories, such as lawmaking, oversight, and constituent service. This "concrete approach" attempts to define the possible outputs that could be examined in macropolitics in ways that are familiar to most legislative scholars. Alternatively, in what Cooper and Brady refer to as a more abstract approach, performance is viewed as the relationship or role that Congress plays vis-à-vis other units in the political system. It remains to be determined whether this conceptualization represents a distinct way to define performance or is really more a mechanism. In other words, exploring the relationship of Congress to other institutions might really belong on the left-hand side of the equation. Of course, better understanding these complex relationships is at the heart of the macropolitics enterprise, as again it will lead to us identifying and understanding the mechanisms that lead to political outcomes.

Again, we agree that evaluations of congressional performance should address output as well as interinstitutional relations. We believe, however, that most of the progress that will be made in this area in the short run will come from studying performance and other productivity-related categories. This is largely due to the fact that most of the existing theoretical work (e.g., Krehbiel 1998; Cameron 2000) deals with lawmaking. Some of this structure clearly requires that we make additional progress in devising adequate measures to properly test theory. This is no simple task. Cooper and Brady contend that this hurdle is probably the fundamental reason why relatively little research on macropolitics has ever been conducted (1981, 999). The good news is that since Cooper and Brady published their article, considerable progress has been made in the area of measuring legislative productivity (Mayhew 1991; Howell et al. 2000; Lapinski 2000; Clinton and Lapinski 2006).

What may encourage scholars to take up the mantle of macropolitics is to construe performance broadly enough to include a variety of outputs, rather than simple counts. For instance, we might think of measuring performance as not merely the amount of legislation but also its direction—liberal versus conservative (see, for example, Erikson, MacKuen, and Stimson 2002). Or, as Mayhew did in *Divided We Govern*, we can explore the extent and type of oversight of federal agencies as it occurs over long swaths of time. Similarly, in the Freedman and Cameron chapter included in this volume, performance can be taken to be the type and direction of government regulation within a given policy arena over time. Expanding beyond simple counts of important legislation will be vital to bringing in scholars from other areas, including American political development and comparative politics, where the content and direction of policy is considered very important (Skowronek 1982; Smith 1997; Skocpol 1992; Orren and Skowronek 2004; Huber and Shipan 2002).

Even if the primary interest of studying macropolitics remains within the subfield of congressional studies, the increased interest in historical research on Congress will require serious thought about what measures can be developed to test ideas that might be best located within particular historical moments. For instance, it is reasonable to think of performance in different periods as a combination of both *change* and *continuity*. For example, if we are interested in studying the period from the mid-1890s through the 1920s, we might focus on the role of political parties within Congress. In some policy areas, however, influence for the Republican Party meant *not* passing legislation.[10] Several Republican lawmakers, including much of the leadership, were often opposed to (or split) when it came to legislative proposals that would change national labor laws during this time period. Consider labor policy. For several years Democratic representative William Sulzer (N.Y.) annually introduced one or more bills that would have created a Department of Labor with a cabinet-level secretary (Chamberlain 1946, 144). These bills languished in committee until the Democratic Party gained control of the House in 1911. Even labor issues that garnered bipartisan support, such as legislation strengthening child labor laws, cut against the Republican leadership's desire to keep the federal government out of issues that impacted business interests. As Chamberlain writes, "President Taft though keenly aware of the need for protecting children in industry was not favorable to the establishment of a federal children's bureau because he disapproved the 'disposition to unload everything on the federal government that the states ought to look after'" (146). Measuring the status quo, coding for policy direction, and disaggregating policy by substantive issue area are all critical steps for studying legislative productivity in this and in many historical periods. Consequently, scholars should not take lightly the conceptualization and construction of appropriate performance measures as they apply to the questions and periods of interest.

We see Brady and Cooper's essay as the first major call for the study of the macropolitics of Congress. Their primary interest in studying Congress across time was that such an approach nicely captures change—including change in rules, norms, and preferences—all of which are likely to impact policymaking. Political change, for Cooper and Brady, might take the form of new institutions (e.g., the Australian ballot, the Seventeenth Amendment, or changes in internal organization spurred by the Legislative Reorganization Act of 1946) or transformations in the preferences of crucial players in the policy process as a result of events like realigning elections (see also Brady 1988; Mayhew 2002). Identification of change in congressional structure and operations holds particular importance to this longitudinal view of congressional scholarship and congressional performance more generally. It leads us to a critical question, does long-term change in institutional organization and congressional interactions with other political actors affect the process of policymaking and subsequent outcomes?

To study Congress in this longitudinal manner, David Brady sketched out what he believes are the necessary components of a theory of macropolitics.[11] Specifically, Brady focuses on the mechanisms that force change in macropolitical outputs. In many ways Brady's concluding chapter in this volume is a sequel to his original essay on the subject. He acknowledges that building such a theory will take time, but that enough work has been completed in macropolitics to begin to outline what a theory might look like. He asserts that a theory would have to address at least the following questions: When will the government be active and what kinds of activities will it undertake? How do the parts of government—elected and appointed—work together or against each other to either limit activity or enhance it? How do moods, opinions, and elections interact with government actors to yield policy activity or inactivity? Regardless of the motivation, we agree that macropolitics must be studied across time and, potentially, across place. How can one adequately assess performance if a particular Congress cannot be compared to another?

IMPORTANT NEW WORK IN MACROPOLITICS

A number of recent works on Congress fall within the macropolitics genre. A few of these studies stand out—some for their theoretical contributions and others for their empirical efforts, and a few for both. As mentioned above, David Mayhew's work on the consequences of divided government was pioneering, not for its theoretical offerings, but for providing a first cut at the complicated task of measuring governmental performance—here, measured as the productivity of important legislation—over a long time horizon. His simple count of public laws makes the critical distinction between landmark legislation and everything else, and challenges the long-standing belief that unified party government leads to moments of high legislative productivity, while divided government contributes to legislative gridlock.

Of course, Mayhew's controversial work opened up an extensive and interesting debate on the effect of unified and divided government, making the study of divided government without question the most active area of research in the macropolitics realm. While some scholars have questioned his measures of legislative importance and, to a certain extent, his conclusions (Kelly 1993; Howell et al. 2000), others have argued that the broader political context is ignored when one analyzes simple counts of important enactments (Binder 1999, 2003; Edwards, Barrett, and Peake 1997).

Krehbiel's theory of pivotal politics (1996, 1998) offers insights as to when we will see individual and aggregate policy activity (see also Brady and Volden 1998). His approach to policy activity is based on micro-level assumptions regarding preference-driven legislative action. In essence he sees the policy positions of two key legislative players—the cloture pivot and veto pivot as the critical factors in determining when there will be activity or inactivity within a given sphere of public policy. The configuration of these vital political actors in relation to the location of the status quo and the president's position for a given policy dictates when changes in that policy will be adopted. The portion of policy "space" within which the key actors are not able to improve their well-being by enacting new policy is considered the "gridlock interval." Crucial to the pivotal politics model is the role of elections as a catalyst for policy change. If we believe that members of Congress do not change their ideological positions across time (Poole 1998),[12] then electoral turnover is the only real mechanism for making significant alterations in the size and location of the gridlock interval and thus increasing the likelihood of policy change. More broadly, however, this configuration of actors also determines the likelihood of sweeping policy changes in the aggregate. For example, according to Krehbiel's theory, we should observe policy surges at the beginning of new presidential administrations (particularly if we observe a party change), as this is likely to have produced a larger shift in the gridlock interval. This work offers one of the strongest supplements to Mayhew's research on legislative productivity as related to the incidence of unified and divided government, which is not considered to be theoretically related to gridlock per se.

While Krehbiel's model is a powerful one—suggesting a number of hypotheses as to when we should expect surges and slumps in overall legislative output—scholars have only begun to test its empirical predictions. In addition, Krehbiel's model leaves considerable room for other approaches to fill in the gaps. For instance, the pivotal politics theory does not tell us why some policies that have status quo points clearly outside of the gridlock interval are not immediately changed once the gridlock interval shifts. Nor does it say anything about what accounts for timing in relation to policymaking. The theory remains silent on such questions.

Other important work falling within the domain of macropolitics that deals more explicitly with the question of interbranch cooperation and conflict is that of Charles Cameron and his colleagues. Again, motivated by rational choice models of political action, Cameron studies veto bargaining by exploring the incentives of both Congress and the president in the process of negotiating policies (Cameron 2000; Cameron, Lapinski, and Riemann 2000). Cameron shows that vetoes do not inevitably spell the demise of policy proposals but are simply a tool in the give-and-take between branches in shaping government outputs.

Also drawing on the separation-of-powers theme, Erikson, MacKuen, and Stimson's (2002) wide-ranging study of citizen preferences and government activity utilizes years of research on the purposive actions of policymakers to examine how changes in public "policy mood" over time influences the legislative activity and liberalism of Congress, the president, and the courts. The notion behind this body of work is that Congress (and the president) is responsive to constituent wishes. Erikson et al. offer a very good first step in the process of measuring ideological direction of policy output over time.

While macropolitics work was quite rare a decade ago, it is becoming ever more common as we attempt to better understand what drives policy outputs. Collectively, the works highlighted here have turned the study of macropolitics in the United States into a more coherent research tradition that seeks understanding of the mechanisms that drive policy outputs. The objective of this book is to help develop this new, important body of work and provide an impetus for a new wave of macro-oriented research, specifically involving Congress.

ORGANIZATION OF THE VOLUME

The timing and structure of this volume is not accidental. Prior to the last decade or so, scholars had made little headway in the study of macropolitics, partially because of the lack of a theoretical infrastructure. We now have the beginnings of good macropolitics theory, the bulk of it coming from micro-level work focused on the behavior and actions of individual MCs. It is no co-incidence that the first part of this volume, "Theoretical Approaches to the Macropolitics of Congress," draws upon the work of three highly regarded po-litical scientists who are best known for their research on formal models deal-ing with legislatures and the separation-of-powers system. Krehbiel's past work, particularly that examining the role of information in a legislative set-ting, often used deductively derived rational actor models to provide testable predictions regarding the purposive behavior of individual lawmakers. In chapter 1, Krehbiel goes beyond thinking about a single model of legislative policymaking, and instead provides the tools necessary to help us develop empirical methods to test "competing models" of macropolitics (along with demonstrating the importance of determining whether alleged competing the-ories produce non-observationally equivalent predictions). His work brings us back to an important and ongoing debate about the role of political parties as organizing cartels inside Congress (and has implications for the role of parties across different types of legislatures).

Huber and McCarty's contribution is an ambitious chapter that demon-strates the relationships between bureaucratic capacity, legislative expertise, and legislative output. This is accomplished by deriving a game theoretic model that truly possesses macro-level predictions. This type of work is im-portant for two reasons. First, the model puts America's evolving political eras into their historical context, as it is designed to predict when institutional change will affect congressional performance. In other words, the model of-fers the conditions under which we are likely see changes in the macro-outputs Congress produces. The "under what conditions" question is tailored to take into account different moments of congressional history. This model-ing is important, because if we are interested in understanding legislative out-puts, preference-based theories of macropolitics work well for the post-1946 United States, but are less useful for earlier eras. Clearly, Congress-centered reforms must matter, including the development of the committee systems in both chambers, the direct election of senators, and procedural reforms like the introduction of cloture in the Senate or the expansion of subcommittee powers in the House. Second, this model offers true macro-level predictions, thus moving away from theoretical work that is centered on individual lawmakers. The Huber and McCarty chapter is an excellent example of the type of theo-retical work we hope to see more of in the future.

Part 2, The Macropolitics of Representation, builds on the idea that Con-gress is the most representative political institution in our separation-of-powers system. Legislators, who must represent the specific interests of their constituencies, make binding decisions on public policy.[13] Erikson, MacKuen, and Stimson argue that public demand plays a formative role in determining the policies enacted. In the words of Heinz Eulau, legislators are "responsive"

(Eulau 1993). Public opinion regarding federal policy is measured through the familiar conceptualization of "mood," which exists in a left-right (liberal-conservative) continuum. Erikson, MacKuen, and Stimson find overwhelming evidence to support the notion that the causal mechanism underlying the enactment of liberal or conservative legislation is public support. If we believe that legislators should receive direct signals from constituents and translate these messages into policy, then this chapter suggests that our political system is working as it should.

Katznelson and Lapinski believe that the substance of policy is a key, and often missing, element in the study of the policy process. In their chapter, they argue that representation and public policy proceed in tandem but that our political institutions often prevent median voter policies from becoming law. Building on a rich history of early public policy research, they introduce a coding scheme to parse statutes into distinct categories by policy area. Arranging policies in distinct categories allows scholars to identify like policies across time and helps us better identify the primary dimension of policy issue areas. Consequently the coding scheme is an empirical device that should help us better understand how the policy process differs across issues (e.g., preference intensity, absent in most theoretical accounts of policymaking, surely varies across issue areas). In other words, Katznelson and Lapinski argue that if we are to analyze theories of macropolitics, such as Krehbiel's theory of gridlock or Huber and McCarty's model that predicts when legislators will legislate, we need to think about how specific policy areas fit into the picture (e.g., what explains the political ordering of the policy agenda in Krehbiel's model of gridlock?).

The part titled "Testing Theories of Macropolitics across Time," introduces new ideas about testing extant theories of legislative productivity across history. As noted earlier, Cooper and Brady lamented that researchers were largely stymied in their effort to examine institutional performance by the difficulty in formulating appropriate variables. The payoff, however, they surmised, would be quite high if we could devise measures that captured institutional performance across such time periods as varied as the Civil War, the Progressive Era, and the New Deal. Heitshusen and Young take a step in the right direction with their chapter. They argue that legislation that changes the U.S. Code denotes a level of legislative significance. Consequently, they are able to leverage this rich source to create a list of significant enactments back in time, which they use to test existing preference-based theories of macropolitics. This suggestive work provides us with many answers (along with a few new questions) about whether it is appropriate to read the present backwards when testing theories of policymaking.

Shipan's work moves away from studying the effect of partisan control on the passage of important legislation toward a more inclusive study of its effect on the political agenda. The agenda in this case is thought of as being endogenous and an alternative conceptualization of system performance. Shipan contends that understanding the denominator (the number of established objectives of the legislature) will allow us to determine the institutional performance of Congress because it allows us to measure how much of the agenda passes (see Binder 1999, 2003). He finds that divided control of government leads to sharp increases in the size of the political agenda.

The fourth part, "Macropolitics and Public Policy," uses the macropolitics framework to examine the course of legislative change in three very different policy environments. Freedman and Cameron offer a new kind of history of the administrative state—one that is theoretically driven yet has a deep understanding of the logic of individual regulatory regimes. Using a simple spatial model to map the relative ideological positions of the principals and agents involved in telecommunications policy, they are able to predict when significant changes in regulation or enactments occur. Their findings indicate that Congress is willing to act when its agent—in this case the Federal Communications Commission—diverges too far from the ideological preferences of the relevant congressional committees.

Taking a slightly different angle on the macropolitics of the congressional-bureaucratic relationship, Canes-Wrone explores the relative ability of Congress *and* the courts to influence bureaucratic decisions with regard to the issuing of permits for the development of wetlands. Again, examining differences in the ideological inclination of representatives on the relevant oversight committees and in the ideological position of district and appellate courts, Canes-Wrone finds that both branches affect the issuance of permits by the Army Corps of Engineers. For our purposes Canes-Wrone's findings have implications beyond the specifics of this case study by demonstrating that the various principals in this separation-of-powers environment are able to greatly influence the decisions of the bureaucratic agent without directly mandating specific kinds of actions.

Adler and Leblang examine the collective governance of the economy by the executive and legislative branches. Dissatisfied with the existing literature on political cycles that often underestimates the role of Congress as a factor in economic performance, they develop models of ideological and partisan compromise between Congress and the president that are tested against existing theories that most often highlight only the partisanship of the president or the existence or absence of unified party government. Performance of the domestic economy is seen as an additional way to gauge performance of the governing structure. Using economic indicators over most of the postwar period, Adler and Leblang find that their measure of interbranch compromise helps to explain peaks and troughs in economic performance. Specifically, the economy performs better—in terms of increased growth and decreased unemployment—when there is a Democrat in the White House and when there is the likelihood of a "liberal" compromise between executive and legislative branches.

Finally, the volume concludes with chapters by David Mayhew and David Brady. In typical fashion, Mayhew provides us with rich insights about the work contained within the volume along with some new data (an update of his landmark legislation for the 107th Congress) and a few fresh ideas of his own. Instead of attempting to summarize an eclectic set of chapters, Mayhew offers extensive thoughts on two chapters that deal with subjects very close to his own work: the effect of divided government on policy agendas and how public opinion affects the direction (liberal or conservative) of policymaking. Giving his conclusion his signature stamp, he brings to the forefront ideas that will engage scholars for the next few years. First, he asks how the status quo policy reversion point is affected under conditions of crisis. This is an interesting question, especially since our country has revisited crisis over and over again. Does crisis make the existing status quo point irrelevant? Mayhew thinks so. He argues that "a shift of the status quo policy outside the congressional 'gridlock interval' can be spectacularly caused by events other than elections." In other words, the status quo point is thrown out of the window under crisis conditions. How we incorporate this discovery into our theoretical and empirical work is left to the discipline to figure out. Second, he argues that the disappearance of partisanship under conditions of crisis is important and deserves our attention. Mayhew urges scholars to dig deeper into the circumstances surrounding the movement of Congress toward unanimous or near unanimous action.

Brady shows that studying macropolitics is compatible with two major approaches to American politics: the rational choice tradition and the American political development approach. He delineates the differences between the two genres: the former puts heavy emphasis on the role of elections and political preferences, while the latter is more interested in social movements and the origins and development of political institutions. He points out that both share an interest in understanding the dynamics of American politics over time. His chapter also sketches out an overview of the progress we have made in developing a theory of macropolitics since he published his initial probe in 1981, and provides a road map for areas of research where good progress can be made in the short term.

NOTES

1. Senator James Jeffords renounced his Republican Party affiliation on May 24, 2001. The "Macropolitics of Congress" conference was held in Boulder, Colorado, June 1–3, 2001.

2. By micro-oriented work we simply mean that the unit of analysis is the individual member of Congress. Most micro-level theories, of course, are ultimately interested in the collective behavior of individuals. The distinction between collective (macro) behavior and macro-outputs is an important one. Aggregate behavior in many

ways serves as a bridge between micro- and macro-oriented work. We return to this linkage later in the introduction.

3. It is even more important in that divided government has been prevalent throughout the post–World War II period, and with the current competitive political environment, the probability is high that it will be with us into the foreseeable future.

4. While Wilson conceded that our separation-of-powers system worked well in a more simple time, he believed that it did not function well as society faced more complex problems than existed at the Founding.

5. See Whittington and Carpenter 2003 for an argument for placing more emphasis on studying the role of the executive branch in public policy.

6. Much recent research has pointed out that Congress, particularly the Senate, is not a majoritarian institution (Krehbiel 1998). See the *Wall Street Journal* editorial "Daschle's Dead Zone" (July 22, 2004, A12).

7. Research on Congress that until the early 1970s had been rooted in social-psychological analyses shifted its focus by embracing rational actor models heavily influenced by economics. This transformation, documented in several excellent review essays (Gamm and Huber 2002; Polsby and Schickler 2002), has lasted until today.

8. The structure-conduct-performance paradigm is as old as the New Deal with roots in the Harvard Department of Economics. See Mason and Lamont 1982 or Tirole 2003 for a historical review of the concept. Cameron (2000) speculates that this paradigm is well suited to studying policy outputs.

9. Cooper and Brady prefer the word *change* to *development* because of the normative component of the latter.

10. This is somewhat of a simplification as Progressive Republicans were interested in many national level reforms. Furthermore, southern Democrats were against intrusions by the federal government across a number of policy issues.

11. Taken from Brady's comments during a roundtable presentation at the Colorado-Yale conference.

12. Redistricting might lead members to change their preferences, as they consider themselves to be delegates of their districts.

13. Of course, representation is provisional in that public policies can be changed by future Congresses (Katznelson and Lapinski 2004).

REFERENCES

Angrist, Joshua D., and Alan Krueger. 2001. "Instrumental Variables and the Search for Identification: From Supply and Demand to Natural Experiments." *Journal of Economic Perspectives* 15 (4): 69–87.

Ansolabehere, Stephen, Alan Gerber, and Jim Snyder. 2002. "Equal Votes, Equal Money: Court-Ordered Redistricting and Public Expenditures in the American States." *American Political Science Review* 96:767–77.

Babington, Charles. 2004. "Some Bush Initiatives Languish in Congress: Follow-up Missing, Lawmaker Says." *Washington Post*, April 5, A1.

Binder, Sarah. 1999. "The Dynamics of Legislative Gridlock, 1947–1996." *American Political Science Review* 93:519–34.

————. 2003. *Stalemate: Causes and Consequences of Legislative Gridlock*. Washington, D.C.: Brookings Institution Press.

Brady, David W. 1988. *Critical Elections and Congressional Policy Making*. Stanford, Calif: Stanford University Press.

Brady, David W., and Craig Volden. 1998. *Revolving Gridlock: Politics and Policy from Carter to Clinton*. Boulder, Colo.: Westview Press.

Cain, Bruce E., John Ferejohn, and Morris P. Fiorina. 1987. *The Personal Vote: Constituency Service and Electoral Independence*. Cambridge: Harvard University Press.

Cameron, Charles M. 2000. *Veto Bargaining: Presidents and the Politics of Negative Power*. New York: Cambridge University Press.

Cameron, Charles M., John S. Lapinski, and Charles Riemann. 2000. "Testing Formal Theories of Political Rhetoric." *Journal of Politics*, 62: 187–205.

Chamberlain, Lawrence. 1946. *The President, the Congress, and Legislation*. New York: Colombia University Press.

Clinton, Joshua, and John S. Lapinski. 2006. "Measuring Legislative Accomplishment." *American Journal of Political Science* 51.

Coleman, John. 1999. "Unified Government, Divided Government, and Party Responsiveness." *American Political Science Review* 93:821–36.

Cooper, Joseph, and David Brady. 1981. "Toward a Diachronic Analysis of Congress." *American Political Science Review* 75:988–1012.

Edwards, George, Andrew Barrett, and Jeffrey Peake. 1997. "The Legislative Impact of Divided Government." *American Journal of Political Science* 41:545–63.

Erikson, Robert S., Michael B. MacKuen, and James Stimson. 2002. *The Macro Polity*. New York: Cambridge University Press.

Epstein, David, and Sharyn O'Halloran. 1999. *Delegating Powers: A Transaction Cost Politics Approach to Policy Making under Separate Powers*. New York: Cambridge University Press.

Eulau, Heinz, 1993. "The Congress as Research Arena! An Uneasy Partnership between History and Political Science" *Legislative Studies Quarterly* 18:569–92.

Fenno, Richard F., Jr. 1973. *Congressmen in Committees*. Boston: Little, Brown.

———— 1978. *Home Style: House Members in Their Districts*. New York: HarperCollins.

Fiorina, Morris P. 1992. *Divided Government*. New York: Macmillan.

Ford, Henry Jones. 1898. *The Rise and Growth of American Politics*. New York: Macmillan.

Gamm, Gerald, and John Huber O. 2002. "Legislatures as Political Institution: Beyond the Contemporary Congress."

In *Political Science: State of the Discipline*, ed. Ira Katznelson and Helen Milner. New York: Norton.

Higgs, Robert. 1987. *Crisis and Leviathan: Critical Episodes in the Growth of American Government*. New York: Oxford University Press.

Howell, William, E. Scott Adler, Charles M. Cameron, and Charles Riemann. 2000. "Measuring the Institutional Performance of Congress in the Post-war Era: Surges and Slumps in the Production of Legislation, 1945–1994." *Legislative Studies Quarterly* 25:285–312.

Huber, John D., and Charles Shipan R. 2002. *Deliberate Discretion? The Institutional Foundations of Beareaucratic Autonomy*. New York: Cambridge University Press.

Jacobson, Gary C. 1990. *The Electoral Origins of Divided Government: Competition in U.S. House Elections, 1946–1988.* Boulder, Colo. Westview Press.

Katznelson, Ira, and John S. Lapinski. 2004. "Congress and American Political Development: Missed Chances, Rich Possibilities." Yale University Typescript.

Kelly, Sean Q. 1993. "Divided We Govern: A Reassessment." *Polity* 25:475–95.

Krehbiel, Keith. 1996. "Institutional and Partisan Sources of Gridlock: A Theory of Divided and Unified Government." *Journal of Theoretical Politics* 8:7–40.

———. 1998. *Pivotal Politics.* Chicago: University of Chicago Press.

Lapinski, John S. 2000. "Representation and Reform: A Congress Centered Approach to American Political Development." Ph.D. diss. Department of Political Science, Columbia University.

Mason, Edward S., and Thomas S. Lamont. 1982. "The Harvard Department of Economics from the Beginning of World War II." *Quarterly Journal of Economics* 97:383–433.

Mayhew, David R. 1974. *Congress: The Electoral Connection.* New Haven: Yale University Press.

———. 1991. *Divided We Govern: Party Control, Lawmaking, and Investigations, 1946–1990.* New Haven: Yale University Press.

———. 2002. *Electoral Realignments: A Critique of An American Genre.* New Haven: Yale University Press.

Myerson, Roger B. 1995. "Analysis of Democratic Institutions: Structure, Conduct, and Performance." *Journal of Economic Perspectives* 9 (1): 77–89.

Orren, Karen, and Stephen Skowronek. 2004. *The Search for American Political Development.* New York: Cambridge University Press.

Polsby, Nelson, and Eric Schickler. 2002. "Landmarks in the Study of Congress since 1945." *Annual Review of Political Science* 5:333–67.

Poole, Keith. 1998. "Recovering a Basic Space from a Set of Issue Scales." *American Journal of Political Science* 42:954–93.

Poole, Keith, and Howard Rosenthal. 1997. *Congress: A Political Economy History of Roll Call Voting.* New York: Oxford University Press.

Skocpol, Theda. 1992. *Protecting Soldiers and Mothers: The Political Origins of Social Policy in the United States.* Cambridge: Belknap Press of Harvard University Press.

Skowronek, Stephen. 1982. *Building a New American State: The Expansion of National American Capacities.* New York: Cambridge University Press.

Smith, Rogers. 1997. *Civic Ideals: Conflicting Visions of Citizenship in U.S. History.* New Haven: Yale University Press.

Stimson, James, Michael B. MacKuen, and Robert S. Erikson. 1995. "Dynamic Representation." *American Political Science Review* 89:543–65.

Tirole, Jean. 2003. *The Theory of Industrial Organization.* Cambridge: MIT Press.

Wilson, Woodrow. 1885. *Congressional Government.* New York: Houghton Mifflin.

Whittington, Keith E., and Daniel P. Carpenter. 2003. "Executive Power in American Institutional Development." *Perspectives on Politics* 1:495–513.

PART I: *Theoretical Approaches to the Macropolitics of Congress*

1

Macropolitics and Micromodels: Cartels and Pivots Reconsidered

Keith Krehbiel

> You like potato and I like potahto
> You like tomato and I like tomahto
> Potato, potahto, Tomato, tomahto.
> Let's call the whole thing off!
> —*George and Ira Gershwin, 1936*

An ongoing debate in contemporary legislative studies centers on whether a good theory of lawmaking in the U.S. national government requires an explicit party component. The main bones of contention have been picked sufficiently elsewhere[1] that some participants or observers may wish to "call the whole thing off." To do so seems ill advised, however. Not only is the issue far from resolved, but it also resides at the heart of obtaining a deeper understanding of dynamic democratic processes. Political parties exist in nearly every democratic system of government; therefore knowledge about the conditions under which political parties affect electoral and policymaking outcomes is vitally important for understanding democracy itself.

Vital importance is one thing. Tangible progress is something else. And while methodological innovations for studying partisanship and preferences in Congress occur semiregularly, confident answers to vitally important questions are in short supply for two reasons. First, improvements are needed in developing, describing, and applying a general framework in which lawmaking is a piece of a larger, dynamic democratic process that includes not only other aspects of policymaking but also extragovernmental processes such as elections. Second, empirical methods for testing theories should be designed to test more than one theory at a time. The pitfalls of the opposite tendency—to test a single theory in isolation from competitors—are roughly proportional to the approximate observational equivalence of other theories that purport to explain the same things as the focal theory. For example, if only one theory is tested but that theory is nearly observationally equivalent to another, untested, but quite different theory, then less is learned than meets the eye. Illustrations will follow.

This essay addresses these two broad methodological shortcomings, albeit with a more specific substantive focus. First, I introduce and illustrate a general framework for the analysis of dynamic democratic processes. The framework is designed to accommodate micro-level models within a macropolitical context. Second, within the framework, I make a concerted attempt to test two theories of lawmaking simultaneously by highlighting the surprisingly rare instances in which the theories make different predictions.

MACROPOLITICS AND MICROBEHAVIOR

Along with many other studies in this book, this one views dynamic democratic processes as instances of macropolitics.[2] Clarification of terms is the first order of business. Macro democratic politics consists of a repeated sequence of governmental and electoral processes. Such processes are *dynamic* because they are repeated. Voters elect politicians at one period; politicians make policy in the next period; voters reelect or replace policymakers in the next election; and so on. The processes are *democratic* because participation rights are broadly dispersed within each phase. Popular sovereignty is characteristic of democratic elections, and parliamentary bodies in democracies allocate rights and resources broadly among their elected members. Finally, such processes take on societal significance at the *macro* level. Electoral and governmental processes and outcomes are regularly discussed and studied at a high level of aggregation. For example, postelection pundits write and discuss what *the* electorate said. Newspaper reporters and Beltway analysts write about the Congress and its intentions. Interest groups adopt strategies that respond to, and try to influence, decisions of *the* judiciary or of *an* executive agency or *the* majority party.

In politics, as in economics, it is natural and common to discuss events in an anthropomorphic fashion, focusing on the figurative big picture. Almost invariably, however, achieving a deep understanding of macropolitics requires a microfoundation—that is, a theory involving strategic interaction between an analytically tractable set of key, individual politicians. For example, it may be useful to know, as a purely descriptive matter, that unified governments are more productive than divided governments (or, perhaps, about equally productive).[3] However, a more satisfactory understanding of democratic processes is obtained when a microanalytic theory is articulated and corroborated that says *why* one form of government is (or isn't) more productive than the other. Likewise, it may be useful to know that the electorate at large is responsive to macroeconomic conditions in congressional elections.[4] However, a higher level of understanding of democratic processes is obtained when a microanalytic

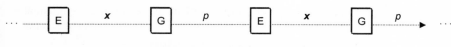

a. Macro Politics (Reduced form – preferences in / policy out)

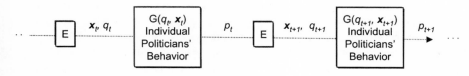

b. Micro foundation for the government phase

Key: E =   macro-level electoral model (unspecified)
          x =   elected officials' induced preferences
          q =   status quo policy
          $p = G(q,x)$ =   new policy

Figure 1.1: Dynamic Democratic Processes: Macro- and Micropolitics

theory is articulated and corroborated that says why individual voters respond to economic stimuli in the observed fashion.

In other words, macro-level and micro-level studies of politics are not competitors in substance or in method. They are complements in the best sense of the word. Micro-level analyses provide depth of understanding to macro-level observations. Macro-level frameworks clarify the system-level significance of micro-level theories.

Figure 1.1 summarizes the components of dynamic democratic processes in a manner conducive to reading and interpreting the various works throughout this book. At the top and highest level of aggregation, elections (E) and governments (G) simply repeatedly succeed one another. Each phase of political behavior is figuratively a black box: individuals reside and take actions within the boxes, but the theoretical analyst does not say much about individuals and the empirical analyst does not see or measure much individual-level behavior. So, for example, although it may well be the case that the descriptive accuracy of a macro-level claim approaches indisputability,[5] a deep understanding of central tendencies of, or variation in, these events is lacking in the absence of an explicit and somewhat disaggregated theory of elections or governments. Specifics about elections or governments, therefore, are essential ingredients in studying effectively the diverse set of phenomena called macropolitics.

Of course, no all-encompassing microanalytic theory of dynamic macropolitics exists, nor is such a theory likely to exist in the short-term future. Instead, we are at a phase in which any given theory of the electoral or governmental process is likely to have competing theories about approximately the same slice of the dynamic framework in figure 1.1. For instance, we have an increasingly rich and diverse set of theories of government, including theories of lawmaking, rule making, and any given pair of branches of strategic interaction: legislative-executive, executive-judicial, and legislative-judicial. All of these can be seen as versions of the preferences-in/policy-out structure, and many such theories are represented in this volume. Likewise, we have a multitude of theories of electoral competition that vary widely in terms of assumptions, results, and what they seek to explain. If presented in a dynamic context, the electoral counterpart to figure 1.1 would have a large $\bar{E}$ box in which parameters, such as voters' preferences, candidates' locations, and policies previously enacted by government, would be specified.

As knowledge accumulates in this necessarily piecemeal fashion, it becomes increasingly feasible and promising to ramp up selectively the level of micro-level specificity while studying dynamic democratic processes. Naturally, studies that focus on elections will tend to increase the specificity within the electoral phases, while depicting the governing phases in a relatively reduced form or black-box fashion (see, for example, Erickson, Mackuen, and Stimson 2002). Conversely, studies that focus on governing will be less concerned with the microfoundations of the electoral process than with the microfoundations of policymaking within the governmental apparatus (e.g., the remainder of this study). At one level, this is simply an instance of specialization. However, with the big picture of macropolitics in mind, successful efforts of specialization in a study of elections and government hold promise as an instance in which the whole might exceed the sum of the parts.

MICRO-LEVEL THEORIES OF LAWMAKING

Any of several theories could be chosen to fill in details within the black box of government decision-making in figure 1.1. Two such theories, however, are particularly useful for addressing the possible roles of parties in government. The Cox-McCubbins *cartel agenda model* has an explicit party component, while the Brady-Krehbiel-Volden *pivotal politics theory* does not.[6] Although this overview identifies several, seemingly major analytic differences, when all is said and done—including taking into account limitations in measurement— the two theories' directly testable implications are often identical. Fortunately, this is not always the case. Therefore, several necessarily indirect tests are developed that leverage off of these relatively subtle differences.

The pivot and cartel theories share many assumptions. They are noncooperative games with complete information. They are both one-period models of collective choice. Players are assumed to have Euclidean preferences over policies, where policies are represented as points on the real line, and the status quo point is given exogenously. If and when legislation receives consideration by the full chamber, legislators are not constrained by party affiliation or party pressures when they cast votes. In terms of macropolitics, the theories comport well with the representation in figure 1.1. Prior to government decision-making, a status quo policy and a set of politicians' preferences are given exogenously. Presumably the real-world counterparts are that any given period's exogenous status quo is an outgrowth of the previous period's policies as implemented, and, likewise, the current period's exogenous preferences are results from an immediately prior electoral process (in turn affected by the previous period's policies). Both theories, in other words, have core analytic properties that are perfectly consistent with the preferences-in/policy-out characteristic of democratic theory. Similarly but more abstractly, this property can be represented by a mapping G that takes a status quo q and a vector of preferences $x = \{x_1, \ldots, x_i, \ldots, x_n\}$ into a new policy p. For any given period t of lawmaking, then,

$$p_t = G(q_t, x_t). \tag{1}$$

The main difference in the implications of the theories can be traced both to players and to procedural assumptions. In terms of equation 1, the mapping $G()$ is different in cartel theory than in pivot theory because, as the level of analysis moves from macro to micro, different theories identify different individuals as key players, and (2) they make different assumptions about which players are able to take certain actions and at which time.

The Cartel Agenda Model

In the cartel model, the key player is the agenda setter, by whom is typically meant the majority party leader(s). The agenda setter has a monopoly over making proposals and, thus, has a unilateral right to kill legislation. The stages of the cartel game are simple. (1) The majority party leadership makes any proposal or decides not to make a proposal at all. (2) If and only if a proposal is made in stage 1, the House considers it under an open rule; otherwise, the game ends and the status quo remains in effect.

The equilibrium in the cartel game is analytically identical to that in Denzau and Mackay (1983) and Krehbiel (1985); simply substitute "leader" for "committee." In stage 1, the agenda setter exercises gatekeeping authority if and only if his utility from the status quo exceeds his utility from the policy equal to the median voter's ideal point. This is because the agenda setter knows that, under the open rule, the equilibrium response to any proposal is to amend the bill to the chamber median voter's ideal point. So, in stage 2, the median voter does nothing if gatekeeping was exercised, and selects his or her ideal point as the final policy otherwise.

The top panel of figure 1.2 graphs equilibrium outcomes as a function of the location of status quo points. Two characteristics of the equilibrium are noteworthy. First, the model exhibits convergent tendencies: whenever a bill is brought to the House, the House amends it, and a median voter outcome results. Second, for one noncentral interval of status quo points—specifically those between the floor median voter and the party leader's reflection point[7]—the exogenous status quo point is the outcome of the game. This is the functional equivalent of the pivot theory's gridlock interval. A majority of the chamber would like to change policy; however, given the procedural assumptions in the model, the majority is unable to do so.

The Pivotal Politics Theory

The pivotal politics theory differs substantially from cartel theory in terms of procedural assumptions; yet it yields a surprisingly similar set of predicted outcomes. Its essential institutional features are the presidential veto and the Senate's filibuster and cloture procedures. The sequence of moves is (1) the median voter makes a proposal; (2) the filibuster pivot decides whether to kill a bill or let it be amended; (3) the median voter selects a bill under an open rule; (4) the president decides whether or not to veto the bill; and, (5) if the president vetoes the bill, the pivot decides whether to sustain or override the veto.

Shown in the middle of figure 1.1, the equilibrium correspondence for the pivot theory exhibits median-convergent tendencies, too. It also has an interval—albeit a relatively centrally located one—in which the requisite supermajority cannot be obtained to break gridlock.

A potentially important difference between the pivot theory and the cartel theory is the notion of partial convergence. Specifically, in the pivot theory, there are instances of status quo points for which a coalition builder must make compromises to get even a diluted bill passed. Supermajoritarianism is the key to this need for a compromise. Specifically, in equilibrium, either a filibuster pivot (the forty-first senator on the side of the spectrum not occupied by the president) or the veto pivot (the thirty-fourth senator from the extreme point on the side that is occupied by the president) must be indifferent between the status quo and the proposed bill. For relatively moderate status quo points, this constraint will bind, and the policy, likewise, will not converge all the way to the median voter's ideal point.

Comparisons of Predictions

Although the pivot theory is arguably more solidly grounded in procedural realities than is the cartel theory,[8] for a wide range of status quo points, there is no observable difference between the theories. This fact is illustrated in the bottom panel of figure 1.2, which is a composition of the previous two panels.

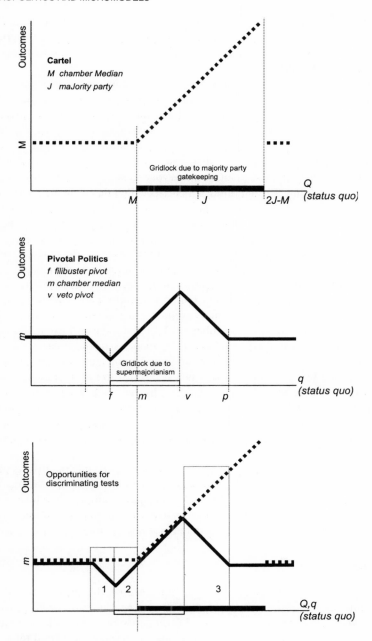

Figure 1.2: Summary of Theories

The three numbered windows represent opportunities to discriminate between the theories. Although, in total, their sills make up a sizable fraction of the horizontal axis, insufficient light shines through for making confident inferences about the theories.

Window 1 represents a situation in which, according to the cartel theory, the majority party will propose a new policy, will succeed, and will succeed in spite of the opposition of a majority of the minority party. Cartel theorists called this a minority party roll (or tomato). According to the pivotal politics theory, on the other hand, window 1 represents situations in which policy gravitates toward the chamber median voter, but does not quite arrive at that point, because the filibuster pivot, and everyone to her left, would successfully oppose such a policy. Pivotal politics theorists called this a situation of partial convergence (or tomahto). Analytically, the behavior is different in the two situations; it is partisan in the cartel theory and nonpartisan in the pivot theory. The outcomes, too, are slightly different. However, in the absence of precise techniques for measuring bill locations with the same metric as ideal points, the theories are, for all practical purposes, observationally equivalent.

Window 2 exhibits somewhat greater differences across theories than is the case in window 1. The cartel theory predicts minority party rolls once again. The pivot theory, in contrast, predicts gridlock via a filibuster, or, more realistically, a credible threat of a filibuster. Differences notwithstanding, it is again difficult to differentiate between the theories in these cases, because evaluators—given measurement limitations—cannot conclusively tell when the status quo lies in window 2, or when it lies just to the right or just to the left of the window. So if the cartel theorist observes what may be an instance of filibuster-induced gridlock, he may defensibly argue that the status quo was really at, or just to the right of, the median voter's ideal point. The real obstruction, in other words, came from the majority party. The cartel theorist's potato is the pivot theorist's potahto.

Window 3 represents the same song, third verse: plausible but divergent interpretations exist but cannot be adjudicated. Generally speaking, the inability to measure accurately bill locations and status quo locations—and to do so on the same scale as ideal points—is the single most important factor that undermines the ability to test the theories in the most transparent and direct manner.

Existing Tests

Existing tests further illustrate these problems. Among the most ambitious and forcefully argued of these is a study by Cox and McCubbins (1999) in which two kinds of evidence are presented: (1) comparisons of the relative frequencies of majority and minority party rolls,[9] and (2) predictions of roll rates as a function of preference distances, such as estimates of the House median voter's ideal point and House party leaders' ideal points. The authors' conclusions are strong and substantive.

The majority party's formal agenda powers allow it to, and are used to, keep issues off the floor agenda that would foreseeably displease significant portions of the party. This *negative agenda power is unconditional* in the sense that its exercise should not theoretically and does not empirically vary with the similarity of the party members' ideas of good public policy. (Cox and McCubbins 1999, 5)

We should note that key assumptions in the methods employed in this study are often unstated, and that the inferences drawn from data, while intuitive, rarely consider a baseline model against which the discovered tendencies can be compared. A specific example is that the central claim of unconditional agenda power rests mainly on the finding that the minority party gets rolled much more often than the majority party. The extent of asymmetry varies depending on the era and on what roll calls are filtered out, but one such ratio is approximately eight to one. The findings seem to fit the model and to justify the authors' inferences. The equation-like logic goes as follows:

Majority-party monopoly agenda-setting + partisan motivations

= asymmetric partisan roll rates.

The theme of partisanship is conspicuous, and the prediction of the theory is borne out. Nevertheless, it is worthwhile to explore alternative explanations. To make this point most striking, consider a theory that essentially negates the main components in the cartel model. Specifically, instead of assuming that the procedural deck is stacked in favor of the majority party, assume there is no agenda setting or gatekeeping whatsoever, and collective choice proceeds under a completely open rule. Instead of assuming that proposal (or nonproposal) making is motivated by partisanship, assume instead that partisanship plays no role in behavior whatsoever. How could such an intrinsically and completely nonpartisan theory—which many readers will recognize is Duncan Black's (1958) median voter theory—be consistent with asymmetric partisan roll rates?

The framework of dynamic democratic politics helps to answer this question. As shown in figure 1.3, the illustration begins with a uniform and unbiased distribution of status quo points at time 0. Without loss of generality, the majority party median initially resides on the left side of the median voter, while the minority party median resides on the right. In the first Congress all status quo points converge to the median voter's ideal point, as represented by the bar in the middle of the line at time 1. These equilibrium outcomes are then inherited as status quo points by the Congress at time 2. Suppose the intervening election causes a rightward shift in preferences and, consistent with the electoral tide, also sweeps the right party into power. Lawmaking in the second Congress has the feature that 100 percent of votes on final passage will not only move the status quo point from q_2 to M but will also constitute minority party rolls. Finally, suppose the next election causes a leftward shift in preferences and a return to majority status the party on the left. Again, with

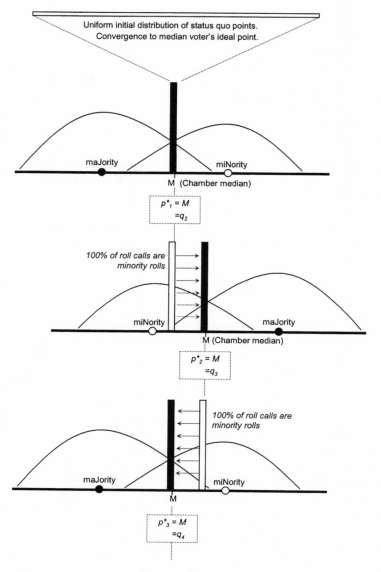

Figure 1.3: Asymmetry in Roll Rates in a Nonpartisan Model with No Agenda Setter

neither gatekeeping nor partisan behavior of any sort, the minority party roll rate will be 100 percent. Accordingly, in this example in which party control coincides with preference swings, the roll ratio exceeds the Cox-McCubbins eight-to-one ratio by a substantial margin: it is infinity.

Admittedly, the illustration is an overstatement of the degree to which non-partisan legislative behavior can manifest itself as what appears to be partisan-ship. For example, electoral tides do not always lead to changes in majority party status. In these cases, a swing away from the majority leads to majority party rolls and would reduce the ratio from the theoretical maximum of infin-ity. Nevertheless, the ability to produce party-asymmetric roll rates at all from a nonpartisan legislature serves to illustrate the need for, and importance of, having some explicit baseline model when interpreting data of this sort. Cox and McCubbins's inferences seem to stem from an implicit baseline expecta-tion of cross-party symmetry in roll rates, or a one-to-one ratio. Their ostensibly compelling evidence for substantive claims suddenly becomes questionable, however, upon searching for—and easily finding—another model that is a substantive opposite yet is nevertheless capable of generating similar expec-tations.[10] Needed, then, are tests that either are more explicit about baseline expectations, or that accommodate two or more theories, or both. Some illus-trations follow.

NEW TESTS

Inferred Status Quo Points

Many of the problems encountered in previous work stem from the unobserv-ability of the theoretical primitives used in theories of lawmaking. For exam-ple, preferences, ideal points, and bill locations in Euclidean space all play a major role in theories. Yet, they are all difficult to observe and measure, so the test that follows is necessarily indirect.[11] Likewise, it is well established that many micro-level theories of government are crucially dependent upon the lo-cation of status quo policy prior to the commencement of any given governing phase. Using the framework of dynamic democratic politics, however, it is possible to recast this problem in a way that salvages testability.

Figure 1.4 formalizes an alternative way of studying roll rates to test the cartel theory.[12] The horizontal axis represents the range of possible status quo points. By assumption of the cartel theory, the bill on which a vote on final passage is taken lies at point M, the chamber median voter's ideal point. The boundaries of the partition are reflection points of the respective party medi-ans voters, N (miNority) and J (maJority), with reference to the chamber me-dian, M. Their substantive significance is as follows. Take the boundary be-tween intervals A and B, namely $2N - M$. To the left of this critical point, a majority of both parties prefers the bill. To the right, and throughout interval B, a majority of the minority party prefers the status quo to the bill. Because the bill has chamber majority support, however, the minority will lose. Or, in the Cox-McCubbins terminology, the minority party gets rolled. The reasoning applies symmetrically on the majority side of the spectrum

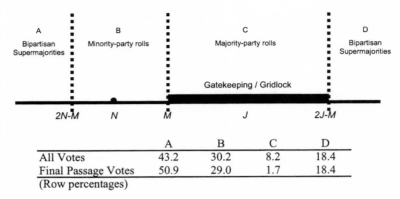

	A	B	C	D
All Votes	43.2	30.2	8.2	18.4
Final Passage Votes	50.9	29.0	1.7	18.4
(Row percentages)				

Figure 1.4: Rolls and Roll Calls in Cartel Theory as a Function of Inferred Status Quo Points

and with reference to the critical point, $2J - M$, on the boundary of intervals C and D.

Previous work has implicitly focused on moderate status quo points, defined here as those in intervals B and C. Within this framework, however, it is also possible—easy, indeed—to consider the substantive significance of status quo points that have the common feature of commanding majorities within both parties en route to the chamber median outcome. Such behavior is reasonably labeled "bipartisan" and is easy to identify empirically by the presence of chamber supermajorities composed of substantial support on both sides of the aisle.

With this indirect but explicit line of reasoning, it is possible to reassess the cartel theory by assuming that real-world legislators were in fact playing the cartel agenda-setting game, that the data we observe is therefore a by-product of that game, and that the coalitional structure on observed roll calls is informative with regard to where, in figure 1.4, the status quo must have been located. Then, not only are we well positioned to put the previous findings about comparative roll rates into perspective, but we are also able to see whether the distribution over all four intervals is consistent with the theoretical premise.

The data below the figure summarize roll calls for two sets of votes in the postwar era: all roll calls, and only roll calls on final passage votes. Cox and McCubbins draw their inferences from the relative frequencies represented as intervals B and C. Notice, however, that only 30 to 40 percent of congressional roll calls lie in these categories. Conversely, 60 to 70 percent of such roll calls are ones in which bipartisan supermajorities form. Could such a high percentage of bipartisan supermajorities have formed in a legislature dominated by majority party agenda control?

The answer is either "no," or, "possibly, under some unspecified assumptions."

The negative answer is supported by reasoning strictly from the assumptions of the model, most notably, complete information. In such a world, after one round of addressing policies for which the status quo lies outside the cartel-theoretic gridlock interval, the only remaining policies that the legislature might address are policies whose status quo points lie within the cartel-theoretic gridlock interval. Therefore, in the absence of exogenous changes in the parameters of the model, the strict prediction of the model is that, after one play of the game, nothing ever happens again. In light of this reasoning, the distribution at the bottom of figure 1.4 does not fit theoretical predictions at all. Nearly 6 or 7 out of 10 observed roll calls are suggestive of status quo points that lie well outside of the boundaries that can be consistently rationalized by a straightforward over-time application of the cartel theory.[13]

The answer, "possibly, under some unspecified assumptions," requires a supplementary model that allows for uncertainty to have a bearing on collective choice, while otherwise preserving the essential behavioral and institutional features of the theory. A sketch of such a model is provided next.

STEADY-STATE OUTCOMES IN MARKOV
MODELS OF GOVERNMENT

The central features of a Markov process are *states, transition probabilities,* and *steady state distributions.* In the context of the theories of lawmaking, a state is a spatial location of the status quo point, which, in turn can be interpreted as public policy in a given jurisdiction at any given time. Given n states (in this context, n intervals partitioning the status quo space), let S represent a probability distribution over those states, ordered low to high.[14]

Transition probabilities for a system with n states are represented by an $n \times n$ matrix P whose cell entries $p_{i,j}$ give the probability that, if the system is in state i at one time period, it will make the transition to state j in the next period. The substantive underpinning of the transition matrix is the theory that is being assessed. Indeed, the contents of the transition matrix P in the Markov framework are exactly the contents of the micro theory mapping $G(\cdot)$ in figure 1.1.

Because the cartel model and the pivot model are both complete information theories, it is reasonable to begin with these special cases. Under complete information, each element of the transition matrix P is either a zero or a one. Given the status quo point in any specific time t, the theories imply with certainty whether the status quo can and will be changed, and, if so, exactly how it will be changed, that is, what the new state will be.

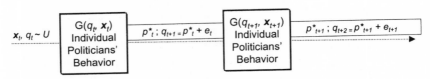

Figure 1.5: The Stochastic Model

Finally, a steady state distribution is a probability distribution over the set of states, S, that has the following property:

$$S \cdot P = S.$$

That is, if a system begins with a distribution over individual states with probabilities as given by the vector S, and then undergoes transitions between states, as specified by the transition probability matrix P, the result will be a return to the distribution of states with which the system began. A steady state distribution, then, has the property that, through the transition probability matrix, it maps into itself. An objective of the analysis of Markov chains is to ascertain if *steady state distributions* (or *limiting distributions*), as defined above, exist and are unique. If so, then empirical analysis can assess the degree to which the distribution of states, which are shown to be steady or stable, are approximated by the real-world frequency distribution of states.

A missing link in the analytic setup is the electoral phase. As described in the introduction, it would be both premature and complicated to test simultaneously micro-level theories of both the electoral and the governmental processes. We can, however, link the focal, governmental processes together with a reduced-form assumption that has either an electoral interpretation or an imperfect policy-implementation interpretation. This is done by postulating that, between stages of play of the games, a random shock to the system occurs.[15] Figure 1.5 provides a sketch of a general framework in which either of two kinds of randomness can be analyzed. First, we can model this situation as one in which a random shock is applied to the policy after the policy has been adopted. This captures the apparent fact that legislators often operate in an environment of uncertainty, so they cannot be sure that the policies they selected will have exactly their intended consequences. Alternatively, this shock can be interpreted as imperfect implementation of the legislative policy by the executive branch. Second, we can model this situation as one in which the randomness occurs outside the governmental arena. More specifically, the electoral process can be interpreted as a mechanism that determines the induced preferences of governmental actors. So, to the extent that there are electoral tides that affect everyone but are subject to commonly shared uncertainty, we can characterize these as between-period shocks that shift all ideal points of the government to the left or to the right. The question of which formulation of

	A	B	C*	D
No shock	0.0	0.0	100.0	0.0
Lo shock	0.0	22.2	66.7	11.1
Hi shock	16.0	20.0	40.0	24.0

	I	II	III*	IV	V
No shock	0.0	0.0	100.0	0.0	0.0
Lo shock	0.0	11.1	77.7	11.1	0.0
Hi shock	6.7	13.3	60.0	13.3	6.7

*Gridlock occurs in intervals C and III; subsequent calculations are rescaled accordingly.

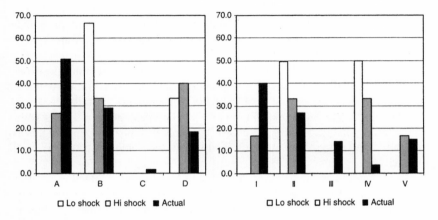

Figure 1.6: Steady States and Implied Distributions of Roll Calls in the Stochastic Model

randomness is most reasonable is addressed in the appendix, where the conclusion is, simply, that it doesn't matter analytically, because both formulations feed identically into the government function.

Application of the stochastic model begins by partitioning the range of possible status quo points into the minimum number of intervals required to capture qualitatively all possible forms of behavior within the model. In the cartel theory, then, for example, there are four such intervals (A–D). In the pivot theory, there are five (I–V). For each theory, three shock scenarios are studied. The first scenario—no shocks—is a complete information version of the models with no between-Congress changes. The second scenario—low shocks—assumes that between each Congress, the policies adopted during that Congress and the status quo points in the gridlock interval are perturbed by a uniformly distributed random variable $\varepsilon \in \{-1, 0, 1\}$, where a nonzero realization represents the direction, and number of intervals, to move the status quo. The third scenario—high shocks—simply expands the range of shocks to plus or minus 2, or uniform $\varepsilon \in \{-2, -1, 0, 1, 2\}$.

Under each of the three scenarios, both the pivot and the cartel theory have unique steady-state distributions. These are summarized in figure 1.6. Once again, it is apparent that the two theories have a lot in common. Convergent tendencies are strong when the exogenous shocks are nonexistent or small. However, convergence is asymmetric in the cartel model but not in the pivot model. Conversely, as the exogenous shocks grow, both theories predict that more legislative activity will occur. The reason is that exogenous shocks of either of the two forms discussed above create out-of-equilibrium status quo points that are ripe for change.

Table 1.1 compares the steady state distributions for the cartel theory under the three shock scenarios with actual data from the House. Columns A–D denote intervals as in the earlier discussion.

Consider first the leftmost four columns of results. If there are no exogenous shocks to the status quo, the limiting distribution has the property that all status quo points are instances of gridlock. Consequently, no bills are considered under these conditions, and the predicted percentage of roll calls within the types is a flat zero across the board. The large discrepancy between this expectation and congressional data was, after all, the impetus for the stochastic model.

In the middle set of columns, a relatively small range of stochastic shocks spreads out status quo points somewhat. An important feature of the equilibrium here, as well as with large shocks (see below), is asymmetry. Specifically, while the random variable is symmetric, its consequences are not, due to the assumption in the model that gatekeepers exist on one side of the aisle but not on the other side. Therefore, a rough expectation of the cartel theory is that there will be more minority party rolls (interval B situations) than bipartisan supermajority coalitions (interval A or D situations).[16]

Among the most revealing findings is that, in spite of the claims based on asymmetric party roll rates, the actual percentage of minority rolls in each of two samples—all votes, and only votes on final passage—is *less* than predicted by a factor of two. That is, the actual level of asymmetry in roll rates is well below what the theory predicts.

Of course, the previous paragraph refers to a small-shock world. Perhaps this is a reasonable assumption, perhaps not. In any case, results are also given for regimes in which interelection forces may cause very large shocks in the status quo. Again, the findings are revealing. The asymmetry mentioned above persists, but a noteworthy change is that now the cartel theory predicts the proportion of minority party rolls almost perfectly. The overall rate of errors in this scenario is less than half of that in the previous two scenarios. So, the tentative conclusion from this application is that the large-shocks scenario produces a steady state distribution that closely approximates the empirical distribution in the postwar period.

Although the Markov framework is useful as an illustration of embedding a micro-level single-period theory into a macro-level framework of dynamic democratic politics, its full potential is not reached here. At present, there is no

TABLE 1.1 Predicted and Inferred Locations of the Status Quo, Cartel Theory

	No Shocks				Low Shock				High Shock			
	A	B	Cᵃ	D	A	B	Cᵃ	D	A	B	Cᵃ	D
Steady state distribution	0.00	0.00	1.00	0.00	0.00	0.22	0.67	0.11	0.16	0.20	0.40	0.24
Predicted percentage	0	0	0	0	0	68	0	33	27	33	0	40
Actual percentage												
All votes	43	30	8	18	43	30	8	18	43	30	8	18
Final passage votes	51	29	2	18	51	29	2	18	51	29	2	18
Errors (actual − predicted)												
All votes	43	30	8	18	43	−38	8	−15	17	−3	8	−22
Final passage votes	51	29	2	18	51	−39	2	−15	24	−4	2	−22
Sum of absolute errors												
All votes	100				104				49			
Final passage votes	100				106				52			

ᵃ Interval C predicted percentage is 0 because of gatekeeping. Other percentages are recalculated accordingly.

straightforward way of making comparative statements about the relative fits of two or more micro-level theories with regard to the distribution of status quo points. For a true, comparative-theoretical test, another approach is needed.

REGIME CHANGES AND PARTY ROLLS

A final test assesses whether changes in party control of government are associated with parties' propensities to win or lose legislative battles. This analysis is somewhat more demanding on the theories than the previous analysis, because now we focus on variance as opposed to central tendencies or so-called stylized facts.

Measures and hypotheses. For the cartel theory, the dummy variable, New Cartel, takes on a value of 1 if and only if the majority regime in the House changed in the recent election. Recall from the theory section that the consequence of such a switching regime is that many policies had been bottled up by majority party leaders acting as gatekeepers. After the election, in contrast, with a new majority party and its agenda-setting power, the floodgates will open, and a deluge of new legislative activity will transform the erstwhile stable-via-gatekeeping status quo points into new policies. In so doing, the new minority party (and erstwhile gatekeepers) will not be able to stop the initiatives, and therefore will get "rolled" with heightened regularly. All such situations are shown in Figure 1.7, which can be read as described in the key.

For the pivot theory, the dummy variable, New Pivot, takes on a value of 1 if and only if the party of the president changed in the most recent presidential election. If so, the analytic consequence is that the gridlock interval flips. The point v, the veto pivot, follows the president to the other side of the median voter, while the more moderate filibuster pivot, point f, is left behind to act as a new, more moderating, constraint on the other side of the spectrum. The anticipated magnitude of this change is quite small relative to, say, that expected in the cartel theory. In the cartel theory, the relevant pivotal player is the majority party's median voter. Suppose that the distribution of ideal points on a relevant policy dimension is uniform. Then a cartel-theoretic change in majority party control is represented analytically by a change in the agenda setter's ideal point by as much as 50 units. In contrast, the gridlock interval in the pivot theory shifts towards the new president by only 7 points—from the thirty-fourth percentile to the forty-first percentile (the positions of the old veto pivot and new filibuster pivot, respectively).

Taken together, these theoretical observations imply the following testable hypotheses.

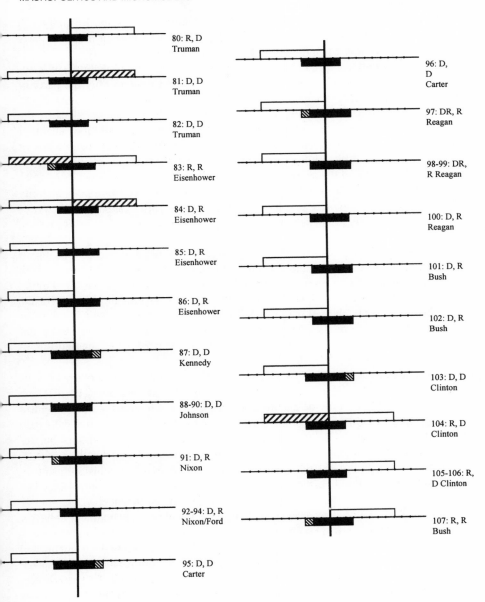

80: R, D
Truman

81: D, D
Truman

82: D, D
Truman

83: R, R
Eisenhower

84: D, R
Eisenhower

85: D, R
Eisenhower

86: D, R
Eisenhower

87: D, D
Kennedy

88-90: D, D
Johnson

91: D, R
Nixon

92-94: D, R
Nixon/Ford

95: D, D
Carter

96: D,
D
Carter

97: DR, R
Reagan

98-99: DR,
R Reagan

100: D, R
Reagan

101: D, R
Bush

102: D, R
Bush

103: D, D
Clinton

104: R, D
Clinton

105-106: R,
D Clinton

107: R, R
Bush

Figure 1.7: Postwar Regime Changes. Striped intervals denote inherited status quo points that are out of equilibrium and thus ripe for new legislation. Bars above the axis are for the cartel theory; below for the pivot theory. Labels at the right refer to Congress, majority party in Congress, and President. If Congress is split, the House's party is listed first.

- Hypothesis 1 (cartel theory). The probability of a minority party roll should be greater in the first Congress after a change in majority party control than when the election reinstates the former majority.
- Hypothesis 2 (pivot theory). Other things equal, the probability of a minority party roll should be greater in the first Congress after the party of the president changes to match that of the Congress than at other times. Note: Cartel theory predicts no increment in these situations because the majority party has not changed; it blocked before and will block again.
- Hypothesis 3 (relative effects). Because of the different magnitudes of changes in the gridlock intervals for the two theories, the estimated effect for the cartel theory should be greater than for the pivot theory.
- Hypothesis 4 (pivot theory). Other things equal, the probability of a majority party roll should be greater in the first Congress after the party of the president changes to match the minority party in Congress than at other times.[17]

Findings. Table 1.2 presents probit estimates for three nested sets of data.[18] The House of Representatives generated 16,711 roll call votes from the 50th through the 104th Congresses, and the first set of analysis includes all of these. The second set of analysis confines attention to over four thousand roll calls that were votes on final passage. The third set further pares down the number of observations by estimating the models only on votes on final passage *and* that were not bipartisan—that is, a majority of one party voted the opposite of a majority of the other party.

The first dataset is not at all selective. Many of these roll calls are on matters whose significance to national policy is, at best, obscure. The first two rows of table 1.2 provide encouragement for the cartel model. As party control changes in the House, the minority party is more likely to lose roll calls than after a regime-maintaining election. In contrast, the pivot model does not account for variation in roll calls as a whole. The coefficient for the variable, New Pivot, in the second equation has the wrong sign and is insignificant. In light of these findings, the third equation—or joint test—is not surprising. The cartel-theoretic effect stands alone in its statistical significance.

Understanding the consequences of amendments and amendment behavior for the nature of, and coalitional support for, final bills is not straightforward. To know this relationship just at the theoretical level requires stringent, and many would say implausible, assumptions about the proposal process, its exogeneity, the information that legislators have about one another's preferences, and their computational abilities (possibly with an "as-if" qualifier). For these reasons, and in light of the related empirical realities, skeptics are likely to be more interested in findings based on a subset of roll calls in which the strategic situations are much clearer. Roll calls on votes on final passage have this property, and there were 4,303 such roll calls during the 50-year period from 1947 to 1996, the 80th to 104th Congresses.[19] The estimates in the middle of

TABLE 1.2 Minority Losses as a Function of Regime Change

Regime	Coefficient	Standard Error	z	p > |z|	N
All motions					
New Cartel	0.155	0.034	4.55	0.000	16,711
Constant	−0.819	0.012	−70.48	0.000	
New Pivot	−0.018	0.028	−0.64	0.524	
Constant	−0.798	0.012	−66.15	0.000	
New Cartel	0.154	0.034	4.51	0.000	
New Pivot	−0.006	0.028	−0.20	0.844	
Constant	−0.818	0.013	−63.50	0.000	
Motions on final passage					
New Cartel	0.195	0.073	2.68	0.007	4,303
Constant	−0.580	0.021	−27.40	0.000	
New Pivot	0.186	0.057	3.25	0.001	
Constant	−0.591	0.022	−26.94	0.000	
New Cartel	0.196	0.073	2.70	0.007	
New Pivot	0.187	0.057	3.27	0.001	
Constant	−0.608	0.023	−26.61	0.000	
Final passage with party opposition					
New Cartel	0.287	0.227	1.26	0.206	1,306
Constant	1.561	0.058	26.81	0.000	
New Pivot	0.448	0.197	2.28	0.023	
Constant	1.531	0.059	25.81	0.000	
New Cartel	0.327	0.229	1.43	0.153	
New Pivot	0.467	0.198	2.36	0.018	
Constant	1.503	0.062	24.40	0.000	

table 1.2 are more balanced in terms of our focal theories than were the esti-mates for all roll calls. Now both regime dummy variables produce significant coefficients of essentially the same magnitude. Interestingly, the regime-change dummy variables are not strongly correlated with one another, so when the joint test is conducted in equation 3 within the middle set, the coefficients are unchanged until the third decimal place. The results—at least if viewed in isolation—suggest that a hybrid theory might be promising.

Before coming to this conclusion, however, it is useful to examine a still smaller set of votes: namely, those that exclude so-called hurrah votes on which, by definition, large, *bipartisan majorities* form. The substantive reason for such exclusion, again, is that many of the roll calls in the analysis thus far—including votes on final passage—focus on measures such as the naming of public buildings, commemoratives, designation of Day, Week, or Month as National This That and The Other, and so on. Accordingly, the bottom third of table 1.2 considers only bills and votes on the final passage and for which majorities of the two parties revealed preferences in opposition with one another. This sample is likely to include the most contentious bills in the historical period, and it is likely to include the more significant bills relative to the other, larger samples too.

The results based on the most discriminating roll call filter bring us to a conclusion much different from that drawn when all motions were considered. First, the coefficient that is essential for a cartel-consistent account of the data is no longer significant, although its magnitude has increased. The coefficient for the pivot variable, however, continues to grow as the set of roll calls shrinks to the most contentious and, presumably, important bills. Although it is statistically significant, the value of .448, has a small substantive effect (.04) because the baseline is very high—.937 to be exact. With a high baseline probability that the minority party will get rolled, there is little room for an additional boost. The effect is, however, statistically significant ($p = .023$).

This analysis in table 1.2 overall is somewhat encouraging for the method in terms of its ability to discriminate between two difficult-to-test theories. Specifically, the findings include qualified support for hypothesis 1 (cartel) that tapers off as the sample becomes more selective; somewhat stronger support for hypothesis 2 (pivot); and little support for hypothesis 3 (implied by the theories jointly). One key stone remains unturned, however: the phenomenon of majority party losses. Recall from the theoretical overview that, according to the cartel theory, a majority party never loses in equilibrium. The reason is that party leaders can identify situations in which noncentral outcomes favor the party, and they can prevent proposals about such policies from reaching the floor for consideration by the House. Recall, also, that, although majority party rolls are rare relative to the other types of roll calls identified, they nevertheless occur. Can the pivot theory also account for some of the cross-Congress variation in such losses?

Table 1.3 suggests that it can. As in the case of minority party losses, here, too, the pivot theory does not perform particularly well when the universe of roll calls is considered. The small but somewhat significant coefficient in the first set of estimates, however, almost quadruples when the analysis is confined to votes on final passage. Furthermore, and consistent with the analysis of minority party losses, the pivot-theoretic variable is most powerful when putative partisanship is most pronounced. Specifically, in the third equation estimated, the coefficient of 0.877 indicates that majority party rolls are about 4.5 times more likely not to occur after a change in the party of the president to a regime of divided government.[20] As shown in figure 1.8 for the 91st and 97th Congresses, when the party of the president changes and the congressional majority remains constant and of the opposite party, the essential ingre-

TABLE 1.3 Majority Losses as a Function of Pivot Regime Changes

Regime	Coefficient	Standard Error	z	p > |z|	N
All motions					
New Pivot	0.131	0.056	2.36	0.018	16,711
Constant	−1.588	0.016	−96.97	0.000	
Motions on final passage					
New Pivot	0.488	0.121	4.03	0.000	4,303
Constant	−2.187	0.052	−41.88	0.000	
Final passage with party opposition					
New Pivot	0.877	0.165	5.33	0.000	1,306
Constant	−1.686	0.062	−27.10	0.000	

dient for the critical test between cartel theory and pivot theory exists. Pivot theory predicts that the change in constraining pivotal voters from unified government's veto pivot to the divided government's filibuster pivot liberates a sliver of formerly gridlocked status quo points for change in the new divided government administration. In cartel theory, however, gridlock is predicted to prevail, because, in spite of the desire of a congressional supermajority for policy change, the so-called Legislative Leviathan unconditionally will not tolerate such change.

Although this most discriminating finding is tentative and perhaps fragile, it seems worth stressing that there are more than a few reasons to have regarded it is unlikely a priori.

First, in addition to running contrary to the expectation given by the cartel theory, hypothesis 4 also runs contrary to conventional wisdom, or "the Beltway theory of divided government," by which I mean the widely held notion among pundits that divided government causes gridlock. This finding suggests that when party control in the White House changes and results in a mismatch between Congress and president, it is more likely than under normal circumstances for the majority party in Congress to get rolled. It is neither less likely, as the Beltway notion of "Congress digging in its heels" loosely suggests, nor impossible as the cartel theory tightly implies. Second, it is surprising that this marginal effect was detectable in the dataset, given that the filters applied at this stage of the analysis are crass, and given that there were only two Congresses in time series for which this key, discriminating condition was met. Third, in spatial terms, recall that when the condition is met, it is, in some sense, just barely met: all that changes in terms of pivots is the constraining member on the majority party side of the aisle switches from the thirty-fourth percentile member to the forty-first. At best, the window of opportunity for picking up the discovered effect is small. On balance, then, the finding might be regarded as unlikely support for the pivotal politics theory.

Finally, and more central to the broader, methodological, thrust of this chapter, the finding, however interpreted, serves as an illustration that, even when two theories seem to be observationally equivalent, it is, nevertheless, sometimes possible to derive analytically, and to test empirically, hypotheses that discriminate.

DISCUSSION

In their recent study, Cox and McCubbins begin with their well-known thesis about majority party power, improve upon it with an explicit formal model, and subject the model to some novel empirical tests. Apropos of Legislative Leviathan, their findings—most notably, a large ratio of minority to majority rolls—seem gigantic. Whether they warrant the inference that majority party agenda-setting power is "unconditional," however, is questionable for several reasons this chapter has attempted to clarify and address. The general research strategy has been to consider otherwise difficult-to-test hypotheses from simple static theories by embedding those theories in a macropolitical framework. In addition to this primary, methodological illustration, the chapter lends itself to a few secondary, and necessarily tentative, substantive conclusions.

First, when modeling Congresses over time as a sequence of cartel-theoretic static games with intervening electoral or policy shocks, the finding is that the cartel theory performs poorly in high-certainty environments, but does much better as the variance of shocks increases. In the highest uncertainty environment, the cartel theoretic prediction of minority party rolls is quite accurate.

Second, the cartel theory also exhibits a modest capacity to explain variation in minority party rolls. This explanatory ability, however, exists only in a dataset that is undiscriminating in its inclusion of roll call votes. When roll calls are filtered, and votes are limited to those on final passage and votes that are contentious as measured by interparty opposition, a change in the regime of party control ceases to have a predictable effect on the fortunes of the majority and failures of the minority.

Third, the theory of pivotal politics has roughly the opposite characteristics. The pivot theory does not help to account for variation in minority roll rates over all unfiltered roll calls. In the case of final passage votes, and especially votes that elicited interparty competition, however, pivot-defined regime changes have statistically significant predictive power for both minority and majority rolls.

Among the limitations of the analysis, the one that most needs to be highlighted is that—yet again—roll call voting data have been the primary bases for inference. Researchers seem to be chronically dependent upon roll calls and have become comfortably numb when methodological assumptions are incomplete, unstated, or inconsistent with the theories the methods purport to test. So, in spite of some recent improvements in these regards (e.g., Snyder and Groseclose 2000; McCarty, Poole, and Rosenthal 2001), we are paradoxically cursed with riches. In addition to the wealth of theories, we also have a wealth of room for improvement in testing theories. The method of embedding micro-level theories into macro-level frameworks of dynamic democratic politics is one promising avenue for improvement that this chapter—and many other chapters in this volume—begins to develop and employ.

APPENDIX : AN EQUIVALENCE RESULT ON TYPES OF RANDOM SHOCKS

Although the distinction between policy-implementation shocks and electoral-process shocks seems to be important, when each random process is formalized in the most transparent way, the distinction is not important. Identical assumptions about the distribution of the random variable in the policy-shock formulation and the analogous distribution of the random variable in the electoral-shock formulation are such that observable behavior after exogenous shocks is identical.

Figure 1.A1 illustrates the two stochastic processes. At the top of each panel is an arbitrary but identical starting point that shows the exogenous status quo q as a shaded triangle, a set of ideal points x^i shown as circles, and with one such ideal point x^v signifying the pivotal voter, given the configuration of ideal points and the location of the status quo. (It is not necessary to stipulate who this voter is; all that is required is for the theory in question to have such an identifiable voter. Clearly, this condition holds for the pivot model and for the

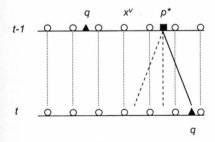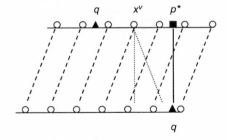

Model A: between-period shocks   Model B: between-period shocks
to the last-passed policy   to preferences of legislators

Figure 1.A1: Observational Equivalence of Stochastic Shocks

cartel model.) Finally, each of the $t - 1$ scenarios generates an equilibrium outcome p^*.

How do the random components of the two models affect the parameters that will define the policymaking stage at time t? In the left panel, representing the policy-shock process, the value of the random variable is applied to the equilibrium policy p^*, which has the effect of moving the status quo q_t one unit to the left or to the right or not at all, depending upon the random draw. Without loss of generality, suppose the random draw is +1. The consequence is that the new status quo is farther to the right, as shown. From the preferences as drawn in the bottom part of the left panel, we can then consult the theory under consideration, identify the pivotal voter in this situation, and proceed.

In the right panel, the shock is applied to all ideal points x_{t-1}^i rather than to the policy chosen, namely p_{t-1}^*. Again, assume that the random draw is +1. Because the functional form as specified negates the draw, all ideal points are shifted to the left, as shown by the dashed lines. The consequence is that the parametric setup in the right panel at time t is identical to that in the left panel, with the exception that, were there numbers applied to the axes, the two scenarios would differ from one another by one unit. This, however, is inconsequential for the decision making that will occur at time t. The proposition shows that the example generalizes.

Proposition 1. *For any arbitrarily selected starting conditions at period t, defined by a status quo q_t and a set of preferences p_t^i, the behavior in the next period $t + 1$ is equivalent under the different intermediate random processes A and B.*

Proof. Observational equivalence of behavior requires that the relative positions between ideal points and the status quo are the same in model A and model B. This is fully stated in an n-tuple of deviations between players' ideal points and the status quo. Formally, $d_t^i = p_t^i - q_t$. We show that, when expressed in terms of parameters at $t - 1$ when the scenarios in A and B are assumed to be identical, and then by applying separately the different random processes, the expression for d_i for period t is identical in models A and B. To make the random processes comparable across models, let $\mu = \epsilon = \pi$ and note that the substitutions that occur below are simply the respective random processes described above.

$$\text{For model A:} \quad d_t^i = p_t^i - q_t$$
$$= p_t^i - (x_{t-1}^* + \mu)$$
$$= p_t^i - x_{t-1}^* - \mu$$

$$\text{For model B:} \quad d_t^i = p_t^i - q_t$$
$$= (p_t^i - \mu) - x_{t-1}^*$$
$$= p_t^i - x_{t-1}^* - \mu$$

NOTES

I am grateful to participants in seminars at the Princeton's Center for the Study of Democratic Politics, at Stanford's Graduate School of Business, and at the University of Colorado's conference "The Macropolitics of Congress." Additional helpful comments were provided by Scott Adler, Jonathan Bendor, Alan Gerber, Nolan McCarty, Adam Meirowitz, and Alan Wiseman.

1. See, for example, Krehbiel 1999b; Snyder and Groseclose 2000; and McCarty, Poole, and Rosenthal 2001.

2. Indeed, they are almost synonymous. The hairs possibly worth splitting are that (1) some—but not many—dynamic political processes are not democratic but nevertheless may qualify as macropolitics; and (2) as argued subsequently, studies of dynamic democratic processes benefit from micro-level as well as macro-level analyses.

3. See, for example, Heitshusen and Young in this book.

4. For more on the so-called sociotropic voting hypothesis, see Kinder and Kiewiet 1981.

5. An example of such a claim—at least up until 1998—is midterm election losses of the president's party.

6. See any of an impressively long list of works by Gary Cox and Matthew McCubbins, beginning with *Legislative Leviathan* in 1993, for the origins and development of the cartel model. See Krehbiel 1996, 1998 and Brady and Volden 1998 for overviews and tests of the theory of pivotal politics.

7. A reflection point for a given player and a given policy or proposal p is defined as the point y such that the utility of the player for y equals his utility for p.

8. The key procedures in pivot theory are the president's veto power (granted in the Constitution) and the Senate's rule XXII (codified in Senate rules for nearly a century now). The key procedure in the cartel theory is gatekeeping power, which, strictly speaking, is nullified by the House's discharge procedure (also codified for nearly a century).

9. Party A is said to be rolled by party B if a majority of party A forms a common position on the vote, a majority of party B forms a common position on the vote that is opposite that of party A, and the outcome of the vote is that position which is favored by party B.

10. The pivotal politics theory also predicts asymmetric roll rates when embedded in an electoral setting.

11. See Kramer 1986 on the necessity of indirect tests.

12. For reasons to be noted, this method is less amenable to pivot-theoretic tests in a way that obtains comparability with the cartel theory.

13. A similar but less severe problem is noted in *Pivotal Politics* (Krehbiel 1998), although it is derived by reasoning about observed coalition sizes rather than party

composition. Specifically, sizes of winning coalitions are systematically greater than the pivot theory predicts. This suggests—like the cartel theory—that many status quo points at any given time have figuratively migrated out of the theory's gridlock interval. The proposed response with this problem is the same as that subsequently proposed for the cartel theoretical equivalent.

14. For purposes of simplicity, accessibility, and analytic tractability, I consider only discrete cases of the theories in question. Little is lost in making this simplification, because the status quo/state space is partitioned sufficiently finely so that each state represents a unique type of behavior, relative to neighboring states.

15. Cox and McCubbins take a similar approach. However, the several important details are lacking.

16. The reason the predicted percentage shows two-thirds of the probability mass in interval B is that interval C status quo points do not generate observations and are thus taken out of the denominator for other probability calculations.

17. The cartel theory predicts that majority party rolls are constant and zero, i.e., nonexistent.

18. Difference in means tests would suffice; however, I am opting for probit estimates because of plans to add control variables and other covariates in future work.

19. I can approximate but not replicate Cox and McCubbins's summary table. The reason for discrepancies almost surely lies either in slightly different definitions of what constitutes final passage, or the well-known fact that ICPSR files are buggy and ICPSR codebooks are abysmal.

20. $\Phi(\hat{a}) = 0.046$. $\Phi(\hat{a} + \hat{\beta}) = 0.209$.

REFERENCES

Black, Duncan. 1958. *The Theory of Committees and Elections.* London: Cambridge University Press.

Brady, David W., and Craig Volden. 1998. *Revolving Gridlock.* New York: Westview Press.

Cox, Gary W., and Mathew D. McCubbins. 1993. *Legislative Leviathan: Party Government in the House.* Berkeley and Los Angeles: University of California Press.

———. 1999. "Agenda Power in the U.S. House of Representatives." University of California, San Diego Typescript.

Denzau, Arthur T., and Robert J. Mackay. 1983. "Gatekeeping and Monopoly Power of Committees: An Analysis of Sincere and Sophisticated Behavior." *American Journal of Political Science* 27:740–61.

Kinder, Donald R., and D. Roderick Kiewiet. 1981. "Sociotropic Politics: The American Case." *British Journal of Political* Science 11:129–61.

Kramer, Gerald H. 1986. "Political Science as Science." *In Political Science: The Science of Politics,* ed. Herbert Weisberg. New York: Agathon Press.

Krehbiel, Keith. 1985. "Obstruction and Representativeness in Legislatures." *American Journal of Political Science* 29:643–59.

———. 1996. "Institutional and Partisan Sources of Gridlock: A Theory of Divided and Unified Government." *Journal of Theoretical Politics* 8:7–40.

————. 1998. *Pivotal Politics: A Theory of U.S. Lawmaking.* Chicago: University of Chicago Press.

———— 1999b. "The Party Effect from A to Z and Beyond." *Journal of Politics* 61:832–40.

McCarty, Nolan, Keith T. Poole, and Howard Rosenthal. 2001. "The Hunt for Party Discipline in Congress." *American Political Science Review* 95:673–87.

Snyder, James M., and Timothy Groseclose. 2000. "Party Influence and Congressional Roll-Call Voting." *American Journal of Political Science* 44:193–211.

2

Bureaucratic Capacity
and Legislative Performance

John D. Huber and Nolan McCarty

Ironically, most studies of the macro performance of Congress are rather micro in their orientation. Existing work focuses almost exclusively on how the distribution of political preferences across parties and branches affects the output of "significant" legislation. It has not focused on longer-term institutional changes that increase or decrease the capacity or willingness of Congress to perform its legislative functions.

If one seeks only to explain the post–World War II time series of legislative enactments, a focus on divided government (Mayhew 1991; et al. 2000), the gridlock interval (Krehbiel 1998), or bicameral polarization (Binder 1999) may be appropriate. However, it is doubtful that party or preference-based approaches can go very far in explaining longer-term national trends in legislative productivity.[1] In the language of time-series econometrics, divided government, gridlock intervals, and bicameral preference differences are roughly stationary, while the amount of legislative activity experienced explosive growth during the first part of the twentieth century (Heitshusen and Young, this volume; Lapinski 2000). It is clear that explaining such a dramatic increase in activity requires a theory of legislative decision-making that incorporates variables that plausibly move in tandem with the series on legislative productivity.

The dominant theoretical approach also seems ill-equipped to explain other important aspects of legislative productivity in American politics. There are vast differences across the American states, for example, in the activism of legislatures. There are even differences at a given point in time in which federal departments or agencies are more or less likely to be affected by new laws.

This chapter develops a model of legislative productivity that we hope can address some of these limitations in the literature. Our goal is to incorporate insights from existing theories of legislative-executive preference conflict into a model that looks explicitly at important nonlegislative aspects of the policymaking process. With the exception of Huber and Shipan (2002), to the extent that existing models of law production analyze nonlegislative actors in the law production process, they typically examine only legislative functions of such actors (such as a presidential veto or the striking down of a law by courts). Nonlegislative policymaking, however, is a central feature of politics and should be incorporated into the study of macro policymaking. Courts, presidential rule-making, legislative oversight, and, perhaps most importantly, bureaucrats have considerable impact on policy outcomes after laws are adopted. We argue that legislative actors will anticipate the impact of such nonlegislative policymaking on policy outcomes, and will incorporate these expectations into their decisions to adopt any new laws.

Bureaucratic actors, of course, typically play the most significant role in turning laws into policy outcomes, and our analysis examines how the practical necessity of delegating implementation responsibilities to bureaucrats affects incentives to adopt new legislation in the first place. There has, of course, been considerable previous work on how legislation is designed to address problems of bureaucratic control, delegation, and implementation (e.g., Banks 1989; Bawn 1995; McCubbins, Noll, and Weingast 1989; Huber and Shipan 2002; Epstein and O'Halloran 1999; and Volden 2002). This work, however, typically focuses on *how* to delegate authority, rather than whether to adopt a new item of legislation in the first place.

The model we develop examines several aspects of nonlegislative policymaking and their impact on legislation, but the central focus is on "bureaucratic capacity." Most existing models assume that bureaucrats can choose effectively the outcomes they most prefer, subject to constraints in legislation or elsewhere in the political environment. We assume that bureaucratic capacity—which we define as the likelihood that bureaucrats can take actions that yield their intended outcomes—varies. Our goal in making this assumption is to analyze a phenomenon that seems central in empirical accounts of bureaucratic politics in the United States. Scholars often argue, for example, that the competence of bureaucrats varies over time in the United States, with reforms such as the Civil Service Reform Act of 1883 and subsequent executive orders leading to increased professionalism in the bureaucracy. They also argue bureaucratic capacity can vary across departments at a given point in time (e.g., Carpenter 2001), and across the American states (e.g., Barrilleaux 1992). We want to understand how variation in bureaucratic capacity affects decisions to adopt new legislation.

Our model therefore examines a phenomenon that is emphasized by Carpenter (2001). His historical study of the Departments of Agriculture, Interior, and the Post Office pays a great deal of attention to how capacity within the bureaucracy affects policy change. But the connection he draws between bureaucratic capacity and policy change is largely nonlegislative. He argues that agencies with reputations for competence have significantly more leeway to innovate and develop new programs *without* explicit legislative approval. By contrast, our analysis examines how bureaucratic capacity influences the *adoption of new legislation*, and we do so within a game-theoretic model that treats institutional features of the nonlegislative environments as variables that influence strategic interaction.

To explore the relationship between bureaucratic capacity and what Adler and Lapinski refer to as legislative performance, we develop a game-theoretic model of legislative delegation of policymaking authority to an administrative agency with varying capacities to implement particular policies. Our model is related to Huber and Shipan (2002), which examines how the broad institutional context affects delegation, and it builds directly on Huber and McCarty (2004), which focuses on how bureaucratic capacity affects delegation and the incentives for political reform.

We emphasize two pathways by which bureaucratic capacity affects the adoption of new legislation. On one hand, there is a straightforward "efficiency loss." If bureaucrats are bad at what they do, the value of adopting new programs will decline, increasing gridlock. On the other hand, there is a less obvious "compliance" effect. If bureaucratic capacity is relatively low, it will be more difficult for bureaucrats to comply with legislative statutes, decreasing their incentives to do so. This forces legislative actors to grant bureaucrats *more* autonomy in the laws that they adopt, decreasing the value of adopting new laws, and thereby increasing gridlock. Thus, as bureaucratic capacity declines, the legislature and executive will be less able to achieve mutually beneficial gains from adopting new legislation.

In what follows, we describe our game-theoretic model. We then use this model to describe our argument about how bureaucratic capacity (and several other variables) can influence law production. While an empirical test of the model is beyond the scope of this chapter, we also develop a number of empirical implications for the study of the macropolitics of Congress, and American politics more generally.

THE MODEL

There are three players in our model: a Legislature (with ideal point $x_L = 0$) that proposes legislation; a President (with ideal point $x_P \geq 0$) who can veto policy proposals; and a Bureaucrat (with ideal point $x_B \in \mathbb{R}^1$) who takes actions to implement policy. The players interact to determine a policy outcome in a single-dimensional policy space. Each of the players has quadratic utility functions over policy outcomes.

Of central interest in our analysis is the impact of bureaucratic capacity on the ability of the Legislature and President to agree on policy change. In our model, bureaucratic capacity is the ability of the Bureaucrat to execute the action he intends. Formally, if the Bureaucrat attempts action a, then the outcome of this action is $a - \omega$ where ω is a random variable with a probability density function $f(\omega) = \dfrac{\Omega - |\omega|}{\Omega^2}$ on the interval $[-\Omega, \Omega]$. Therefore, ω is distributed symmetrically around a mean of 0 with a variance $\sigma_\omega^2 = \frac{1}{6}\Omega^2$.[2] Since it is directly related to the variance of ω and therefore the Bureaucrat's ability to control the realized action, Ω represents bureaucratic *incapacity* in our model. When Ω is very small, the Bureaucrat's capacity is large (because the maximal errors in implementation are small). As Ω increases, so too does the possibility of large errors in implementation. Since we assume that all players have quadratic preferences, the utility from any action that is not overturned is $-(l-a)^2 - \frac{1}{6}\Omega^2$ for $l \in \{L, P, B\}$.[3]

Our assumption, then, is that bureaucrats take actions, but the result of these actions will often be other than what was intended. For some bureaucrats, this will be a bigger problem than for others. It may be the case, for example, that a bureaucrat charged with administering a pension system will attempt to establish a clear set of rules about eligibility and payments. But this bureaucrat may be unable to enforce adequately the application of these rules, as subordinates in the agency may favor particular individuals over others, may refuse pensions where they are deserved, may provide pensions to individuals who are ineligible, or may simply fail to show up for work. Similarly, a senior bureaucrat may attempt to limit imports of a particular product to a specific amount, but be unable to execute this limit because government agents at the docks allow too many, or too few, of a product to enter a country. In general, then, we think of large Ω as corresponding to situations where senior bureaucrats are unable to control subordinates, corruption is rampant, or bureaucrats are simply incompetent to carry out the tasks they have been assigned. In the context of American political development, it useful to think of Ω as varying across states (in state-level bureaucracies), across agencies in the federal government, and over time as general administrative capacities wax and wane.

The game begins when the Legislature decides whether to adopt a bill. If no bill is adopted, the final policy is the reversion policy Q, which enforces the status quo outcome, Q. If the Legislature adopts a bill, the bill specifies the upper and lower bound on policies that the Bureaucrat can implement while remaining compliant with the law. Formally, this bill is $x = [\underline{x}, \bar{x}]$. If x is adopted, the President must decide whether to accept or veto the legislation. If he exercises a veto, the status quo is in the outcome. Thus, policy change requires the consent of both the Legislature and the President.

If the President accepts x, the Bureaucrat adopts an action, a, to implement the legislation. The outcome of this action is $a + \omega$. The final policy outcome, however, depends not only on a and ω, but also on other institutional factors that can move policy to the ideal point of the Legislature or the President. In this respect, our model follows Huber and Shipan (2002), who argue that nonstatutory factors such as the decisions of courts and presidential rule-making authority can influence policy outcomes, *independent* of the language of legislation. There are also factors that can influence whether legislatures can achieve their desired policy outcomes by means other than legislative statute. These would include favorable court decisions and effective oversight opportunities.

We treat these alternative influences on policy outcomes as variables in our model. For any x, we assume that there is an exogenous probability β that the outcome moves to the President's ideal point. This parameter, β, therefore captures variation in the powers of the president over time and across policy areas with a large β representing situations where presidents have greatest ability to influence policy directly. Similarly, we assume that γ is the probability that the outcome moves to the Legislature's idea point, where $\beta + \gamma < 1$. A large γ represents a situation where the Legislature can be reasonably confident of obtaining desired policy outcomes independent of the language of statutes or the actions of bureaucrats.

We also assume that γ measures the probability the Bureaucrat will be caught if $a - \omega \notin [\underline{x}, \bar{x}]$. Our model does not assume, then, that bureaucrats must comply with the law. They may try to do so, but fail because of a large error in their action. Or they may not even try to comply with a statute, taking instead an action that they know will be out of compliance with the statute. If, however, the Bureaucrat does not comply with the law ($a - \omega \notin [\underline{x}, \bar{x}]$), then with probability γ the Bureaucrat is caught out of compliance, and must pay a cost δ of noncompliance. The parameters γ and δ therefore capture the effectiveness of the Legislature at uncovering and punishing inappropriate actions by the Bureaucrat.[4]

It is useful to note in this regard that punishment is based on the outcome of the Bureaucrat's attempted action, $a - \omega$. We assume that politicians cannot observe a, the Bureaucrat's intended action. They can only observe the outcome from these actions. Thus, if the Bureaucrat "accidentally" complies with the statute (i.e., $a \notin [\underline{x}, \bar{x}]$ but $a - \omega \in [\underline{x}, \bar{x}]$) he cannot be punished, and if he tries to comply but fails (i.e., $a \in [\underline{x}, \bar{x}]$ but $a - \omega \notin [\underline{x}, \bar{x}]$), he can be punished.

Our model, then, can be summarized as follows:

- The Legislature begins the game by deciding whether adopt to new legislation, $x = [\underline{x}, \bar{x}]$, which establishes the domain of actions that the Bureaucrat can take while complying with the law. Failure to adopt a new statute enforces the status quo, Q.
- If the Legislature adopts new legislation, the President either accepts or vetoes it. A veto enforces the status quo.
- If a new statute is proposed and accepted by the President, the Bureaucrat

attempts an action to implement policy. The outcome of this action will diverge from what the Bureaucrat intended, and the variation in this divergence is a function of the Bureaucrat's (in)capacity, Ω.

- The final policy is the Legislature's preferred policy (with probability γ), the President's preferred policy (with probability β), or the outcome of the Bureaucrat's action, $a - \omega$ (with probability $(1 - \beta - \gamma)$.
- If the outcome of the Bureaucrat's action $(a - \omega)$ does not comply with the law $(a - \omega \notin [\underline{x}, \bar{x}])$, then with probability γ, the Bureaucrat pays the penalty for noncompliance, δ.

In the next section, we begin analyzing the solution to the model by focusing on the best strategy the Bureaucrat can adopt during policy implementation.

BUREAUCRATIC CAPACITY AND INDUCIBLE
BUREAUCRATIC ACTIONS

Scholars have long recognized that policy change in presidential systems cannot occur unless policies exist that the legislature and president mutually prefer to the status quo. In this section, we describe how strategic incentives in the delegation process make the existence of "mutually preferred policies" necessary but not sufficient for policy change to occur. It may be that such mutually preferred policies exist but cannot be implemented. To understand what policies can actually be implemented, we have to consider the actions of bureaucrats. In proposition 1, we describe how the strategy of the Bureaucrat in our model influences the feasible set of alternatives that could be implemented following the adoption of a statute.

Proposition 1: *Let* $\theta = 2(1 - \beta - \gamma)$ *and* $\pi = \gamma\delta$. *There exists some statute* $[\underline{x}, \bar{x}]$ *that will induce any action in the interval*

$$
A = \left[x_B - \min\left\{ \frac{\pi}{\theta\Omega} \sqrt{\frac{2\theta\Omega^2}{\pi + \theta\Omega^2}}, \frac{\pi}{\theta\Omega} \right\}, x_B + \min\left\{ \frac{\pi}{\theta\Omega} \sqrt{\frac{2\theta\Omega^2}{\pi + \theta\Omega^2}}, \frac{\pi}{\theta\Omega} \right\} \right].
$$

No other action is inducible.

Proof. See appendix.

To understand the intuition underlying proposition 1, consider the Bureaucrat's best response to any statute, which is described in the proof of proposition 1. Figure 2.1a depicts an example where ω (the distance between the Bureaucrat's action and the outcome from this action) is distributed according to $f_1(\omega)$, with a maximum value of $\Omega = 1$. Consider two possible actions by the Bureaucrat. The first is when the Bureaucrat adopts the policy she most prefers

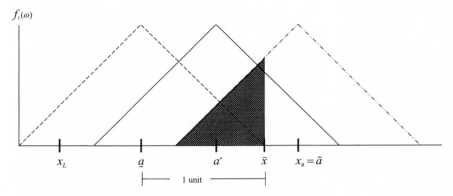

Figure 2.1a: The Bureaucrat's Incentives for Compliance

from those actions that always ensure compliance with the statute (for any re-alization of ω). Given that $\Omega = 1$, if the upper bound of the statute is at $\bar{x}$, the best "always compliant" action is at $\underline{a} = \bar{x} - 1$. The distribution of the consequences from this action are depicted by the dashed triangle with an apex above $\underline{a}$. In this case, the Bureaucrat's action never results in noncompliance, but the policy outcome ($\underline{a} + \omega$) is always relatively distant from his ideal policy, x_B.

Next consider what happens if the Bureaucrat takes an action to implement his most preferred policy, $\tilde{a} = x_B$. Following this action, with some probability (depicted by the shaded area under the dotted triangle and to the left of $\bar{x}$ in figure 2.1a), the outcome from the Bureaucrat's action complies with the statute. The rest of the time it will not. The expected cost of the noncompliant outcome for the Bureaucrat depends not only on the magnitude of this probability of noncompliance (the area under the dotted curve to the right of $\bar{x}$), *but also* on the probability noncompliant actions are detected (γ) and the cost of being caught in noncompliance (δ). As the expected cost of noncompliance grows, the Bureaucrat can be induced to move his action away from his ideal point.

The Bureaucrat's optimal action during policy implementation is thus determined by weighing the relative value of compliance and noncompliance. As the Bureaucrat moves his action from $\underline{a}$ to $\tilde{a}$ in figure 2.1a, the expected cost of noncompliance increases (because the probability of noncompliance increases), but the expected policy benefits (when noncompliance does not occur or is undetected) also increase. In equilibrium, the Bureaucrat will choose the action where the marginal expected policy benefits of moving his action toward his ideal point are exactly equal to the marginal expected costs of this movement. Given the location of $\bar{x}$, for example, for certain values of the other parameters in the model, the Bureaucrat's optimal action could be at a^*, which

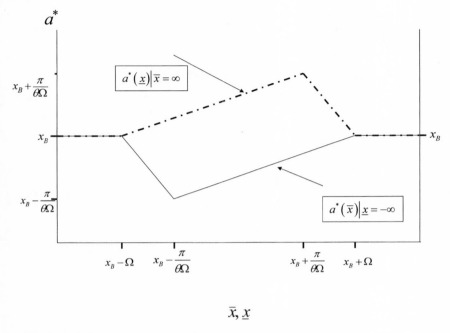

Figure 2.1b: The Bureaucrat's Best Response

yields the distribution of outcomes depicted by the solid triangle. Note that in equilibrium, the Bureaucrat often takes an action that he knows will result in some noncompliant outcomes (i.e., outcomes under the solid triangle and to the right of $\bar{x}$).

Obviously, the Bureaucrat's action will be influenced by the location of $\bar{x}$. As $\bar{x}$ moves to the left, the Bureaucrat must move his action to the left to maintain the same expected probability of noncompliance, which reduces the Bureaucrat's policy utility. Proposition 1 shows that there is a limit to how far the Bureaucrat is willing to move his action away from his ideal point. If the policy costs of achieving some level of compliance are sufficiently large (because $\bar{x}$ is sufficiently far to the left, for example), then the Bureaucrat will prefer adopting his most preferred action, $\bar{a}$, to adopting any other action.

In the model, the specific range of outcomes that the Bureaucrat can be induced to take depends on the relationship between $\theta\Omega^2 = 2(1 - \beta - \gamma)\Omega^2$ and $\pi = \gamma\delta$. Although this relationship affects the precise location of the boundary, it does not affect the intuition from the model (or the substantive results about the impact of bureaucratic capacity on gridlock, discussed below). Figure 2.1b depicts one example of the Bureaucrat's best response, a^*, to statutes adopted by the Legislature and President—and thus the range of actions that the Legislator can induce for the case when the expected cost of noncompliance is relatively small (i.e., when $\pi\delta < \theta\Omega^2$). This ensures that the range of inducible actions is $A = \left[x_B - \dfrac{\pi}{\theta\Omega}, x_B + \dfrac{\pi}{\theta\Omega} \right]$ as in proposition 1.

One way that actions smaller than x_B can be induced is to set $\underline{x}$ very low (so that it does not affect the Bureaucrat's actions), leaving $\bar{x}$ as the only constraint on the Bureaucrat. The Bureaucrat's optimal action as a function of $\bar{x}$ is depicted by the solid line in the figure. If $\bar{x}$ is too low ($\bar{x} < x_B - \Omega$), the Bureaucrat's optimal action will be at his ideal point (case 10 in the proof of proposition 1). Similarly, for any $\bar{x}$ above $x_B + \Omega$ (and $\underline{x}$ very low) (case 4), the Bureaucrat will take the action at his ideal point (because this action never can result in noncompliance). For any $\bar{x}$ such that $x_B - \Omega \le \bar{x} \le x_B - \dfrac{\pi}{\theta\Omega}$, the Bureaucrat's best response is to adopt $a^* = \dfrac{\theta\Omega^2 x_B - \pi(\bar{x} + \Omega)}{\theta\Omega^2 - \pi}$ (case 9). Thus, the upper bound of the statute can be used to induce any action in the interval $\left[x_B - \dfrac{\pi}{\theta\Omega}, x_B \right]$. Alternatively, if $x_B - \dfrac{\pi}{\theta\Omega} \le \bar{x} \le x_B + \Omega$, the Bureaucrat's best response is to adopt $a^* = \dfrac{\theta\Omega^2 x_B + \pi(\bar{x} - \Omega)}{\theta\Omega^2 + \pi}$ (case 3). Again, the statute can be set so as to induce any action in the interval $\left[x_B - \dfrac{\pi}{\theta\Omega}, x_B \right]$. Although the Legislature and President will be indifferent between which of two possible statutes is used to induce a particular outcome, the Bureaucrat will not since more noncompliance as the statute's upper bound moves away from the Bureaucrat's ideal point.

By a similar logic, by setting $\bar{x}$ very high (so that it does not constrain the Bureaucrat), the Legislator can use the location of $\underline{x}$ to induce any action in the interval $\left[x_B, x_B + \dfrac{\pi}{\theta\Omega} \right]$. The dashed line in figure 2.1b depicts these actions. As in the previous example, if the lower bound is sufficiently low ($\underline{x} < x_B - \Omega$), it will not constrain the Bureaucrat from adopting his ideal point (case 4), and if the lower bound is too high ($\underline{x} > x_B + \Omega$), the Bureaucrat will ignore it and attempt to implement his ideal point (case 7). But using $\underline{x} \in [x_B - \Omega, x_B + \Omega]$, the statute can induce any action in the interval $\left[x_B, x_B + \dfrac{\pi}{\theta\Omega} \right]$. For example, if $\underline{x} \in \left[x_B - \Omega, x_B + \dfrac{\pi}{\theta\Omega} \right]$, then the conditions for case 2 in the proof of proposi-

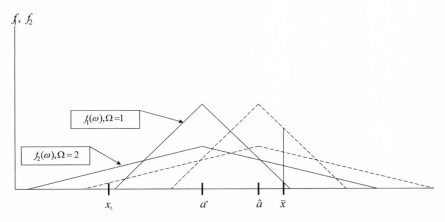

Figure 2.1c: The Relationship between Bureaucratic Capacity and the Set of Inducible Actions

tion 1 are satisfied, implying, $a^* = \dfrac{\theta\Omega^2 x_B + \pi(\underline{x} + \Omega)}{\theta\Omega^2 + \pi}$, and the action can be

anywhere in the interval $\left[x_B, x_B + \dfrac{\pi}{\theta\Omega} \right]$. Similarly, for $\underline{x} \in \left[x_B + \dfrac{\pi}{\theta\Omega}, x_B + \Omega \right]$,

case 6 is satisfied and $a^* = \dfrac{\theta\Omega^2 x_B - \pi(\underline{x} - \Omega)}{\theta\Omega^2 - \pi}$. Again, $\underline{x}$ can be set to yield

any action in the interval $\left[x_B, x_B + \dfrac{\pi}{\theta\Omega} \right]$.

Clearly, the set of actions that the Bureaucrat can be induced to take will have an impact on the incidence of gridlock. As the size of this set increases, there will be a greater possibility that the Legislator and President can find a statute that yields an expected outcome that each prefers to the status quo, Q. Importantly, the size of the set of inducible actions decreases as Ω increases.

Figure 2.1c illustrates the logic of the relationship between bureaucratic capacity (the magnitude of Ω) and the size of this set of inducible actions. As in figure 2.1a, given $f_1(\omega)$ and $\bar{x}$, the Bureaucrat's optimal action is at a^*. But what if Bureaucratic capacity declined and was distributed according to $f_2(\omega)$, with the maximal shock now being $\Omega = 2$? This decrease in Bureaucratic capacity decreases the Bureaucrat's marginal cost (in terms of increased probability of getting caught in noncompliance) of moving his action toward his ideal policy. Consider, for example, a small adjustment in the Bureaucrat's action from a^* to $\hat{a}$. Given the relatively high level of bureaucratic

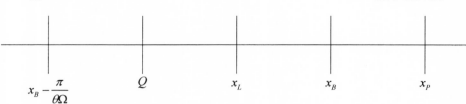

Figure 2.2a: Example 1

capacity described by $f_1(\omega)$, the move to $\hat{a}$ has a substantial impact on the probability the Bureaucrat's action results in noncompliance (the area under the curve to the right of $\bar{x}$ has increased substantially). If $f_2(\omega)$ describes bureaucratic capacity, by contrast, the same move has a much smaller relative impact on the percentage of all realized outcomes that are noncompliant. Since the marginal policy benefit to the Bureaucrat of moving from a^* to $\hat{a}$ is the same under both distributions of ω, and since the increase in the marginal cost of noncompliance is lower given $f_2(\omega)$, then given $f_1(\omega)$, the Bureaucrat's optimal action following the adoption of a statue will move closer to his ideal point as the Bureaucrat's capacity to achieve intended actions declines.

LEGISLATIVE GRIDLOCK

We now turn to the main object of analysis, the relationship between legislative gridlock and the variables in our model—in particular, the level of bureaucratic capacity. We begin by characterizing the size of the "gridlock interval" for all possible parameter values in our model. This interval is the set of all status quo points that cannot be changed through equilibrium behavior in the model. To characterize the interval, it is useful to consider its upper and lower bounds separately.[5]

As in standard models of gridlock, whenever the status quo lies between the ideal points of the Legislature and President, no policy change can occur.[6] In our model, however, the gridlock interval will always be larger than $[x_L, x_P]$. To see why, consider example 1, illustrated by figure 2.2a, where we assume the parameters in the model yield a set of inducible policies in $\mathbf{A} = \left[x_B - \dfrac{\pi}{\theta\Omega}, \, x_B + \dfrac{\pi}{\theta\Omega} \right]$. In this example, $Q < x_L$ and $x_B - \dfrac{\pi}{\theta\Omega} < x_L < x_B + \dfrac{\pi}{\theta\Omega}$. Since the Legislature can induce any action in the interval $\mathbf{A}$, it can write a statute that induces the Bureaucrat to adopt the Legislature's ideal point. If the Legislature prefers this to Q, so will the President, so the veto does not constrain the Legislature. But if the Legislature adopts a statute that induces $a^* = x_L$, with some probability (γ) the policy outcome will be the Legislature's ideal point with certainty, with some probability (β) the outcome will be the President's ideal point, and with some probability $(1 - \beta - \gamma)$, the outcome will be the Legislature's ideal point plus the random shock due to bureaucratic incapacity. Thus, the Legislature's expected utility from adopting this new program (which induces the Bureaucrat to adopt the Legislature's most preferred policy) is given by

$$-\beta x_P^2 - (1 - \beta - \gamma)\sigma_\omega^2.$$

The expected utility of not adopting the new program is simply $-Q^2$. The Legislature therefore prefers adopting its optimal statute only if $Q < -\sqrt{\beta x_P^2 + (1 - \beta - \gamma)\sigma_\omega^2}$. Clearly, the right-hand side of this expression is less than 0 (the Legislature's ideal point) whenever there is any bureaucratic "incapacity" (i.e., whenever $\Omega > 0$). It is also interesting to note that even if $x_P = x_L = 0$ (so that there is no policy disagreement between the Legislature and President), there will be gridlock for status quos lying to the left of their ideal points.

How is the lower bound of the gridlock interval determined? First note that for all $Q < x_L$, any statute that the Legislature prefers to the status quo is also preferred by the President (because $x_L \leq x_P$). Since policy change is constrained by the set of actions the Bureaucrat can be induced to take, we need only consider the three policies that might represent the Legislature's most preferred inducible action (which are determined in this example by the location of the set $\mathbf{A} = \left[x_B - \dfrac{\pi}{\theta\Omega}, x_B + \dfrac{\pi}{\theta\Omega} \right]$ relative to the Legislature's ideal point). The first possibility is the one we have just considered: $x_B - \dfrac{\pi}{\theta\Omega} < x_L < x_B + \dfrac{\pi}{\theta\Omega}$, which allows the Legislature to induce an action at its ideal point. Second, if $x_L < x_B - \dfrac{\pi}{\theta\Omega}$, then $x_B - \dfrac{\pi}{\theta\Omega}$ is the best action that can be elicited from the Bureaucrat. Finally, if $x_B < x_L$, then it is possible that $x_B + \dfrac{\pi}{\theta\Omega} < x_L$, which means that the Legislature's best inducible action is $x_B + \dfrac{\pi}{\theta\Omega}$. For each of these cases, the lower bound of the gridlock interval is determined by defining which status quo policies of those lower than x_L that the Legislature prefers to the best action the Bureaucrat can be induced to take.

The logic for identifying the upper bound of the gridlock interval is identical, only now we must consider the preferences of the President. Again, there are three cases to consider, which are determined by the location of the set $\mathbf{A}$ relative to the President's ideal point. A full characterization of the gridlock interval is given in proposition 2.

Proposition 2: *The upper and lower bounds of the gridlock interval are given below.*

1. If $0 < x_B - \dfrac{\pi}{\theta\Omega}$, $\underline{Q} = -\sqrt{\beta x_P^2 + (1-\beta-\gamma)\left[\left(x_B - \dfrac{\pi}{\theta\Omega}\right)^2 + \sigma_\omega^2\right]}$.

2. If $x_B - \dfrac{\pi}{\theta\Omega} < 0 < x_B + \dfrac{\pi}{\theta\Omega}$, $\underline{Q} = -\sqrt{\beta x_P^2 + (1-\beta-\gamma)\sigma_\omega^2}$.

3. If $x_B + \dfrac{\pi}{\theta\Omega} < 0$, $\underline{Q} = -\sqrt{\beta x_P^2 + (1-\beta-\gamma)\left[\left(x_B + \dfrac{\pi}{\theta\Omega}\right)^2 + \sigma_\omega^2\right]}$.

4. If $x_B + \dfrac{\pi}{\theta\Omega} < x_P$, $\overline{Q} = x_P + \sqrt{\gamma x_P^2 + (1-\beta-\gamma)\left[\left(x_P - x_B - \dfrac{\pi}{\theta\Omega}\right)^2 + \sigma_\omega^2\right]}$.

5. If $x_B - \dfrac{\pi}{\theta\Omega} < x_P < x_B + \dfrac{\pi}{\theta\Omega}$, $\overline{Q} = x_P + \sqrt{\gamma x_P^2 + (1-\beta-\gamma)\sigma_\omega^2}$.

6. If $x_P < x_B - \dfrac{\pi}{\theta\Omega}$, $\overline{Q} = x_P + \sqrt{\gamma x_P^2 + (1-\beta-\gamma)\left[\left(x_B - \dfrac{\pi}{\theta\Omega} - x_P\right)^2 + \sigma_\omega^2\right]}$.

Proof. See appendix.

Having established the boundaries of the gridlock interval for all possible parameter values in the model, it is straightforward to explore how variables in our model affect the size of this interval. First note that in all possible cases, the gridlock interval will increase in size as bureaucratic capacity decreases. There are two reasons, both of which are alluded to above, for this relationship. The first and most obvious is the "efficiency effect"—lower levels of bureaucratic capacity produce greater errors in implementation, reducing the value of new legislation to all the actors in the model. As noted in the discussion of figure 2.2a, for example, even if the Legislature can induce an action at its ideal point, it may prefer no action at all if there is considerable uncertainty about how close the actual outcome from the intended bureaucratic action is to the Legislature's ideal point. As bureaucratic capacity declines, the value of an action at the Legislature's ideal point will decline, which means that the status will have to become even more extreme before the Legislature will wish to undertake a new program. Consequently, low levels of bureaucratic capacity can force the Legislature and President to forgo the creation of new programs even when there exist programs that both prefer to the status quo. This dynamic corresponds almost directly with Carpenter's (2001) argument that

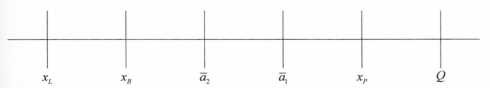

Figure 2.2b: Example 2

a reputation for competence is necessary for a department to obtain greater policy authority.

However, the relationship between capacity and gridlock exists for an additional reason that is unrelated to the straightforward efficiency loss associated with low-capacity bureaucrats. We call this the *compliance effect*. As shown in proposition 1, the set of inducible actions shrinks towards the Bureaucrat's preferred policy as bureaucratic capacity declines (because as capacity decreases, the policy costs to the Bureaucrat of ensuring a particular level of compliance with the statute will increase). Thus, for any location of the Bureaucrat's ideal point, as bureaucratic capacity declines, the best inducible action will move away from the Legislature, the President, or both actors. This makes it more difficult for the President and Legislature to design legislation inducing a bureaucratic action that both prefer to the status quo.

Consider example 2, illustrated by figure 2.2b, where $x_P < Q$. The figure depicts two different upper bounds on the set **A**. If bureaucratic capacity is sufficiently high, this upper bound could be at $x_B + \dfrac{\pi}{\theta\Omega} = \bar{a}_1$. Given the location of Q, it may well be the case that the President prefers a new program that induces an action at $\bar{a}_1$ to maintaining the status quo, and if the President prefers it, so too will the Legislature. But suppose that bureaucratic capacity were lower, moving the upper bound of the set **A** to $\bar{a}_2 < \bar{a}_1$. In this case, since the best action the Bureaucrat can be induced to take has moved away from the President's ideal point, the President may now prefer to maintain Q rather than adopting the new program. Thus, the low level of bureaucratic capacity has prevented the Legislature and the President from implementing a new program even though there are many outcomes that both actors prefer to the existing policy.

It is important to note that the compliance effect produces a relationship between gridlock and capacity even in the absence of the efficiency effect. To see this, suppose that rather than implementing a new program, the political actors were considering modifying an existing one, so that bureaucratic capacity affects both the implementation of new programs and the implementation of the status quo. In this model, the "efficiency effect" does not influence the choice between the status quo and the new program because the same variance in implementation errors occurs for either policy choice. But the "compliance effect" will still influence the size of gridlock interval. As bureaucratic capacity declines, the best inducible action will become less attractive to at least one political actor.

On this point, our argument diverges somewhat from Carpenter's. He stresses that reputations for competence increase bureaucratic autonomy, allowing agencies to take on more policy tasks without explicit legislative approval. In our model, as bureaucratic capacity increases, the Legislature and President have more opportunities to delegate authority to the Bureaucrat, but they are able to do so because they can adopt new policy statutes that ensure a sufficient level of influence over which action the Bureaucrat attempts to take. This legislative route to delegating authority becomes less attractive as bureaucratic capacity *diminishes*.

Other factors influencing gridlock. One factor that can help offset the negative impact of bureaucratic capacity on gridlock is the penalty of non compliance(δ). As this penalty increases, the set of inducible actions expands (because the Bureaucrat will be willing to take actions farther from his ideal point to avoid the penalty). Thus, whenever the set of inducible actions constrains the gridlock interval (e.g., $x_B + \frac{\pi}{\theta\Omega} < x_P$ or $x_B - \frac{\pi}{\theta\Omega} > x_L$), increases in δ will decrease the size of the gridlock interval.

Another variable that receives considerable attention in studies of gridlock is policy conflict between the Legislature and President. As in most models, as x_P moves away from x_L in our model, there will be an increase in the size of the gridlock interval. Such an increase in conflict always diminishes the value to the Legislature and the President of adopting a new program (because with positive probabilities given by β and γ, the outcome will be at the other political actor's ideal point). It also increases the range of policies between the ideal points of the two political actors that can never be changed, as in standard models of gridlock. The one interesting exception to this result occurs when both the status quo and the best inducible action are to the right of the President's ideal point. In this case, as x_P increases, the value of the best inducible action also improves for the President, which can expand the circumstances under which policy change is attractive to the President.

Finally, consider the effect of the Bureaucrat's policy preferences on gridlock. If the set of inducible actions does not constrain the gridlock interval (as in the example of figure 2.1a), the Bureaucrat's preferences have no effect on its size. But if this set does determine a boundary, then the gridlock interval varies with changes in the Bureaucrat's ideal point. If the Bureaucrat's ideal point is "extreme" (e.g., $x_B + \frac{\pi}{\theta\Omega} < x_L$ or $x_B - \frac{\pi}{\theta\Omega} > x_P$), then as his ideal point moderates toward the political actors, the gridlock interval will diminish in size (because the best inducible action will improve for both political actors). More interestingly (and counterintuitively), if a centrist Bureaucrat becomes more liberal, reforms in a liberal direction become more difficult.[7] Consider the case, for example, where the President's most preferred inducible action is lower than her ideal point and the status quo is rather conservative. If x_B moves to the left, the President's best obtainable action does as well. This makes her less inclined to agree to allow liberal changes to conservative status quos, thereby expanding the gridlock set upward.[8]

These substantive results regarding the size of the gridlock interval are summarized in proposition 3.

Proposition 3: *The size of the gridlock interval*

- Always increases as bureaucratic capacity declines.
- Decreases as the Bureaucrat's penalty for noncompliance increases, but only if the set **A** of inducible actions by the Bureaucrat defines a boundary of the gridlock interval (cases 1, 3, 4, and 6 in proposition 2).
- Increases as policy conflict between the Legislature and President increases, except when the lower boundary and the status quo are both to the right of the President's ideal point (in which case increased conflict can lead to decreased gridlock).
- Decreases as the ideal point of "extreme" Bureaucrats become more centrist and increase as the ideal point of "centrist" Bureaucrats become more extreme.

Proof. See appendix.

CONCLUSION

In this chapter, we have presented a model of several previously neglected features of legislative and bureaucratic institutions and their effect on legislative gridlock. We have focused in particular on bureaucratic capacity, a feature of bureaucracies that varies over time in the U.S. federal government, across federal agencies, and across the U.S. states. We argue that there is a strong positive relationship between increases in bureaucratic capacity and the adoption of new policy programs.

Our analysis focuses on two mechanisms by which bureaucratic capacity encourages new legislation. The "efficiency effect" is straightforward and unsurprising: as the competence with which agencies implement new programs increases, the payoff to all actors of adopting new programs also increases. This expands the possibility of executive-legislative agreement on new policies.

The second mechanism, the "compliance effect," is more subtle, and represents what we feel is the more interesting insight from our model. We do not assume that bureaucrats automatically comply with policy guidelines in statutes. They must choose to do so, and their capacity to realize the outcomes intended by their actions affects their willingness to try to do so. This link between bureaucratic capacity and compliance incentives influences the extent to which politicians can design statutes that yield desirable bureaucratic actions. Since declines in bureaucratic capacity make it more difficult for bureaucrats to comply with statutes, low-capacity bureaucrats are less willing to make the policy sacrifices that may be necessary to ensure compliance. Consequently, politicians delegating to low-capacity bureaucrats have to design statutes that allow these bureaucrats more latitude to pursue their own preferred policies rather than those of politicians. This clearly affects macro policymaking as it decreases the incentives of politicians to adopt new programs.

Politicians, then, should always prefer high-capacity bureaucrats. And when there is policy disagreement between the legislature and executive in American politics, this preference for high-capacity bureaucrats exists independent of whether the bureaucrats share the preferences of any particular politician. A Democratic-controlled legislature, for example, would prefer high-capacity "Republican" bureaucrats to low-capacity "Republican" bureaucrats because this capacity facilitates mutually beneficial policy bargains between Republicans and Democrats.

These observations about the compliance effect focus our attention on two empirical issues regarding the relationships between politicians, bureaucrats, and policy change. First, as noted in the introduction, the vast majority of formal and quantitative empirical research on policy change focuses on how policy conflict between legislature and executive influences law production. Our analysis suggests the value of incorporating measures of bureaucratic capacity into such analyses. Conflict across the legislative branches, for example, could be high, but policy change could nonetheless occur if bureaucratic capacity is sufficiently high. Conversely, policy conflict across branches could be low, but policy change difficult if bureaucratic capacity is low. Thus, our empirical understanding of law production should improve if we interact measures of bureaucratic capacity with measures of preference divergence across political principals.

Second, our model suggests a correlation between bureaucratic capacity and the use of policy details in statutes that create new programs. When capacity is low, statutes must give bureaucrats more policy leeway so that bureaucrats will not be inclined to ignore the policy instructions all together. As capacity improves, politicians are better able to use policy details to micromanage bureaucratic behavior. Thus, not only the production of new legislation, but also the nature of new legislation should be influenced by bureaucratic capacity.

While a full-scale empirical test of these hypotheses is beyond the scope of this chapter, Heitshusen and Young's (this volume) measure of legislative productivity in the late nineteenth and early twentieth centuries may be useful in determining the extent to which enhanced bureaucratic capacity associated with civil service and Progressive Era bureaucratic reforms contributed to increased legislation during this period. By counting changes to the U.S. Code, their measure reflects both the production of new laws and their scope and specificity, and is thus an ideal indicator for assessing our hypotheses.

While not establishing any causal link, changes in Heitshusen and Young's measure seem to readily track Johnson and Libecap's (1994) measure of the percentage of the federal workforce covered by the provisions of the Civil Service Reform Act of 1883. In the 10 years prior to the Pendleton Act, the number of changes to the code ranged from 200 to 300 with an average of 240. In the decade following the Pendleton Act, the number of changes increases markedly to around 340 per biennial congress. However, there is reason to believe that the full effects of civil service reform were not felt immediately. Coverage as a percentage of the federal workforce was low, and numerous loopholes left open the possibility for patronage appointments.[9] Even 10 years after the act, only 20 percent of the federal workforce was covered by its provisions.[10] However, following numerous executive orders reclassifying positions and closing loopholes, coverage reached 80 percent by 1920 before leveling off. Over this same period the average number of code changes crept above 1,300 until leveling off with very little change until the New Deal.

While these patterns certainly should not be mistaken for hard evidence of a causal link between bureaucratic capacity and legislative output, our hypotheses hold up at least as well as competing explanations for increased legislative activity over this time period. As Heitshusen and Young point out, critical elections fail to provide a suitable explanation for increased legislative output. Indeed, changes to the code began trending upward in the early 1890s, well before the Democrats were routed in 1896. The emergence of Progressivism also provides an incomplete explanation. The upward trend began under the conservative presidencies of Grover Cleveland and William McKinley and accelerated dramatically prior to Progressivism's high-water mark, the presidency of Woodrow Wilson.[11]

Finally, in concluding, we should also point out an important avenue for further development of the theoretical argument. Our model assumes that bureaucrats and politicians are equally informed about which policies will yield desired outcomes. By contrast, most existing theories of delegation quite reasonably assume that bureaucrats have an informational advantage—that is, bureaucrats are assumed to have greater policy expertise than legislators. In such models, the challenge for legislators is to exploit the bureaucrats' expertise by delegating in a way that encourages bureaucrats to use it on the politicians' behalf, rather than against the politicians. It seems reasonable to assume that in many instances, bureaucrats at the top of an agency do have an informational advantage, but that there nonetheless may also exist variation across agencies in their capacity to implement their intended actions. It would therefore be useful to explore how policy expertise and bureaucratic capacity interact to influence delegation and policymaking processes.

APPENDIX

Proof of Proposition 1. The bureaucrat's expected utility of attempting to implement the policy a is given by

$$-\int_{a-\bar{x}}^{a-\underline{x}} \beta(x_P - x_B)^2 + \gamma(x_L - x_B)^2 + (1-\beta-\gamma)(a-\omega-x_B)^2 f(\omega)d\omega$$

$$-\int_{-\Omega}^{a-\bar{x}} [(1-\beta-\gamma)(a-\omega-x_B)^2 + \beta(x_P - x_B)^2 + \gamma(x_L - x_B)^2 + \gamma\delta] f(\omega)d\omega$$

$$-\int_{a-\underline{x}}^{\Omega} [(1-\beta-\gamma)(a-\omega-x_B)^2 + \beta(x_P - x_B)^2 + \gamma(x_L - x_B)^2 + \gamma\delta] f(\omega)d\omega.$$

Evaluating the integrals in Bureaucrat's expected utility yields

$$EU_B(a \mid \bar{x}) = -(1-\beta-\gamma)(a-x_B)^2 - (1-\beta-\gamma)\sigma_\omega^2 - \beta(x_P - x_B)^2$$
$$- \gamma(x_L - x_B)^2 - \gamma\delta[1 - F(a-\underline{x}) + F(a-\bar{x})],$$

where $F(\cdot)$ is the cumulative distribution function for ω. The first-order condition for a maximum is

$$\frac{\partial EU_B(a)}{\partial a} = -2(1-\beta-\gamma)(a-x_B) - \gamma\delta[f(a-\bar{x}) - f(a-\underline{x})] = 0. \quad \text{(A.1)}$$

Because of the $f(a-\bar{x}) - f(a-\underline{x})$ term, this first-order condition depends on the position of a relative to $\underline{x}$, $\bar{x}$, and Ω. For example, suppose (as in case 1, below) that $a > \bar{x} - \Omega$ and $a < \underline{x} + \Omega$ so that $f(a-\bar{x})$ and $f(a-\underline{x})$ are positive. Then the first-order condition is

$$\frac{\partial EU_B(a)}{\partial a} = -2(1-\beta-\gamma)(a-x_B) - \gamma\delta\left[\frac{\Omega - |a-\bar{x}|}{\Omega^2} - \frac{\Omega - |a-\underline{x}|}{\Omega^2}\right] = 0$$

or

$$\frac{\partial EU_B(a)}{\partial a} = -2(1-\beta-\gamma)(a-x_B) - \gamma\delta\left[\frac{|a-\underline{x}| - |a-\bar{x}|}{\Omega^2}\right] = 0.$$

Because of the absolute value signs, this expression will depend on whether or not a lies between $\underline{x}$ and $\bar{x}$. If $\underline{x} < a < \bar{x}$, it reduces to

$$\frac{\partial EU_B(a)}{\partial a} = -2(1 - \beta - \gamma)(a - x_B) + \gamma\delta\left[\frac{\bar{x} + \underline{x} - 2a}{\Omega^2}\right] = 0.$$

If $a > \bar{x}$, it is

$$\frac{\partial EU_B(a)}{\partial a} = -2(1 - \beta - \gamma)(a - x_B) - \gamma\delta\left[\frac{\bar{x} - \underline{x}}{\Omega^2}\right] = 0.$$

The first-order condition would also be effected by $a < \bar{x} - \Omega$ and/or $a > \underline{x} + \Omega$ since one or both of the density functions would be zero.

In total, there are ten different possible expressions depending on conditions on a, $\underline{x}$, $\bar{x}$, and Ω. Each set of conditions is listed below, along with optimal action a^*, which satisfies (A.1). For example in case 1 below, a^* is a solution to A.1 if and only if $\underline{x} < a^* < \bar{x}, a^* > \bar{x} - \Omega,\ a^* < \underline{x} + \Omega$, and $a^* = \dfrac{\theta\Omega^2 x_B + \pi[\bar{x} + \underline{x}]}{\theta\Omega^2 + 2\pi}$.

1. If $\underline{x} < a^* < \bar{x},\ a^* > \bar{x} - \Omega,\ a^* < \underline{x} + \Omega,\ a^* = \dfrac{\theta\Omega^2 x_B + \pi[\bar{x} + \underline{x}]}{\theta\Omega^2 + 2\pi}$

2. If $\underline{x} \le a^* < \bar{x},\ a^* < \bar{x} - \Omega,\ a^* \le \underline{x} + \Omega,\ a^* = \dfrac{\theta\Omega^2 x_B + \pi(\underline{x} + \Omega)}{\theta\Omega^2 + \pi}.$

3. If $\underline{x} < a^* \le \bar{x},\ a^* \ge \bar{x} - \Omega,\ a^* > \underline{x} + \Omega,\ a^* = \dfrac{\theta\Omega^2 x_B + \pi(\bar{x} - \Omega)}{\theta\Omega^2 + \pi}.$

4. If $\underline{x} < a^* < \bar{x},\ a^* < \bar{x} - \Omega,\ a^* > \underline{x} + \Omega,\ a^* = x_B.$

5. If $a^* < \underline{x}$ and $a^* > \bar{x} - \Omega,\ a^* = x_B + \dfrac{\pi}{\theta\Omega^2}[\bar{x} - \underline{x}].$

6. If $a^* < \underline{x},\ a^* < \bar{x} - \Omega,\ a^* > \underline{x} - \Omega,\ a^* = \dfrac{\theta\Omega^2 x_B - \pi(\underline{x} - \Omega)}{\theta\Omega^2 - \pi}.$

7. If $a^* \le \underline{x} - \Omega,\ a^* = x_B.$

8. If $a^* > \bar{x}$ and $a^* < \underline{x} + \Omega,\ a^* = x_B - \dfrac{\pi}{\theta\Omega^2}[\bar{x} - \underline{x}].$

9. If $a^* > \bar{x}$ and $\bar{x} + \Omega > a^* > \underline{x} + \Omega,\ a^* = \dfrac{\theta\Omega^2 x_B - \pi(\bar{x} + \Omega)}{\theta\Omega^2 - \pi}.$

10. If $a^* \ge \bar{x} + \Omega,\ a^* = x_B.$

The second-order conditions are $-1 - \dfrac{2\pi}{\theta\Omega^2}$ *for case* 1, $-1 - \dfrac{\pi}{\theta\Omega^2}$ *for cases* 2

and 3, $-1 + \dfrac{\pi}{\theta\Omega^2}$ *for cases* 6 *and* 9, *and* -1 *for the remaining cases.*

To solve for a^* we first must examine whether any of cases 1–10 can be satisfied simultaneously. It is straightforward to show that if $\pi < \theta\Omega^2$, then all cases are mutually exclusive. Therefore, given that the second-order conditions are satisfied in all cases, a solution that satisfies any first-order conditions and the corresponding case constraints represents a global maximum.

If $\pi > \theta\Omega^2$, the cases are no longer mutually exclusive. For example, case 6 requires that $a^* > \underline{x} - \Omega$ and $a^* = \dfrac{\theta\Omega^2 x_B - \pi(\underline{x} - \Omega)}{\theta\Omega^2 - \pi}$. These two conditions can only be satisfied simultaneously if $a^* \leq \underline{x} - \Omega$, which is the condition for case 7. Thus, whenever case 6 is satisfied, case 7 is satisfied as well. Similar analyses reveal that cases 9 and 10 are satisfied simultaneously, cases 2 and 7 are satisfied simultaneously, and cases 3 and 10 are satisfied simultaneously. To determine the optimal action by the Bureaucrat in these cases, first note that the second-order conditions for a maximum are not satisfied in cases 6 and 9 when $\pi > \theta\Omega^2$. Thus, the optimum action is computed by comparing the solutions for each remaining pair of cases directly. Comparing 2 and 7 reveals that the solution to case 2 is optimal if and only if

$$x_B + \Omega\left[\sqrt{2\left(\frac{\theta\Omega^2 + \pi}{\theta\Omega^2}\right)} - 1\right] \geq \underline{x}. \tag{A.2}$$

Similarly, the solution to case 3 is optimal is

$$x_B - \Omega\left[\sqrt{2\left(\frac{\Omega^2\theta + \pi}{\Omega^2\theta}\right)} - 1\right] \leq \bar{x}. \tag{A.3}$$

Given that the 10 cases plus equations A.2 and A.3 characterize the optimal bureaucratic action, we can compute the maximum and minimum actions that the bureaucrat can be induced to take. Note that in cases 4, 7, and 10, the maximum and minimum action is x_B. In the remaining cases, the optimal action is a linear function of either $\bar{x}$ or $\underline{x}$ or both. Therefore, the largest and smallest a must come at a boundary point contained in the constraints on $\bar{x}$ and $\underline{x}$. However, in all of these cases except 2 and 3, the constraints on $\bar{x}$ and $\underline{x}$ are open intervals that do not contain their boundaries. Therefore, the maximum and minimum actions must either be x_B or lie on the extreme points of case 2 or 3.

First, consider $\pi < \theta\Omega^2$. The extreme values on case 2 occur when $a^* = \underline{x}$ or $a^* = \underline{x} + \Omega$, which lead to $a^* = x_B + \dfrac{\pi}{\theta\Omega}$ and $a^* = x_B$. Since a^* is linear in $\underline{x}$ for case 2, any action in $\left[x_B, x_B + \dfrac{\pi}{\theta\Omega} \right]$ can be induced. Similarly, in case 3, the

extreme values occur at $a^* = \bar{x}$ and $a^* = \bar{x} - \Omega$ or $a^* = x_B - \dfrac{\pi}{\theta\Omega}$ and $a^* = x_B$.

The linearity of a^* in $\bar{x}$ suggests that $\left[x_B - \dfrac{\pi}{\theta\Omega}, x_B \right]$ is inducible. Combining

case 2 and 3, the inducible set is $\left[x_B - \dfrac{\pi}{\theta\Omega}, x_B + \dfrac{\pi}{\theta\Omega} \right]$.

Now consider $\pi > \theta\Omega^2$. Given equation A.2, the upper boundary of a for

case 2 occurs when $\underline{x} = x_B + \Omega\left[\sqrt{2\left(\dfrac{\theta\Omega^2 + \pi}{\theta\Omega^2} \right)} - 1 \right]$ so that $\left[x_B, x_B + \dfrac{\pi}{\theta\Omega} \right.$

$\times \left. \sqrt{\dfrac{2\theta\Omega^2}{\pi + \theta\Omega^2}} \right]$ is inducible. Similarly, equation A.3 implies that $\left[x_B - \right.$

$\dfrac{\pi}{\theta\Omega}\sqrt{\dfrac{2\theta\Omega^2}{\pi + \theta\Omega^2}}, x_B \Big]$ is inducible from $\bar{x}$ satisfying case 3.

The fact that $\dfrac{\pi}{\theta\Omega}\sqrt{\dfrac{2\theta\Omega^2}{\pi + \theta\Omega^2}} > \dfrac{\pi}{\theta\Omega}$ if and only if $\theta\Omega^2 > \pi$ implies that we

can write the inducible set as

$$A = \left[x_B - \min\left\{ \dfrac{\pi}{\theta\Omega}\sqrt{\dfrac{2\theta\Omega^2}{\pi + \theta\Omega^2}}, \dfrac{\pi}{\theta\Omega} \right\}, x_B + \min\left\{ \dfrac{\pi}{\theta\Omega}\sqrt{\dfrac{2\theta\Omega^2}{\pi + \theta\Omega^2}}, \dfrac{\pi}{\theta\Omega} \right\} \right].$$

Proof of Proposition 2. Let $\hat{a}_j$ be the most preferred inducible policy for $j \in \{L, P\}$. Given proposition 1 and the fact that preferences are single peaked, $\hat{a}_j \in \{\underline{a}, x_j, \bar{a}\}$. The set of status quo changes that each principal will veto are given by

$$-\beta(x_p - x_j)^2 - \gamma(x_L - x_j)^2 - (1 - \beta - \gamma)[(\hat{a}_j - x_j)^2 - \sigma_\omega^2] \le -(Q - x_j)^2. \quad \text{(A.4)}$$

The set of status quos that satisfy equation A.4 can be written as $[\underline{Q}_j, \overline{Q}_j]$, where

$$\underline{Q}_j = x_j - \sqrt{\beta(x_p - x_j)^2 + \gamma(x_L - x_j)^2 + (1 - \beta - \gamma)[(\hat{a}_j - x_j)^2 + \sigma_\omega^2]}.$$

$$\text{(A.5)}$$

and

$$\underline{Q}_j = x_j + \sqrt{\beta(x_p - x_j)^2 + \gamma(x_L - x_j)^2 + (1 - \beta - \gamma)[(\hat{a}_j - x_j)^2 + \sigma_\omega^2]}.$$

(A.6)

Since it can be shown that $\underline{Q}_L < \underline{Q}_P$ for all values of $\hat{a}_L$ and $\hat{a}_P$, $\underline{Q} = \underline{Q}_L$. Similarly, $\bar{Q} = \bar{Q}_R$. Cases 1–3 represent $\underline{Q}$ for all possible values of $\hat{a}_L$: $\underline{a}$, 0, and $\bar{a}$. Cases 4 – 6 represent $\bar{Q}$ for all values of $\hat{a}_P$.

Proof of Proposition 3. In addition to the conditions defining each of the cases, the following implications of proposition 2 are useful in signing the derivatives for the various comparative statics:

1. $\underline{Q} < 0.$

2. $\bar{Q} > x_p.$

3. $\dfrac{\partial \underline{a}}{\partial \Omega} = -\dfrac{\partial \bar{a}}{\partial \Omega} = \left\{ \begin{array}{l} \dfrac{\pi}{\theta \Omega^2} \\[2ex] \dfrac{\pi}{\theta} \dfrac{4\theta\Omega}{(\pi + \theta\Omega^2)^2} \left(\dfrac{2\theta}{\pi + \theta\Omega^2} \right)^{-\frac{1}{2}} \end{array} \right\} > 0.$

4. $\dfrac{\partial \underline{a}}{\partial \delta} = -\dfrac{\partial \bar{a}}{\partial \delta} = \left\{ \begin{array}{l} -\dfrac{\gamma}{\theta \Omega} \\[2ex] -2\gamma \left[\dfrac{2\theta}{\theta\Omega^2 + \pi} \right]^{-\frac{1}{2}} \dfrac{\theta\Omega^2}{(\theta\Omega^2 + \pi)^2} \end{array} \right\} < 0.$

5. $\dfrac{\partial \underline{a}}{\partial x_B} = \dfrac{\partial \bar{a}}{\partial x_B} = 1.$

Bureaucratic Capacity:

Case 1: $\dfrac{\partial \underline{Q}}{\partial \Omega} = \left[2\underline{a} \dfrac{\partial \underline{a}}{\partial \Omega} + \dfrac{\theta\Omega}{6} \right] \underline{Q}^{-1} < 0.$

Case 2: $\dfrac{\partial \underline{Q}}{\partial \Omega} = \dfrac{\theta\Omega}{6} \underline{Q}^{-1} < 0.$

Case 3: $\dfrac{\partial \underline{Q}}{\partial \Omega} = \left[-2\bar{a} \dfrac{\partial \bar{a}}{\partial \Omega} + \dfrac{\theta\Omega}{6} \right] \underline{Q}^{-1} < 0.$

Case 4: $\dfrac{\partial \overline{Q}}{\partial \Omega} = \left[2(x_P - \underline{a}) \dfrac{\partial \underline{a}}{\partial \Omega} + \dfrac{\theta \Omega}{6} \right] [\overline{Q} - x_P]^{-1} > 0.$

Case 5: $\dfrac{\partial \overline{Q}}{\partial \Omega} = \dfrac{\theta \Omega}{6} [\overline{Q} - x_P]^{-1} > 0.$

Case 6: $\dfrac{\partial \overline{Q}}{\partial \Omega} = \left[2(\underline{a} - x_P) \dfrac{\partial \underline{a}}{\partial \Omega} + \dfrac{\theta \Omega}{6} \right] [\overline{Q} - x_P]^{-1} > 0.$

Penalty:δ

Case 1: $\dfrac{\partial \underline{Q}}{\partial \delta} = 2\underline{a} \dfrac{\partial \underline{a}}{\partial \delta} \underline{Q}^{-1} > 0.$

Case 3: $\dfrac{\partial \overline{Q}}{\partial \delta} = 2\overline{a} \dfrac{\partial \overline{a}}{\partial \delta} \underline{Q}^{-1} > 0.$

Case 4: $\dfrac{\partial \overline{Q}}{\partial \delta} = -(x_P - \overline{a}) \dfrac{\partial \overline{a}}{\partial \delta} [\overline{Q} - x_P]^{-1} < 0.$

Case 6: $\dfrac{\partial \overline{Q}}{\partial \delta} = (\underline{a} - x_P) \dfrac{\partial \underline{a}}{\partial \delta} [\overline{Q} - x_P]^{-1} < 0.$

President's ideal point:

Cases 1–3: $\dfrac{\partial \underline{Q}}{\partial x_P} = -2\beta x_P \underline{Q}^{-1} < 0.$

Case 4: $\dfrac{\partial \underline{Q}}{\partial x_P} = 1 + 2[\gamma x_P + (x_P - \overline{a})][\overline{Q} - x_P]^{-1} > 0.$

Case 5: $\dfrac{\partial \underline{Q}}{\partial x_P} = 1 + 2\gamma x_P[\overline{Q} - x_P]^{-1} > 0.$

Case 6: $\dfrac{\partial \underline{Q}}{\partial x_P} = 1 + 2[\gamma x_P - (\underline{a} - x_P)][\overline{Q} - x_P]^{-1} \lessgtr 0.$

This last result is caused by the ambiguity of having x_P move both toward Q and $\underline{a}$.

Bureaucrat's Ideal Point:

Case 1: $\dfrac{\partial \underline{Q}}{\partial x_B} = 2\underline{a}\underline{Q}^{-1} < 0.$

Case 3: $\dfrac{\partial \underline{Q}}{\partial x_B} = 2\overline{a}\underline{Q}^{-1} > 0.$

Case 4: $\dfrac{\partial \overline{Q}}{\partial x_B} = -2(x_P - \overline{a})[\overline{Q} - x_P]^{-1} < 0.$

Case 6: $\dfrac{\partial \overline{Q}}{\partial x_B} = 2(\underline{a} - x_P)[\overline{Q} - x_P]^{-1} > 0.$

NOTES

We would like to thank Stuart Jordan for research assistance.

1. Even in the short postwar series, Howel et al. (2000) find statistically significant time trends after controlling for shifts in partisan control and other control variables.

2. For our results, only the unimodality of ω is crucial. The density of ω is that of the sum or difference of two uniform random variables with 0 mean.

3. The separability of the utilities of the mean and variance is a property of quadratic utility functions.

4. It would be straightforward to assume that β also affects the probability of noncompliance, and such an assumption would not change our results regarding bureaucratic capacity. We focus here on legislative oversight, which we feel is more important given that bureaucrats in American politics typically have preferences that are more aligned with the executive.

5. It is quite easy to show that the set of unaltered status quos will always be a single interval.

6. See, for example, Brady and Volden 1998 and Krehbiel 1998.

7. Because of symmetry, the same can be said for conservative policy changes when the bureaucrat becomes more conservative.

8. The model of McCarty (2004) exploits a similar trade-off. In that model, a president might wish to use his appointment power to move an agency in the direction of the legislature to increase the legislature's willingness to fund the activities of the agency.

9. See Skowronek 1982 and Johnson and Libecap 1994.

10. Johnson and Libecap 1994, fig. 3.2.

11. We certainly do not completely discount the role of Progressivism. First of all, like all models of legislative productivity, our model associates increased productivity

with changes in political preferences. Second, a major objective of Progressive reformers was implementing reforms to enhance bureaucratic capacity.

REFERENCES

Barrilleaux, Charles. 1992. "Measuring and Comparing American States' Administrative Characteristics." *State and Local Government Review* 24:12–18.

Banks, Jeffrey S. 1989. "Agency Budgets, Cost Information, and Auditing." *American Journal of Political Science* 33:670–99.

Bawn, Kathleen. 1995. "Political Control versus Expertise: Congressional Choice about Administrative Procedures." *American Political Science Review* 89:62–73.

Binder, Sarah A. 1999. "The Dynamics of Legislative Gridlock." *American Political Science Review* 93:519–33.

Brady, David W., and Craig Volden. 1998. *Revolving Gridlock: Politics and Policy from Carter to Clinton*, Boulder, Colo.: Westview Press.

Carpenter, Daniel P. 2001. *The Forging of Bureaucratic Autonomy: Reputations, Networks, and Policy Innovation in Executive Agencies, 1862–1928*. Princeton: Princeton University Press.

Epstein, David, and Sharyn O'Halloran. 1999. *Delegating Powers*. New York: Cambridge University Press.

Howell, William, E. Scott Adler, Charles M. Cameron, and Charles Riemann. 2000. "Divided Government and the Legislative Productivity of Congress, 1945–94." *Legislative Studies Quarterly* 25:285–312.

Huber, John D., and Nolan McCarty, 2001. "Legislative Organization, Bureaucratic Capacity, and Delegation in Latin American Democracies." Typescript.

———. 2004. "Bureaucratic Capacity, Delegation, and Political Reform." *American Political Science Review* 98:481–94.

Huber, John D., and Charles R. Shipan. 2002. *Deliberate Discretion: Institutional Foundations of Bureaucratic Autonomy in Modern Democracies*. New York: Cambridge University Press.

Johnson, Ronald N., and Gary Libecap. 1994. *The Federal Civil Service System and the Problem of Bureaucracy*. Chicago: University of Chicago Press.

Krehbiel, Keith. 1998. *Pivotal Politics: A Theory of U.S. Lawmaking*. Chicago: University of Chicago Press.

Lapinski, Johns S. 2000. "Representation and Reform: A Congress Centered Approach to American Political Development." Ph. D. diss., Columbia University.

Mayhew, David R. 1991. *Divided We Govern: Party Control, Lawmaking, and Investigations, 1946–1990*. New Haven: Yale University Press.

McCarty, Nolan. 1999. "Bargaining over Authority: The Case of Appointment and Removal Power," Typescript.

———. 2004. "The Appointments Dilemma." *American Journal of Political Science* 48:413–28.

McCubbins, Mathew D., Roger G. Noll, and Barry R. Weingast. 1987. "Administrative Procedures as Instruments of Political Control." *Journal of Law, Economics, and Organization* 3:243–77.

————. 1989. "Structure and Process, Politics and Policy: Administrative Arrangements and Political Control of Agencies." *Virginia Law Review* 75:431–82.

Skowronek, Stephen. 1982. *Building a New American State: The Expansion of National Administrative Capacities, 1877–1920.* New York: Cambridge University Press.

Volden, Craig. 2002. "A Formal Model of the Politics of Delegation in a Separation of Powers System." *American Journal of Political Science* 46:111–33.

PART II: *The Macropolitics of Representation*

3

Public Opinion and Congressional Policy: A Macro-Level Perspective

Robert S. Erikson, Michael B. MacKuen,
and James A. Stimson

What role does public opinion play in congressional policymaking? Considering the limited attention that the average voter pays to congressional goings-on, one might be tempted to answer, "not much." The voter at the average or median level of political information and awareness speaks with a weak voice when it comes to current congressional policy issues. At best, such a voter is capable of evaluating policies only after the fact, retrospectively evaluating their political agents from the perceived consequences of their actions. If the whims of our uninformed typical voter were to govern electoral outcomes, politicians would be free to enact public policy unconstrained by constituency preferences. It would follow that public opinion in the aggregate would be largely unconnected to the content of congressional policymaking.

Fortunately, this gloomy depiction of how democracy *might* be practiced does not fit the actuality of national politics in the United States. Students of public opinion are becoming increasingly aware that the same voters who appear so unprepared for their citizen role as individuals (Delli Carpini and Keeter 1996) display considerable rationality in the aggregate (Page and Shapiro 1992). As we have argued at length in *The Macro Polity* (Erikson, MacKuen, and Stimson 2002), the voter of average information, who typically is the focus of micro-level studies, is not the decisive voter in American democracy at the macro level. Simply put, those voters who are disproportionately informed and attentive to national politics exert a disproportionate influence on the tides of both public opinion and election outcomes. A little reflection should indicate why this must be so. When Congress considers or makes new policy, most voters are ordinarily inattentive and electorally unresponsive. Only an attentive minority actively makes policy demands and reacts to the actions and nonactions of Congress with their votes. Thus, when public opinion changes in the aggregate, informed and attentive voters are the ones who generate the change. When members of Congress attend to public opinion, they are responding mainly to people beyond the fiftieth percentile in terms of political information and attention. In sum, while the net influence of public opinion is depressed by the electorate's limited information, public opinion matters because of the contribution of informed voters who are more influential than their limited numbers would indicate.

In this chapter, we discuss the connection between macro-level public opinion and the macropolitics of Congress. We frame the representation question in terms of the time-serial causal linkages between public opinion and national policy, with opinion and policy both conceptualized in terms of the left-right dimension. Thus the empirical investigation centers on the connection between the relative liberalism or conservatism of voters' ideological preferences on the one hand and of the policies they get on the other.[1] The electorate's ideological preferences are estimated using the measure of "Mood" introduced by Stimson (1991, 1999). This index, a weighted composite of virtually all available polls on domestic policy issues, measures the liberalism-conservatism of public policy preferences in the United States, starting in the year 1952. We measure policy as the cumulation of liberal (positive) minus conservative (negative) major laws over the years, where major laws are the ideologically scoreable subset of Mayhew's (1991) "Laws" (Erikson, MacKuen, and Stimson 2002). The analysis that follows updates our earlier analysis to incorporate data through 2000.[2]

THE MACROPOLITY ON REPRESENTATION:
THE EXECUTIVE SUMMARY

Our central argument is that the liberalism-conservatism continuum of public opinion is an important influence on the liberalism-conservatism of congressional policy. Although the statistical evidence for a net causal connection is impressive, it is equally important to understand the links in this causal chain. The four links are these:

1. In national elections, relative party fortunes are influenced by the parties' ideological proximity to the electorate; i.e., the electorate votes to a significant degree based on its ideological proximity to the parties.
2. Party fortunes help to determine the ideological direction of national policy. Because Democratic politicians have liberal tastes and Republican politicians have conservative tastes, Democratic control leads to more liberal policies than Republican control.
3. Elected leaders anticipate the effects of ideological proximity in subsequent elections, and are aware that this affects their electoral futures. Thus, they respond to shifts in public opinion, moving leftward when lib-

eral demands increase and rightward when conservative demands increase.[3]

4. If politicians try to assuage voters by giving them the legislation they want, the behavior makes sense only to the extent it can be appreciated by attentive constituencies. The electorate does take notice of policy changes; shifting its policy demands (i.e., Mood) accordingly. Mood represents the public's demand for "error correction"—the discrepancy between the electorate's unobserved ideological preferences and the accumulation of policy.

Links 2 and 3, involving the behavior of the agents in the principal-agent relationship, are straightforward and hardly controversial. Certainly the political parties stand for different goals, although it would be nice to see this verified in terms of policy consequences of party control as well as indictors like roll call votes. And certainly national politicians such as members of Congress worry about public opinion and care about elections, although one might want reassurance that shifts in public opinion are not too subtle for politicians to detect.

Of these potential links, the first and the fourth are most likely to attract controversy, for the reason that they assign some responsibility to the principals—the voters themselves. These links require a level of attention by the American electorate in the aggregate that would seem to defy the textbook description of the American voter (e.g., Campbell et al. 1960). But if these links fail, elected officials—the agents—would lack the motivation to follow public opinion.

One's expectations for the amount of policy representation achieved must fall far short of the perfect representation of the median voter position as in the pure Downsian (Downs 1957) model of electoral politics. But the positions of the parties and the changing demands of the voters work to make policy proximity an important determinant of party fortunes in national politics. In turn, party control matters in policymaking, as Democratic and Republican politicians have different policy priorities when elected. These priorities are tempered by the desire to stay in office, which forces politicians to attend to shifts in public opinion. The public notices sufficiently to affect future elections.

Of course, representation would be enhanced further if more voters were attentive or if politicians did less shirking and more pandering. And even the politicians' most earnest desire to represent the median voter can be thwarted by the difficulty of discerning what the median voter wants, and by the roadblocks inflicted by Madisonian checks and balances. Despite the obstacles, policy representation at the national level is stronger than one might have initial reason to believe.

An important aspect of the interpretation is the depiction of a dynamic public opinion. If the public's underlying preferences were static, opinion and policy would be in equilibrium once the politicians figured out what the median voter wanted. Instead, new exogenous shocks to public opinion emerge faster than governments can respond. Still, policy does eventually respond. Policy at any one time represents the demands of public opinion cumulated over time, albeit with a certain delay.

The details follow. The third section starts with the search for time-serial evidence of ideological voting in presidential and congressional elections, a requirement to set the process in motion. The fourth section examines the empirical connection between Mood and Laws. The fifth section examines the response of the electorate to changing Laws. The sixth section discusses the process as a system of equations, with Mood representing "error correction." The seventh section concludes.

ELECTORAL IDEOLOGY AND ELECTION OUTCOMES—
THE TIME-SERIES EVIDENCE

The literature on the time-series analysis of U.S. national elections (e.g., Lewis-Beck and Rice 1992; Campbell and Garand 2000) is dominated by the goal of forecasting. That is, the central obsession, understandably, is on predicting the next data point. Explanation takes a back seat to forecasting, not due to scholarly indifference but due to the nature of the data available for forecasting. For forecasting purposes, models must be limited to indicators that are observable before the election. The set of indicators always includes some measure of economic prosperity plus, usually, observable political indicators such as the approval rating of the current president.

To the extent forecasting models can predict presidential and congressional elections, it is tempting to visualize a micro-level model of individual-level voting whereby people decide based on the competence indicator of retrospective performance (particularly in the economic realm) plus, perhaps, affect toward the current regime. The electorate's ideology (liberal-conservative policy preferences) has no part in forecasting equations. Is there any additional room for ideology to explain some of the variance?

A strong time-serial causal connection between opinion and policy requires that ideology (or "policy preference" if you prefer) helps to determine election results. Let us redo the election model from scratch, abandoning the seemingly dominant variables of income growth and approval. We start with the two variables that dominate the micro-level discussions of elections—ideology and partisanship. The former we measure via Stimson's Mood for the election year. The latter is "Macropartisanship"—Gallup's reading of relative party strength measured for October of the election year. Macropartisanship is entered as a control, with our interest centered on the parameter estimates for Mood as an independent variable affecting elections.

TABLE 3.1 Presidential Vote and Congressional Seats as function of Mood and Macropartisanship. 1952–2000

	Dependent Variable		
	Democratic Percentage of Presidential Vote	*Democratic Percentage of House Seats*	*Democratic Percentage of Senate Seats*[a]
Mood in Election Year	0.95**	0.43*	1.61***
	(3.86)	(2.50)	(3.95)
Macropartisanship, October, election year	1.12***	0.53**	1.25**
	(4.43)	(2.88)	(2.89)
Midterm (1 = Dem. Pres., −1 = Rep. Pres., 0 = Pres. Year)		−5.11***	−8.08**
		(−4.64)	(−3.24)
Lagged Democratic Percentage of House Seats		0.67***	
		(5.08)	
Constant	−75.23	−39.74	−117.45*
	(−3.02)	(−2.11)	(−2.42)
Adjusted R^2	.66	.66	.47
Root MSE	3.71	3.60	8.52
DW	1.19	2.15	2.34
Number of cases	(13)	(25)	(25)

Note: T-values are in parentheses. Based on national elections, 1952–2000.
[a] For the Senate seat equation, the dependent variable is the Democratic percentage of Senate seats up in the specific election cycle.
*$p < 0.05$.   **$p < 0.01$.   ***$p < 0.001$.

Table 3.1 summarizes our findings. As measured by Stimson's Mood, the electorate's ideological preferences matter as a statistically significant contributor to the outcome of national elections, and as a (JL) predictor of election outcomes for the president, House, and Senate. The more liberal (or conservative) the nation's Mood, the more Democrats (or Republicans) who get elected. We should also note the size of the parameter estimates.

In presidential elections, a point of Mood (roughly 1 percent switching ideological sides) is worth almost 1 percent of the presidential vote. From the coefficients for congressional elections, we can also work the numbers in terms of seats won or lost. In House elections, each switch of one Mood point causes a switch of about 2 seats (out of 435). For Senate elections, each Mood point switch converts about half a seat (out of about 33).[4]

The models selected for table 3.1 are simple in construction, with only a few independent variables and estimation via basic OLS. More complex models and more exotic methodologies only serve to bolster the contribution of ideology (as measured by Mood) as a serious cause of national election outcomes.[5] Clearly, shifts in the nation's ideological mood matter sufficiently to alter election outcomes. By itself, this is sufficient for Mood to be a contributing factor in deciding the ideological composition of government. Further, these effects are of sufficient magnitude to capture the attention of politicians. We turn next to the relevant evidence in terms of national policy.

THE MOOD-LAWS CONNECTION

"Policy" is the body of law that remains in place forever—or until reversed by other permanent changes. Given its cumulative character, policy cannot be a simple response to *current* public demands. Thus we focus on change, asking what happens in each biennium that leaves a lasting residue. Our measurement strategy is an adaptation of David Mayhew's compilation of important laws—which we have coded for direction (liberal or conservative) and extended in time.

We measure "Policy" as the accumulation of "Laws." The Laws index is constructed in simple fashion from Mayhew's (1991) compilation as the number of liberal (important) laws minus the number of conservative (important) laws for the Congress (biennium), from 1953–54 through 1995–96 (extended here through 1999–2000). Policy is measured by adding up the Laws scores, cumulatively, from 1953–54 through 1999–2000. Since liberal important laws outnumber conservative important laws by about nine to one, we detrend the measure. On average, the net change (Laws) is between five and six major laws in the liberal direction, each Congress.[6]

We now are ready to seek an answer to the question: "Does government respond to public demands?" With measures of Mood (the independent variable) and Laws (the dependent variable), we seek first to observe the net causal connection. Then we decompose it into two components. How much is due to the electorate determining the party composition of its government and how much is due to the government responding directly to public opinion? For this exercise, we measure government composition on a scale of the three elected institutions, House, Senate, and presidency, 0–3 for the number in Democratic hands.

The estimates in table 3.2 present the relevant equations, using Congresses (biennia) as the units of analysis.[7] Figure 3.1 shows the pattern of Mood leading Laws over time. The liberalism of laws produced by the U.S. government is very much a function of lagged Mood; Mood lagged one biennium accounts for 40 percent of the variance in the liberalism of Laws; the average Mood

TABLE 3.2 Policy Change (Laws) as a Function of Mood and Party Control

	Dependent Variable = Δ Policy (Laws)			
	(1)	(2)	(3)	(4)
Mood,$_{t-1}$	0.61**	0.78**		
	(2.99)	(4.06)		
Mean Mood,$_{t-1,t-2}$			0.90***	0.61**
			(5.13)	(3.03)
Party Control,$_t$				2.38*
				(2.44)
Laws,$_{t-1}$	0.32			
	(1.89)			
Number of cases	24	24	24	24
Adjusted R^2	.47	.40	.52	.61
RMSE	3.75	3.97	3.54	3.20
DW		1.58	1.74	1.63

Note: Bienniel data, 1953–2000. Change (Δ in Policy = Laws. Democratic Party Control = the number of the three institutions (presidency, House of Representatives, Senate) controlled by Democrats; *t*-values are in parentheses. Intercepts not shown.
*$p < 0.05$.   **$p < 0.01$.   ***$p < 0.001$.

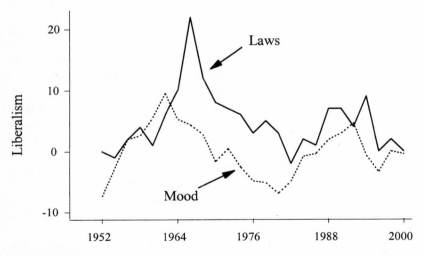

Figure 3.1: Mood and Laws over Time

over the prior two biennia accounts for more than 50 percent of the variance in Laws.

The equations also show that this effect is both indirect (via party control) and also the direct anticipation of public opinion as measured by Mood. Liberal Laws come from Democratic governments. But holding party control constant, what government does is also responsive directly to public opinion, captured in lagged Mood. Of course the public's ideological voting encourages elected officials to respond directly to Mood. Without an electoral incentive, officials would have no need to respond.

THE FLOW FROM POLICY TO OPINION

Our interest in opinion and policy goes beyond how government responds to public opinion. It is also important to understand how people react to the government response. We expect citizens to want more government when government in fact does little, to want less when it does much.

This feedback from Laws to Mood is required for the representation system to work. Why would elected officials change policy in response to Mood unless by doing so they could affect Mood? Consider the case of a liberal Mood and congressional Republicans. For them, a liberal electorate is electorally threatening. The solution of catering to the liberal Mood makes sense if a consequence is to lower the liberal Mood, which eases the electoral threat. For Democrats, a liberal Mood brings a different motivation. A liberal Mood lowers the electoral cost of enacting the liberal policies Democrats like to pass. Thus, like Republicans but for a different reason, Democrats are more willing to pass liberal legislation when Mood is liberal. (Similar reasoning explains why Democrats and Republicans act conservative when Mood is conservative.)

From this theorizing, the expectation is a negative relationship between what government does (Policy) and how citizens respond (Mood). We model such a relationship in table 3.3. We ask whether public opinion (Mood) responds to Policy; alternatively whether Mood change responds to Policy change (Laws). We see that it does. The more liberal the lagged Policy, the more conservative the Mood; the more liberal the lagged Laws, the more conservative the turn in Mood.

Thus we complete the loop. Government action responds to public opinion, and that public opinion responds to government action. These two dynamics are related in a system of equations. We start the system with a shock to Mood—say an exogenous "conservative" shock. Politicians adopt more conservative postures; eventually, actual Policy becomes more conservative. In response, the public lowers its demand for more conservatism and, barring further disruptions, the system returns to equilibrium.

TABLE 3.3 Mood as a Function of Policy and Laws

	Dependent Variable = Mood	
Mood$_{t-1}$	0.83***	0.50**
	(6.11)	(3.58)
Laws$_{t-1}$	−0.26*	
	(−2.31)	
Policy$_{t-1}$		−0.20***
		(−4.74)
Constant	11.85	37.99***
	(1.47)	(5.42)
Number of cases	24	24
Adjusted R^2	.607	.762
RMSE	2.52	1.96

Note: Bienniel data, 1953–2000; *t*-values are in parentheses.
*$p < 0.05$.   **$p < 0.01$.   ***$p < 0.001$.

THE REPRESENTATION SYSTEM: MOOD AS ERROR CORRECTION

The representation system consists not of a single equation but instead a system of interrelated equations. The parameters of these equations are themselves contingent on other variables we have ignored. The size of the Mood effect on elections, for instance, is ultimately a function of the ideological attentiveness of individual voters and the diversity of ideological choices presented by the two major parties. Widen the ideological gulf between the parties, for example—or enlighten the electorate—and the parameters capturing the electorate's responsiveness will change.

The anticipatory Policy response of elites to Mood in turn depends on the degree to which the electorate responds to policy issues. It also depends on their balancing of electoral versus policy considerations in the politicians' optimizing equations. At one extreme, professional politicians striving only to stay elected follow their constituencies at the expense of personal preferences. At the other extreme, elected officials (perhaps when term-limited) follow their preferences and shirk their responsibilities to their constituents.

An important element of the system is the feedback from Policy to Mood. Liberal Policy causes conservative Mood and vice versa. We should pause a moment to figure out why this should be. It is not that legislation generates a boomerang of disillusionment. And it is not that politicians spend their capital passing unpopular legislation. (Available poll data shows that although major laws are often controversial, they are usually favored by the median voter.) Rather, liberal Policy breeds conservative Mood and vice versa for the reason that popular liberal legislation lessens the perceived need for more liberal legislation and popular conservative legislation lessens the perceived need for more conservative legislation. To take an example, Johnson's Great Society was popular but lessened the perceived need for further liberal activism. Similarly, Reagan's conservative revolution was popular but lessened the perceived need to increase the dosage of conservatism.

The Mood measure represents the *relative* judgment by the American electorate. When the electorate is in a liberal Mood, the median voter sees existing Policy as too conservative and welcomes more liberal legislation. When the electorate is in a conservative Mood, the median voter sees Policy as too liberal and welcomes more conservatism. In either case, Mood then responds "negatively" to Policy because liberal (conservative) legislation lowers the demand for liberalism (conservatism).

This theorizing suggests still another aspect to the system. If Mood measures the difference between policy and preferences, we should introduce Preferences as a further latent (or unmeasured) variable. Mood can change when Policy changes, but sometimes Mood can change in a way that is not readily attributed to Policy; the other source would be exogenous changes in the electorate's Preferences.

At this point we push the modeling to the limit. A potentially useful way to model the representation process has Mood as a thermostat, with public opinion registering its view that policy should be "more liberal" or "more conservative" (see Wlezien 1995). The unmeasured Preferences then is the electorate's set point, but one that can vary over time. Restating the model in the language of time-series statistics, Policy equals Preferences plus error in an error correction model, where Mood represents the error. By this formulation one can visualize a graph of Policy and Preferences over time, where Mood represents the net difference—Preferences minus Policy.

If one pursues this idea to the next step, Mood represents a parameter k times the quantity "latent Preferences minus Policy" where Preferences is measured in Policy units. The value of k calibrates how many units of major legislation (the Policy measure) comprise one unit of Mood. That is, one unit of Mood is a demand for k major laws. But what is k?

We can offer a speculative answer, based on imputing rational expectations to politicians. Rational expectations does not mean the absence of error, but rather the absence of *systematic* errors. Actors do not persist in making the same mistake; they are able to learn. For instance, if voters have rational expectations, they will cast partisan votes based on their personal issue positions (liberals vote Democratic, conservatives vote Republican) only if the political parties actually pursue different policies in office. Similarly, if politicians have rational expectations they will not act *as if* the electorate were paying attention

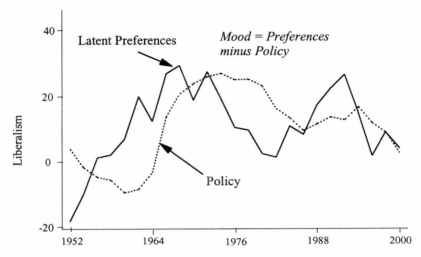

Figure 3.2: Latent Preferences and Policy over Time

to their policies unless the electorate is paying attention.[8] Finally, if politicians have rational expectations, they learn the magnitudes of the signals sent by the electorate when the electorate changes its Mood. This is the key for calibrating Mood and Policy on a common scale.

Using this rational expectations framework, we see a k value of about 3, meaning that one unit (percentage point) of Mood is equivalent to a demand for three major laws. If, say, Congress enacts three extra major liberal laws, Mood moves conservative one percentage point. If k is less than 3, according to the pattern of the Mood and Policy time-series data the Policy response to Mood would be too strong—Congress would move policy farther than the public's target, requiring a spiral of overcorrections each direction that would imply that politicians are unable to learn.[9] If k is greater than 3, then the data suggest the Policy response to Mood would be too weak—Congress would always underestimate the public demand and never reach the public's target.[10] It is in this sense that a k value of about 3 is just about right.[11]

The potential payoff of this theorizing is the speculative depiction of the time series of public Preferences overlaid with actual Policy. Figure 3.2 presents the picture. Here, Mood equals the "Preferences minus Policy" gap. The greater the gap, the more liberal the Mood. By this depiction of figure 3.2, Preferences moves quite a bit. The contemporaneous correlation between hypothetical Preferences and measured Policy is not great (a mere .41), but Preferences does correlate at an impressive .78 with Policy six years later.[12] If figure 3.2 approximately depicts reality, the response of Policy is slow. This is exactly what we expect given a Madisonian system of checks and balances. Policy responds surely but slowly so that Preferences sometimes change faster than the system can respond.

THE CYCLE OF POLITICAL CHANGE

With a rough calibration that one Mood unit corresponds to three Laws units, it is possible to estimate the speed with which demands translate into legislation. The idea is simple conceptually. Suppose we regress Laws on lagged Mood, with Mood calibrated in terms of the demand for legislation (one unit of Mood equals three Laws). The regression coefficient is 0.26, indicating that about one-quarter of current demands get met during the following Congress. We might project from this that one additional quarter of demand gets reduced each biennium. For instance, a unit shock to Mood results in policies that lower the unfulfilled proportion of the unit shock to 0.74 units (that is, $1.00 - 0.26$) the next biennium, 0.55 $[1 - (0.74 \times 0.26)]$ the biennium after that and so forth. The actual responsiveness may be considerably stronger than these projections. The regression of Laws accumulated over m Congresses ($t + 1$ through $t + m$) on Mood (in biennium t) indicates the degree of responsiveness after m Congresses. These regressions indicate responsiveness of .75 after three Congresses, .85 after four Congresses, and .98 after five Congresses. In other words, after roughly a decade, the policy demand is fully transmitted into legislation.

The autocorrelation of Mood is another indicator of responsiveness. Over one biennium, the autocorrelation is .74, perfectly consistent with the .26 estimate of responsiveness. Over two, three, or more biennia, this autocorrelation drops at a faster rate—to .44 with a lag of 2, .17 with a lag of 3, and −22 with a lag of 4 biennia. The implication from seriously applying theory to fragile data is that Mood shocks dissipate in six to eight years—as if this is sufficient time for new shocks to public opinion to result in legislation that fully satisfies the original demand.

Much of the translation from Mood to Laws is via the electorate's control of the party composition of its leaders. If we isolate the policy response from elite anticipation (rather than party control), the biennial Laws response is only .15 of the Mood from the previous biennium. Elections induce an important element of speed to the rate of responsiveness. Relative party strength is a particularly important source of representation when viewed over the brief time span of a biennium or, especially, a mere year of time. Over the longer term such as a presidency, party control matters relatively little in terms of the long-term policy result.[13] The interpretation is that while Policy eventually catches up to (lagged) Mood, no matter who is elected, it catches up quicker if the party in power is the one ideologically compatible with the public's ideological temperament.

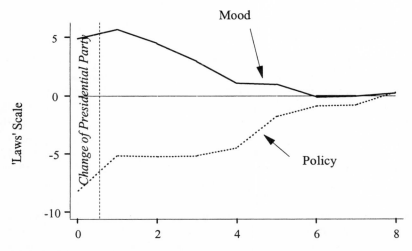

Figure 3.3: Mood and Policy, Averaged over Five Eight-Year Presidential Terms

We close this section with one revealing simple analysis, aggregating Mood and Laws over the course of five eight-year spans of presidential control by one party. The last half of the twentieth century saw six changes of presidential power, with five of these newly elected party regimes lasting at least two terms (eight years) and only one (Reagan–Bush I) lasting three terms. Only Carter did not make the cut. Counting the first eight years of a party regime, we have three Republican administrations (Eisenhower, Nixon/Ford, and Reagan) and two Democratic ones (Kennedy-Johnson, Clinton). We can ask, why (usually) two terms and also, why (usually) not three? The cycles of Mood and Laws helps to provide an answer.

Figure 3.3 aggregates *annual* readings of Mood and Laws over the eight years of the five eight-year "presidencies," plus (for comparison) the pretransition presidential election year. For a reference point, the zero points on Mood and Policy are set to their historical means. Relative to the mean, Mood and Laws are scaled so that positive numbers are liberal for Democratic regimes and conservative for Republican ones.

Figure 3.3 shows that presidents come to power when Mood favors their party and Policy (the accumulation of Laws) is lagging. For Republicans this entry condition is a conservative Mood and liberal Policy; for Democrats it is the reverse. Once a new party is elected, Policy changes and Mood follows in reaction. By the end of the eight years, Policy and Mood are restored to their historical averages. With the electorate in a blissful Mood (at the historical mean), the electorate is not in an ideologically charged state and the election is (for our purposes) a crapshoot.[14]

CONCLUSION

Our thesis is that public preferences govern congressional policy, albeit sometimes slowly. The electorate's chief mechanism of control is the electoral process—voting Democrats into office for liberalism and Republicans for conservatism. But in addition, congressional lawmaking anticipates public opinion in advance of its potential impact on elections. The process is most clearly seen at times when Mood is near its conservative or liberal extreme. Reagan-era policymaking was a response to the conservatism of Mood circa 1980. Earlier, the Great Society was a response to the liberalism of the early 1960s. Part of our understanding of the process is that policy responds slowly, while opinion changes perhaps more rapidly than we would anticipate. And governing parties are pulled in the direction of their ideological agenda independent of a more moderate public opinion. Despite these complications, public opinion (i.e., Mood) has in the past been a strong predictor of future policy (Laws) when future policy is measured over the stretch of several years.

In 2000, when our time series ended, the electorate's Mood reading was within a single digit of its long-term mean, suggesting an ideologically content median voter with a preference for moderation. With an ideologically satisfied median voter, putting either party in charge of government works against policy representation, as the governing party indulges in ideological policymaking that drives policy off its equilibrium path. For instance, if the razor-thin margin of 2000 had put the Democrats in control, their temptation would have been to enact liberal policies in the short run that would hurt their electoral chances in the long run. With the Republican team in power (as of this writing), the opposite temptation is the reality. A Republican Congress, emboldened by a popular Republican president, is poised to press its conservative agenda that includes items with less than majority support within the public. In the short run, this scenario suggests a shock to the process of representation. Yet the safe prediction is the restoration of equilibrium, at least in the long run. Our emphasis on the long run is meant to be more than an escape hatch. Over the past half-century, when measured in left-right terms, public preferences and congressional policy have been interconnected (if not cointegrated) rather than wandering on their separate temporal paths. There is no reason to suspect that the future will be different.

NOTES

1. For the liberal-conservative dimension, we freely use the convenient shorthand term *ideology* here. Some political scientists may object to this usage out of a belief that even "informed" voters lack coherent ideologies and hold, at best, vague unorganized ideas about such matters as the scope of government.

2. Some of the parameter estimates reported here differ slightly from those reported in *The Macro Polity*. The major reason was the updating with four more years of data. In addition, the measurement of Mood changed slightly with each update of the measure.

3. Links 2 and 3 should not be considered as contradictory, but rather part of a trade-off. Politicians care both about policy (2) and about winning (3). Their task is to optimize by nudging policy in the desired direction at minimal electoral risk.

4. Mood and partisanship are negatively correlated (−.41) in the time-series aggregate, so that each suppresses the effect of the other. The reason may be that over the course of a presidency, the president's party tends to gain in party identification but lose ground on the direction of Mood, as it spends its political capital.

5. For presidential elections, the inclusion of measures of party platforms further enhances the t-value of the Mood coefficient. For both presidential and congressional elections, the variables of our models dominate economic prosperity when all variables are entered together. For the two congressional equations, the t-values for Mood become stronger with fancy statistical extensions beyond OLS. Given the negatively autocorrelated errors, the Prais-Winsten GLS estimates sharpen the estimates slightly over their OLS counterparts. The dual House and Senate races also create the appropriate setting for SUR (seemingly unrelated regression) estimates. With SUR, the |t|-values surge when sources of error common to House and Senate elections in the same year are taken into account. As an additional twist, as *The Macro Polity* observes, the congressional equations are strengthened when partisanship is measured by "equilibrium" macropartisanship, discarding the short-term effects of "transient" partisanship. The result again is a boost in the significance of Mood. With SUR, and the equilibrium version of partisanship in the equation, the t-values for mood are 5.86 for Senate elections and 4.00 for House elections.

6. See Erikson, MacKuen, and Stimson 2002, particularly chapter 9, for discussion of the Laws and Policy measurement. Mayhew's original list stops with 1990. For 1991–96, see *The Macro Polity*, updated using a list compiled by Jay Greene using Mayhew's protocols. For the 1997–2000 extension here, our list is from David Mayhew's website. For Clinton II the extension of mass transit funding and the reform of public housing (both 1998) are coded as "liberal" major laws.

7. When measured biennially, Mood is measured as the Mood for the two-year period, rather than the average of two annual readings. For 1997–2000, biennial Mood is projected from the annual readings.

8. The early representation studies by Miller and Stokes (1966; see also Stokes and Miller 1966) were often interpreted to mean that politicians paid far more attention to their constituents than was justified by the public's limited awareness of their actions. Rather than dismiss representatives' preoccupations with constituency as irrational, perhaps stemming from politicians' deluded sense of self-importance, we think it more profitable to ask whether it might be a clue that constituency attention is indeed electorally warranted (see Mayhew 1974).

9. Imagine, for instance, a liberal Mood that the government interprets as a more liberal mandate than the electorate intends. Policy then becomes too liberal for the public, whose new Mood signals trigger an overly conservative spate of policies, which makes the public ask for more liberalism, etc. The problem with this scenario is that it implies that politicians (and perhaps the public) are not able to learn from past errors.

10. With $k = 3$, the policy response is "just right"—each unit of recalibrated Mood yields one unit of Laws, although not immediately. The wait for full satisfaction is perhaps as long as a decade. See the subsequent discussion.

11. Still another reason for setting $k = 3$ is that with a higher value, lagged Policy would be correlated with shocks to Preferences, whereas the theoretical correlation is zero.

12. In a related correlation involving observable variables, biennial Mood correlates at .82 with Policy change over the subsequent six years.

13. With time in years, Mood lagged one year is only on the cusp of statistical significance when in competition with party control as a predictor of Laws (for the year). Over four years (presidencies), party control loses significance entirely, while lagged Mood reigns as the Laws predictor.

14. The astute reader will ask how (on average) the variables can appear to be out of equilibrium at the beginning of the cycle but at their historic means at the end of the cycle, when end-points also serve as beginnings. Part of the answer lies in averaging process; another part lies in the asymmetries of beginning and ending conditions. The beginning conditions include the atypical 1952, 1980, and 1992 elections, none of which are at the end of eight-year cycles. The astute reader will also note that the short four-year Carter presidency presents an annoying selection problem, with Carter's phantom second term "censored." There is no obvious solution.

REFERENCES

Campbell, Angus, Philip E. Converse, Warren E. Miller, and Donald E. Stokes. 1960. *The American Voter*. New York: Wiley.

Campbell, James E., and James C. Garand, eds. 2000. *Before the Vote: Forecasting American National Elections*. Thousand Oaks, Calif.: Sage.

Delli Carpini, Michael X., and Scott Keeter. 1996. *What Americans Know about Politics and Why It Matters*. New Haven: Yale University Press.

Downs, Anthony. 1957. *An Economic Theory of Democracy*. New York: Harper and Row.

Erikson, Robert S., Michael B. MacKuen, and James A. Stimson. 2002. *The Macro Polity*. New York: Cambridge University Press.

Lewis-Beck, Michael, and Thomas W. Rice. 1992. *Forecasting Elections*. Washington D.C.: CQ Press.

Mayhew, David R. 1974. *Congress: The Electoral Connection*. New Haven: Yale University Press.

———. 1991. *Divided We Govern: Party Control, Lawmaking, and Investigations, 1946–1990*. New Haven: Yale University Press.

Miller, Warren E., and Donald E. Stokes. 1966. "Constituency Influence in Congress." In Angus Campbell, Philip E. Converse, Warren E. Miller, and Donald E. Stokes, *Elections and the Political Order*. New York: Wiley.

Page, Benjamin I., and Robert Y. Shapiro. 1992. *The Rational Public*. Chicago: University of Chicago Press.

Stimson, James A. 1991. *Public Opinion in America*. Boulder: Westview.

————.1999. *Public Opinion in America*, revised ed. Boulder: Westview.
Stokes, Donald E., and Warren E. Miller. 1966. "Party Government and the Salience of Congress." In Angus Campbell, Philip E. Converse, Warren E. Miller, and Donald E. Stokes, *Elections and the Political Order*. New York: Wiley, 1966.
Wlezien, Christopher. 1995. "The Public as Thermostat: Dynamics of Preferences for Spending." *American Journal of Political Science* 39:981–1000.

4

The Substance of Representation: Studying Policy Content and Legislative Behavior

Ira Katznelson and John S. Lapinski

Elected representatives, equipped with the authority conferred by mandates of their constituents and the legitimacy bestowed by the regime's constitutional design, make binding decisions across an enormous range. In choosing which public statutes, resolutions, and treaties to enact, they are guided by the organizational routines and rules of the legislature, steered by party commitments and ideologies, directed by agendas established outside and inside their institution, and motivated by the desire to both stay in office and make contributions in the public good. Empirically and normatively, outputs of the state made authoritative by the legislative approval of representatives—what this volume calls macropolitics—define what states do, how they act, and what they are.

If it thus is necessary for students of liberal democracies to make studies of representation a core feature of political analysis, politics in the United States especially requires this emphasis. Though students of comparative politics conventionally situate the country within the universe of presidential, as opposed to parliamentary, regimes, such a characterization is misleading (Lijphart 1999; Shugart and Carey 1992). In a system marked by a separation of powers, Congress possesses uncommon, even unique, powers over policy outputs. Even after the vast enlargement in the scope and capacities of the executive branch since the New Deal, the American political system still fits Woodrow Wilson's designation as a congressional government (Wilson 1885).[1] Relations connecting the United States to other countries, international organizations, and large-scale economic and geopolitical processes in the global arena, the ties joining the national state to its citizens, and the manner in which rules are prescribed within which the private economy functions are all shaped decisively by legislative sanction and decision.

Representation and public policy thus go hand in hand, but not, as a rule, in recent scholarship by political scientists on Congress. Among other key subjects, scholarship on gridlock, divided government, polarization, and the growing importance of ideology, the electoral connection and the purposive orienta-tions of members, the impact of public opinion, the role of information, legisla-tive productivity, delegation, the relative and shifting importance of committees and parties, institutional change in the nineteenth and twentieth centuries, and roll call behavior over the entire course of the country's history has progressed by leaps and bounds. Nowhere in studies of American politics has there been more scientific advance. Notwithstanding, we are struck by how little focus there is on the relationship between representation and public policy, as cause or as effect. It is this zone of present stillness we wish to rouse.

Now at best a minor site of research, when congressional studies took off in the 1960s and 1970s a good many scholars did place the substance of policy at the heart of their work in two principal ways. First, seeing policy as an inde-pendent variable, this literature sought to discern how shifts from one type of issue to another shaped voting blocs and political coalitions. The central no-tion was that alterations to policies under consideration tapped into different party and constituency pressures to produce particular, often dissimilar, coali-tions. Building on earlier studies on party and regional bases of roll call be-havior (Turner 1970) that had analyzed how the content of policies under con-sideration in Congress affects the choices and partisanship of its members, Mayhew (1966) probed the effects of farm issues, urban questions, labor con-cerns, and regional matters on the abilities of the parties to forge inclusive co-alitions. This question also was taken up in a series of theoretically ambitious articles by Lowi, who offered a more abstract classification of policy sub-stance from which he projected political outcomes, including those in Con-gress (Lowi 1964, 1970, 1972). This substantive orientation peaked with the publication of Clausen's *How Congressmen Decide: A Policy Focus*, where he proposed a five-sided "policy-dimension theory of congressional decision-making," arguing that "congressmen develop categories which subsume spe-cific legislative motions so that a common response can be made to all items of legislation included in a more general category" (1973, 8; also see Clausen and Cheney 1970).[2] On this view, members begin their process of decision making by assessing the area of policy content into which the legislation falls.

The second way policy substance entered legislative studies was as a de-pendent variable. Scholars sought to understand how big shifts in environmen-tal conditions—wars, economic shocks, social conflagrations—and large al-terations to political conditions caused by electoral realignments transformed the salience of issues and the substance of congressional policymaking. Writ-ing in this mode, Sinclair (1978, 1982) applied factor analysis to the policy-coding scheme Clausen had developed to show how major external forces overcoming tendencies to inertia and fragmentation had transformed the pol-icy character of the legislative agenda and roll call behavior to produce dis-tinctive policies over the course of a half-century. At the same time, David Brady began to produce landmark scholarship on the mechanisms and content by which critical elections (Key 1955) managed to transform congressional parties and thus produce policy changes that clustered both in the distinct substantive areas identified by Clausen, which he thought to be appropriate for the New Deal realignment, and in distinct areas of legislative significance he identified inductively for both the Civil War and 1890s realignments (Brady 1978, 1985, 1988; Brady and Bullock 1980; Cooper and Brady 1981a, 1981b; Brady and Stewart 1982; Brady and Sinclair 1984). In short, as they studied the preferences of members, the dimensions of roll call voting, the formation of coalitions, the impact of political parties, elections, and realignments, and ties to constituents, this lively research orientation placed front and center the content and character of the issues under consideration. Scholars were curious about how the types and content of issues under review shape political behavior and, in turn, how the congressional process works to produce particular policy results.

This big wager on substance produced contributions still worth attending, but this type of scholarship did not move ahead as its authors had hoped or that we, in retrospect, would have wished. Mayhew soon went on to address other themes, not least member rationality and the electoral connection (1974). Lowi's suggestive classification proved very difficult to operationalize. In turn, the work based on Clausen's substantive typology proved to be limited by the high level of aggregation produced by its small number of policy categories, and, as Brady showed, by its time-bound qualities. Further, at a time when deductive theory had begun to play an important role in studies of Congress, this body of behavioral work suddenly seemed a tad old-fashioned and largely limited to descriptive objectives.

The result was that as other emphases in studies of Congress moved ahead, the substantive dimension underscoring linkages between policy content and legislative behavior dropped away as other trends in the empirical study of Congress soon overtook the focus on policy content. Landmark work on small-group behavior and member motivations in committees, the electoral connection, constituency services, the organization of the House and Senate and especially the reforms of the 1970s, workloads, bureaucratic oversight, legislative productivity, and pioneering, highly aggregated studies of roll call behavior came to dominate the agendas of scholars at just the time congressional studies were exploding, leaving behind the study of the substance of policy in Congress.[3] Subjects that have concentrated the attention of Americanists, including major work on party systems and realignment (Burnham 1970; Brady 1988; see Mayhew 2002 for a critique) and on policy production (Mayhew 1991; Binder 1999; Coleman 1999; Howell et al. 2000; Lapinski 2000a, 2000b), as examples, do not really take policy substance seriously as units of analysis as they rely, for the most part, on simple counts of aggregated significant legislation.

For all the achievements of congressional scholarship, this intellectual history of setting aside the focus on the substance of representation has been costly. Notwithstanding past limitations, the challenges Lowi posed still stand: to find a way of coding policy "to suggest generalizations sufficiently close to the data to be relevant and sufficiently abstract to be subject to more broadly theoretical treatment," and to probe, via such an approach, how "a political relationship is determined by the type of policy at stake, so that for every policy there is likely to be a distinctive type of political relationship" (Lowi 1964; 688). Indeed, each of the topics that has come to define important pivots of congressional research, including still active debates about the role of information, distribution, and parties in shaping how committees are composed and what they do, and about the role of left-right ideological space in structuring roll call voting, could benefit quite a lot from more direct engagement with policy substance. Based on our own work on issue dimensionality, legislative significance, and historical dynamics (Clinton and Lapinski Forthcoming, Katznelson, Geiger, and Kryder 1993; Katznelson and Lapinski 2005; Lapinski 2000a), we believe a return to policy substance can become a constitutive part of current scholarship on such subjects as legislative pivots and the extent of polarization. Moreover, and perhaps even more important, unless this line of study is revivified, some of the most fundamental questions about representation in the ambit of democratic theory, taking in understandings about the distinctive traits of the American regime and the qualities of the country's liberal tradition, cannot be addressed, let alone resolved, adequately.

The main feature of this chapter, a new classification to orient the study of policy substance as both an independent and a dependent variable, is offered as a contribution to the kitbag of tools to recover and advance a more substantively oriented research program. Our task, we came to realize, was that of designing an original coding scheme more fine-grained, theoretically directed, and systematically organized than prior classifications of congressional roll calls. Picking up where others have stopped, we take what we understand as the indispensable first step to rectify the absence of such an analytically directed method for coding the content of congressional roll calls and public laws and, in consequence, the lack of a dataset across American history recording member behavior organized by such an approach to classification.

Our tiered typology, introduced below, is premised, first, on a view about why and how congressional representation should be placed at the center of larger understandings of American politics and history; second, on our understandings about why earlier policy-centered congressional studies faltered and how best to bring policy substance back into the study of politics; and, third, on a set of theoretical considerations about the meanings and purposes of useful coding schemes, guided especially by scholarship on policy and politics within the ambits of historical institutionalism and American political development. We thus begin with these issues before moving on to explain our approach to the classification of policy subjects. We close by describing recent work that has begun to utilize this scheme, and by highlighting other potential payoffs for this endeavor.

REPRESENTATION AND THE AMERICAN REGIME

As the central feature of all modern notions of popular sovereignty, political representation is a complex hybrid. Arguably the most novel contribution to nontyrannical political practices by the liberal political tradition since the publication of Locke's *Second Treatise*, representation, based on consent, simultaneously is elitist, in the sense of delegation to specialists in rule, and democratic, in the sense that this delegation is by election. Modern forms of representation, as distinct from republican forms of rule (Elster 1999), concentrate in the legislature a mechanism for re-presenting the preferences of members of civil society inside the state by semiautonomous members of the institution (Pitkin 1967). Legislatures thus provide the two-way institutional hinge connecting a permeable state to the constellation of its citizens who indicate what they would like legislators to do. In turn, legislators who receive such signals subject them to critical evaluation, make binding policy judgments by sorting out these signals, attend to them, deliberate about them, and reach authoritative decisions. Legislators, who always have a double role of representing both the whole of the sovereign people and the particular proclivities of their specific constituencies, can legislate responsively either by being receptive directly to signals coming from outside the institution or by acting in ways they impute citizens would want if only they could possess as much information as members do in their privileged governmental location. Representation, further, is provisional in at least two senses. Serving for terms, members of a legislature can be replaced by the votes of their constituents, and policies they enact can be revised by subsequent decisions, neither of which can be understood if policy substance is put aside (Manin 1997; Preworski, Stokes, and Manin 1999).

Representation, in short, always is institutional, processual, and substantive in character. It takes place in a particular organizational location characterized by rules, formal and informal, and practices that help shape its capacity, responsiveness, accountability, and productivity. In democracies, representation is an interactive and dynamic process (Erikson, MacKuen, and Stimson 2002). And, central to our efforts, it is concerned with real-world substantive decisions about public policy. Studies of Congress, whether historical or contemporary in focus, have been strongly oriented to institutional analysis, attentive, for example, to how endemic problems of cycling can be inhibited or overcome by institutional arrangements (Weingast and Marshall 1988). There also has been a good deal of fine work on such matters as the relationship of Congress to public opinion, elections, and other key features of the democratic process. Conspicuously missing in the recent past, however, is the third member of the triad of representation, specific policy content.

This substantive aspect of representation is vital if we are to be able to grapple with a deep set of tensions that provide inevitable sources for disagreement and conflict about what governments should do and which policies they should mandate. Political representation assumes the political equality and rationality of those being represented. These suppositions raise questions that legislatures decide. These deal with membership—who gets to be considered sufficiently rational to qualify as an equal citizen—and with how to manage the combination of equal political status and manifest social and economic inequality. Moreover, the types of interests, the scope of ideas, the patterning of discourse, and the range of identities that find their way into a process marked by a territorial organization of representation (as well as issues of wide variations in information, attentiveness, and intensity of preferences, and unequal skills at bargaining and negotiation, all of which are important subjects for students of Congress) are always entwined in a braid with policy. These questions, central to the character of political representation, never appear abstractly, but as integral parts of debates and decisions about such matters as war and peace, tax policy, the welfare state, and civil liberties. Representation makes no sense when divorced from such substantive considerations.

Because of its central place in the constitutional design of the United States, a fully developed treatment of congressional representation is vital to address key issues central to our understanding of American political development. Louis Hartz famously identified the regime as so deeply and pervasively liberal in the Lockean sense that the country's politics have been flat, limited to a relatively confined left-right issue space (Hartz 1955). He mounted this argument almost exclusively in the realm of ideas, missing the chance to place the country's most liberal institution, Congress, at the center of his analysis. Likewise, some of the most important challenges to Hartz, including the recent argument by Rogers Smith (1997) that the United States is better characterized as possessing multiple traditions, have looked at noncongressional discourse, including jurisprudence, rather than to Congress as the key location where political thought is made flesh. These elisions, broadly characteristic of work in American political development,[4] identify a missed chance to advance the long-standing discussion of the special qualities of political life in the United States by linking it to the content as well as the character of political representation over the sweep of American history.

Ironically, there is a mirror-image quality in the vast literature on Congress that not only has become relatively uninterested in policy substance but also is remarkably unreflective about the import of congressional studies for the big regime questions that have been so central to American political development. As scholarship on long-term congressional behavior, most notably the work of Poole and Rosenthal (1997), has characterized the content of the issue space that has defined American politics as gauged in many thousands of roll calls over the long haul of the country's history, no connections have been made to debates about the centrality of Lockean liberalism as the defining axis of the country's discourse, ideas, and choices. This, too, is a missed opportunity. After all, Poole and Rosenthal are most noted for their finding that one dimension, defined by strong loyalty to one or another of the two main parties, has been the central consistent hallmark of congressional representation. Side by side with this empirically grounded claim, and entirely consistent with it, sits the writing of Hartz. In both sets of work, the distinction between left and right exists, but is constrained by a broad consensus about rights and rules of the game, so that political conflict essentially is located almost exclusively on a single ideological axis mapped best by party competition. From this perspective, shifts within American political life may occur from time to time in the form of party system realignments (Burnham 1970), yet the basic limits and contours of the country's issue space remain broadly constant as unidimensional.

This view about hegemonic liberalism and its limited spectrum has been deeply controversial amongst students of American thought and ideology. Interestingly, this dispute has a good deal of unexploited resonance within the now dormant substantive orientation to work on Congress. The early writing of Lowi, Mayhew, and Clausen and other contributors to policy-focused congressional research began to provide analytical and empirical guideposts for examining claims about the valences of American politics. Mayhew (1966) and Clausen (1973), for example, discovered that variations in classes of policy produced quite different political coalitions, tapping into quite distinct sets of preferences, empirically confirming an insight argued more abstractly by Lowi (1964) that variations in policy can reshape politics. Though none of these works sought to question the Hartz hypothesis explicitly, and while each left open the issue as to whether the variations they associated with the content of policy ascended to his synoptic level of analysis, they left us a large and unrealized agenda that could far better place congressional studies in a compelling relationship with basic questions about the character of the country's political tradition and key features of its political development.

WHY THE SUBSTANTIVE TRADITION WAS ECLIPSED AND IMPEDIMENTS TO ITS REVIVAL

Because we wish to revive the substantive research program with stronger conceptual and empirical bases as an integral part of, and not as an alternative to, more recent trends in the study of Congress, we have been reflecting on why the substantive research tradition proved both so short-lived and unable to make a meaningful return. We think there are three main reasons. The first concerns problems in conceptualization and measurement that plagued past researchers and helped bring this body of work to a halt. The tradition petered out in part due to the lack of a sufficiently robust coding scheme that avoids problems of categories that are too bulky or unguided by theory and that can be applied across time without losing gains to historical specificity. The second concerns the strong claim mounted most persuasively by Poole and Rosenthal to the effect that policy variation has little impact on the basic contours of roll call behavior, thus seeming to infirm the orientation regarding policy preferences as an independent variable seeking to discover the mechanisms by which the type of policy shaping member preferences produces legislative politics. The third concerns the course work on legislative outputs has taken, less in the direction of treating specific public policies as the object of analysis than highlighting the role of institutions and environmental factors that influence legislative behavior and productivity.

Every serious student of Congress knows that appropriate coding is the sine qua non for linking substantive policies to the behavior of members. But the operationalization of this truism has been impeded by the absence of satisfactory frameworks for coding public policy. There has been no shortage of coding classifications for roll votes, committee hearings, public statutes, and vetoes; we hardly are the first to try to build an empirical edifice based on the idea that policy content matters. Unfortunately, the main categorizations suffer from at least one of the three pitfalls of overaggregation, the absence of a motivating and orienting theoretical compass, and a dependence on time-bound policy categories. A corollary issue we found insufficiently attended is whether a categorization scheme should be mutually exclusive; that is, whether roll votes or public statutes should be assigned a single policy code or whether it is possible to attach multiple codes to them. This issue is particularly important when public statutes are multifaceted, as in omnibus legislation (see Krutz 2001).

Of prior attempts to classify roll calls and statutes, the most durably influential is the five-tier policy coding created by Clausen (1967, 1973), who first developed his categories to search for policy domains characterized by unidimensionality and stability in the period spanning 1953 to 1964. Important research based on this classification demonstrated the distinct existence and effects of economic and social welfare policy dimensions in roll call voting, hypothesizing the former is influenced more by partisan differences and the latter by constituency constraints (Clausen and Cheney 1970), and showed how the content of policy affected a shift from partisan to regional voting between 1933 and 1956 (Sinclair 1978). Despite these contributions, the bulk of Clausen's highly aggregated coding categories limited its utility and precision, making it difficult, at times impossible, to specify the independent impact of important policy distinctions and differences.[5] By inserting labor votes inside the category of social welfare, for example, the scheme obscures the distinctiveness of roll call behavior in this policy domain (Katznelson, Geiger, and Kryder 1993; Poole and Rosenthal 1997, 111), thus making suspect the findings by Clausen and Cheney that lump these issues together under this single banner. The same problem, of course, applies when we study legislative performance with policy serving as a dependent variable. The boxes into which enactments are sorted simply hold too many different kinds. Because so much substantive research adopted this mode of classification, it found itself bound up with, and limited by, its inherent drawbacks.

There are, of course, other extant approaches to coding. These, however, tend to err on the other side, projecting long, often very long, inductive lists. As an important instance, the remarkable personal effort to code every roll call vote between the 1st and 98th Congresses by Keith Poole for his joint work with Howard Rosenthal arranges them by utilizing an extensive but unsorted inventory of policies. This approach yields such anomalies as categories for World War I and the Korean War but not for World War II, and an oddly nonequivalent set of classifications, placing "Mediterranean pirates," "slavery," and "public works" on the same scale (Poole and Rosenthal 1997, 259–62). By their nature, such inductive lists lack implicit or explicit theoretical rationales. Thus, when applied over time, they manifest a certain lumpiness in their categories. Another impressive research program that falls under the inductive approach is the Policy Agendas Project by Frank Baumgartner and Bryan Jones. The design they adopt is two-tiered, marked by 19 major topics and 225 subtopics. This serviceable codification was developed inductively by first working on congressional hearings, and has been designed specifically for the post-1946 legislative environment (Baumgartner, Jones, and MacLeod 1998; see also Baumgartner and Jones 1993). So even this fine project replicates a rather common feature of congressional coding schemes—the restriction of substantive categorization to categories based on the substance of discussion, debate, and legislation at particular historical periods. As a result, unless modified after being put to a historical test, they cannot claim utility across the full swath of American political history.

Pioneered by Clausen,[6] the bulk of such work in the field has focused on the post-1946 "modern Congress" and thus has classified roll calls and statutes legislation by period-specific categories. For this reason, Brady and Stewart's work on the policy import of realignment (1982) created two other "time-bound" classifications appropriate, respectively, for the Civil War era and the 1890s. For each period, they replicated the method Clausen had used to identify the small number of issue areas he found to be central in the 1950s and 1960s; not surprisingly, their lists across periods have virtually no overlap. This approach to historicity solves the problem of porting inapplicable categories to various time periods, but it leaves scholars dependent on controversial periodization templates (Mayhew 2002). Further, the punctuated and iterated character of the Brady-Stewart approach precludes consistent measurement of the substantive ebb and flow of legislation by policy categories because its historical character both leaves out routine periods and produces an incomplete time series across policy domains.

Whereas all these practitioners of substantive coding are convinced that policy variations have an independent impact on political behavior, one of the most important recent research programs has mounted a powerful case that cuts the other way. Despite Poole's own inductive typology, their work on dimensionality has attempted to show that policy content either does not matter, or, at best, belongs on the periphery of congressional studies. This important work has had a profound effect on how we study many topics within American politics, particularly in how we study lawmaking. For if a single ideological dimension defined by strong loyalty to one of two main political parties has been the central and nearly unwavering hallmark of congressional behavior irrespective of policy content across the full range of American history, then it makes little sense to ask how different policy arenas convene dissimilar patterns of partisanship and choice.

Much empirical work is needed to test the robustness of Poole and Rosenthal's main finding, especially because their suggestion that many policy issue areas are likely to characterized by a single or low-dimensional model is based on such an ambitious and synoptic research program. Notwithstanding this achievement, we are still at a relatively early stage in the effort to empirically discern whether, when, and to what extent public policies, irrespective of content, almost always map into a single dimension of conflict. Nor are we quite comfortable with the level of abstraction about the dominant right-to-left dimension that is required to confidently reach this conclusion. One possibility demanding further investigation is that the strategy of aggregating all roll calls might incline toward the discovery of similarities despite differences while potentially impeding the reverse. It remains to be seen whether Poole and Rosenthal's estimable demonstration of how robustly a low-, usually one-, dimensional spatial model can account for roll call voting might also obscure differences across policy domains.

This might especially be the case when gatekeeping is present, because in such circumstances, we are more likely to observe votes that are characterized by a single left-right (party) dimension. Non-first-dimension issues might not achieve a roll call on the floor, and thus would not be captured by attempts to measure ideal points through such votes. In other words, strong agenda control may allow only for roll call votes on issues that the agenda setter (i.e., the majority party) supports. This would imply that Poole and Rosenthal's findings are more about political opposition and less about the dimensionality of the policy space. Poole and Rosenthal, of course, acknowledge that gatekeeping might pose a problem for their work. Yet they too quickly dismiss this potential problem. They point to the fact that a low-dimensional model is present in both the House (where they assume gatekeeping to be much more prevalent) and the Senate (where they assume a relatively weak committee system and the lack of gatekeeping ability). These interchamber comparisons are potentially helpful, but they are not sufficient to demonstrate that gatekeeping does not happen in the Senate. The postulation that the committee system in the Senate is weak is, in fact, an assumption that is not likely to hold across all American political history. Moreover, other rules and norms might facilitate gatekeeping in the upper chamber through means other than the committee system. Exploring this issue further seems to be prudent.

Poole and Rosenthal do consider specific policy issues, including the minimum wage and interstate commerce, but they tend to do so one issue at a time outside of the ken of any approach to classification, including their own. Further, on the basis of a close examination of the 95th House, Poole and Rosenthal explicitly reject Clausen's argument that congressional voting can be parsed into substantive policy arenas, finding, empirically, that his categories "represent highly related, not distinct, dimensions" (Poole and Rosenthal 1997, 56). Confined to one brief moment (a single Congress with a large number of roll calls), and limited by Clausen's coding, their conclusion that different policy issues do not produce variety in member behavior is premature.

In preliminary work applying our own coding scheme that in part has been motivated by the debate between Heckman and Snyder (1997) and Poole and Rosenthal over the size of congressional issue space, we have begun to discover why not taking the substance of policy into consideration can be problematic. In research regarding policy issue space in Congress between 1931 and 1952, we have learned that many policies are second-dimension issues and a few appear not be well characterized by either a one- or two-dimensional model (Katznelson, Lapinski, and Razaghian 2001a). In this period spanning the start of the New Deal and the conclusion of the Fair Deal, as policy areas shifted, different sets of member preferences were tapped, producing variations in the formation of congressional coalitions as recorded in roll call behavior. From year to year, individual legislator preferences did not change very much. There was much short-term stability. Yet both as new members entered Congress and especially as historical circumstances altered and different issues came to the fore with the effect of changing the content of voting space, the ideal positions of legislators, new and old, changed, if only slightly from Congress to Congress, and unevenly across policy areas. Variations in subject matter thus advanced and sanctioned different, often dramatically distinct, features of roll call behavior.

These findings, especially when read in tandem with recent theoretical work on legislative behavior like Krehbiel's scholarship on pivotal politics (1998), help us see how policy variation can matter. In pivotal politics, status quo points deal with specific policies, at least in theory. "For a given lawmaking situation," Krehbiel suggests, "identify a single primary dimension of conflict," and ask, "Which and how many lawmakers (including the president) want to change policy, and in what direction?" (1998, 235; also see Katznelson and Weingast 2005) In this approach, member preferences, which are always preferences about particular policies, determine whether new legislation becomes law or not. In other words, policy preferences affect legislative production and performance. Our findings regarding the dimensionality of the issue space combined with our work on scaling legislative preferences suggest that one must take care in correctly measuring preferences via their substantive location if one is to conduct a meaningful test of the pivotal politics model of policymaking. The only way to avoid such pitfalls is to measure preferences by coding and analyzing the relevant data substantively by policy area.

Similar observations are relevant for the burgeoning literature on polarization (DiMaggio, Evans, and Bryson 1996; McCarty, Poole, and Rosenthal 1997; Poole and Rosenthal 1984, 1997). Presently, polarization is treated as the result of the growing ideological polarities between the political parties. But this kind of aggregate measure may well mask quite wide variations across policy areas. Even as net polarization is widening, for example, it is possible that the parties may be moving closer together in particular policy domains. We should not assume, say, that when polarization increases regarding domestic welfare policy or policies concerning labor they are also increasing regarding geopolitics or defense. The better the coding scheme the more capable it is of searching for the bases and sources of a rather congested conceptual and empirical phenomenon like polarization. Thus in order to create better, more nuanced independent variables that measure policy preferences more exactly, we require a compelling approach to policy coding.

Much the same case can be made for studies of policy as a dependent variable. Despite this aspect of the tradition of congressional research placing policy at the center of an interest in how behavior and institutions affect policy outputs, the explicit study of legislative outputs has not developed nearly as fast as research that focuses on the role of institutions and environmental factors influencing legislative behavior. We now possess a considerable bank of knowledge on how the quest for election and reelection influences how legislators design internal institutions and how such things as constituency and party pressures affect roll call voting behavior by members of Congress. The imbalance of what we know about member behavior compared to macro-level policymaking has not gone unnoticed. Indeed, a call for more balance through the explicit study of policy as a dependent variable was made in an underappreciated review essay written two decades ago by Cooper and Brady (1981b), arguing that to better understand and pinpoint the effects of institutional changes on the policy process, Congress must also be studied as an independent variable with the output side of the equation including surges and slumps in important legislation.

Cooper and Brady's call for macro-level analysis did not go unheeded. Mayhew's *Divided We Govern* (1991) provided social scientists with a time series of significant legislation that has been used to test a number of important theories dealing with congressional policymaking. Mayhew's measure of significant legislation consists of simple counts of public laws, making a distinction between landmark legislation and everything else. His findings based on this data challenged the long-standing belief that unified party government leads to moments of high legislative productivity while its counterpart, divided government, contributes to legislative gridlock. His work created a small cottage industry for the study of legislative production. Suggestive follow-up scholarship has included work by Sarah Binder (1999), arguing that in examining the effects of institutions and elections on policymaking and to meaningfully test theories related to responsible party government it is important to look not only at the production of important enactments, but at the ratio of failure to success. Binder finds that divided government, and especially party polarization within Congress, affects legislative production. Another important extension of Mayhew's work has comes from John Coleman (1999) on legislative production, who shows how improvements to the dominant model of responsible government, including a range of measures of important postwar legislative enactments, demonstrates, contra Mayhew, that unified government has an important effect on legislative production. Manifestly, this body of work cries out for better policy specification in order to inquire about how the competing predictions of Mayhew and Coleman and the measures of ratios advocated by Binder move across the range of public policies. Here, too, there is no reason to assume a priori that legislative outcomes are consistent across this expanse.

CONSIDERATIONS ON CODING

When we think of policy as an independent variable, we are assuming that legislators hold distinctive preferences about different types of policies, treating preferences as multidimensional, polyvalent, and keenly affected by the substance of policy issues. If we are interested in explaining what government does, policy serves as the dependent variable. The coding scheme we have developed is an instrument to parse and organize both. Research that attempts to determine the role of policy in the study of Congress in each regard cannot be accomplished, of course, without being able to parse policy into meaningful discrete categories.

No taxonomy is innocent. Acts of classification, even when they seem unguided or purely inductive, at once are statements of theory maintaining that this is the way the world might be studied fruitfully within the ambit of a particular perspective on social reality and empirical claims asserting this is how the world actually is organized. In developing the coding scheme we describe below, we were motivated by self-conscious goals in both respects on the understanding that good categorization requires motivating principles and a high degree of recognition by those who share in the experience being catalogued. We also were guided by a series of practical, instrumental, considerations geared to make the scheme both useful and reliable.

Measurement cannot be divorced from theory. Three central ideas impel our classification of policy. As a representative democracy, the United States enacts public policies that define its character as a state. Though its legislature may be sui generis, its assertions of sovereignty over people and territory, its ensemble of institutions and rules of governance, its patterns of transaction with other states in a world of states, and its terms of exchange with its citizens and the economy are hallmarks of stateness the United States shares with other countries. Our first goal, then, has been to construct a way of organizing policy that makes it possible to understand the particularities of state formation in the United States in comparative perspective. This, of course, has been a core goal of studies on American political development since the publication of Stephen Skowronek's *Building a New American State* (1982), but, as we have noted, it has only rarely been pursued in this research tradition by way of systematic studies of congressional agendas and policy choices.

The United States, moreover, is not just a state but, given the centrality of representation to its constitutional design, arguably the globe's most liberal state. Rather than take this feature of its character as fixed or given, we wish to make it possible to probe the contours, limits, and contested content of this liberalism. We make no a priori assumptions about its special place in the realm of ideas or ideology. Rather, we conceptualize liberalism, first, as an open doctrine based on a small number of core values, including government by consent, political representation, toleration, and irreducible rights for its citizens, that can bond, as it has, with a wide variety of other clusters of ideas, including those that are republican, democratic, authoritarian, racist, populist, religious, and socialist; and second, as organized and regulated relationships linking the state to other states, to the economy, and to citizens in civil society. Both aspects are contested and changeable. Both pivot on configurations of public policy. By focusing on Congress and policy it thus becomes possible to chronicle these contests and assign them empirical content both at particular moments and across wider expanses of historical time.

The aim of providing a new way of studying American political history thus constitutes the third core goal of our approach. We do not lack ways to parse the past. Historians and political scientists have access to a variety of descriptive and analytic periodizations, ranging from presidential labels ("the age of . . .") to atmospheric tags ("the Gilded Age") to sets of animating movements ("Progressive Era") to long swaths of time before and after key events ("antebellum") to scientific claims about temporality ("realignment"). Hoping to contribute tools for fresh approaches to the fundamental task of periodization, we have sought to develop an approach to policy coding that, while not time-bound, is sensitive to variations to the content of policy at different historical moments. By making a detailed mapping of the policy landscape of the United States possible over time it should also be possible to better understand such temporal concepts as critical junctures, path dependence, and the import of sequencing.

In combining a focus on representation and public policy, thoughtful coding can advance our understandings of American state formation, the status of liberalism, and the character of temporality in the American experience. If these goals are to be secured, we believe, it is best to break with the convention that forces policy substance into a single level of aggregation and to refuse the choice between deductive and inductive approaches. As research questions shift, so do appropriate constellations of policy and strategies of inquiry. More specifically, we think it important that scholars can classify either by coding at a very particular level and then move up a ladder by combining these particulars or by starting with large categories and move down a ladder toward more particularity and historical specificity. For these reasons, our approach appears in tiers. The first, with only four categories, seeks to capture basic features of state policy found in all modern states and adjudicated by legislatures in all representative democracies. The third, with 69 categories, is intended to be an inclusive set of "experience-near" classifications at a comparable level of analysis that contain the full range of policies in American history. As a hinge between these there is a 14-category middle tier that acts as a buckle connecting the deductive and analytical first tier with the inductive and descriptive third. It is both a specification of the theory underneath the coding at the first level and a more summative statement of policy activity than the third. Here, the focus on state formation, liberalism, and historicity are joined to an inclusive and logically consistent set of fine-grained policy categories.

Guided by the work of historians, political theorists, and scholars of American political development, we thus have sought to create categories appropriate to a representative democracy building a modern national state and creating public policies across time. Resolutely institutional and substantive, this approach centers on what the national state is, what it does, and how it structures key sets of linkages that define the character of its regime. Working in this way, we also had in mind yet another objective, concerned with the character of political science and the place of American political studies within it. We have been particularly keen to organize an approach to policy coding that will be of interest and use outside of the confines of congressional studies or American politics more generally. Colleagues who work in comparative politics, political theory, and international relations should be able to find their questions and categories accessible in our approach. For this reason, as one example, we were not content to limit ourselves in our first tier to the familiar dualism of domestic and international affairs, that, in effect, treats the domestic category as a residual lumping of everything that does not qualify as international, a move that, among other deficits, leaves out of consideration policies like those concerning membership and boundaries that clearly overlap these arenas.

A NEW POLICY TYPOLOGY

Our first tier designating four basic elements common to modern states reserves "domestic affairs" to a specific zone of policies distinct from those that define the characteristics of sovereignty or the organization and scope of the state as an institution, but which designate policy substantive policy outputs (see table 4.1).

Within tier 1, the fittingly first category is sovereignty, the defining characteristic of states from those fashioned after feudalism in early modern Europe to the present membership of the United Nations. Though a rich and contested term, it refers to the state's indivisible claim to rule legitimately over particular people and places. Hence it is concerned with the very existence, boundaries, and membership of the national regime. So the first cluster of policies we consider are those that bear directly on the state as a sovereign entity. To our knowledge, no other coding scheme designates this field of policy for particular consideration.

The second category, *organization and scope*, concerns the substantive reach and range of activities and the institutional elaboration of the national government's instruments for governing, including its basic constitutional rules, norms, formal organization, and terms of political participation. This, too, is a category of policies not ordinarily separated out this way and should facilitate the research of scholars who wish to understand how institutional change maps into policy outputs. In identifying policy specifically related to the institutions that constitute the policymaking apparatus, the possibility opens to systematically measure when, and why, institutions change. Though not limited to the organization of Congress, this category helps advance research focusing on how this institution organizes itself while drawing on other categories to trace links between how Congress sets its own rules and what it produces as policy outputs. Of course, policymaking takes place within a separation-of-powers system in the United States, so this category also allows us to track formal rule changes that relate to the office of the president and the

TABLE 4.1 Policy Coding Schema

Tier 1	Tier 2	Tier 3
Sovereignty	Liberty	Loyalty and expression
		Religion
		Privacy
	Membership and nation	Commemorations and national culture
		Immigration and naturalization
	Civil rights	African Americans
		Native Americans
		Other minority groups
		Women
		Voting rights
	Boundaries	Frontier settlement
		Indian removal and compensation
		State admission/union composition
		Territories and colonies
Organization and scope	Government organization	Congressional organization, administration, and personnel
		Executive organization, administration, and personnel
		Impeachment and misconduct
		Judicial organization, administration, and personnel
	Representation	Census and apportionment
		Elections
		Groups and interests
	Constitutional amendments	Federalism and terms of office
		Political participation and rights
		Other
International relations	Defense	Air force organization and deployment
		Army organization and deployment
		Conscription and enlistment
		Militias
		Naval organization and deployment
		General military organization
		Military installations
		Civil and homeland defense
	Geopolitics	Diplomacy and intelligence
		Foreign aid
		International organizations

TABLE 4.1 (*continued*)

Tier 1	Tier 2	Tier 3
	International political economy	Maritime Trade and tariffs Economic international organizations
Domestic affairs	Agriculture and food	Agricultural technology Farmers and farming support Fishing and livestock
	Planning and resources	Corporatism Environment Infrastructure and public works National resources Social knowledge Post Office Transportation Wage and price controls Interstate compacts and federalism Urban, rural, and regional development
	Political economy	Appropriations Omnibus legislation (double tier 3 code) Business and capital markets Fiscal and taxation Labor markets and unions Monetary Economic regulation
	Social policy	Children and youth Crime Disaster Education Handicapped and disabilities Civilian health Housing Military pensions, benefits, and civilian compensation Public-works employment Social regulation Social insurance
District of Columbia Housekeeping Quasi-private		

judiciary (Cameron 2000; Cameron, Lapinski, and Riemann 2000a, 2000b). Taken together, the first two categories, by bearing on the character and institutional composition and rules of government, make it possible to develop systematic measures that place congressional decision-making at the center of the historical development of the national state without reducing "statemaking," as some literatures do, to a single continuum running from weak to strong, where "strong" too simply connotes a capable executive.

The remaining two categories in our first tier of coding concern the outputs of government. *International relations* refers, of course, to the geopolitical and economic transactions between the United States as a unit in the global system of states and other sovereign states (as well as the international system and its formal and informal organizations), while *domestic affairs* is the category concerned with public policies shaping both the ties between government and the economy and between government and the welfare of its citizens.

The first tier of coding, therefore, is tied to what modern sovereign states are and do across time. By keeping these large categories constant, we can see both what the relative emphasis of lawmaking has been in distinct periods and probe whether policy coalitions vary from one domain to the other.

But these four categories are bulky. At a second tier, we divide each into three or four "blueprint" subcategories. That is, for each class of policies in the first tier, we identify the layered elements that, together, compose its constellation. Thus, sovereignty in a representative democracy entails—indeed, always entails—decisions about liberty, membership, and the demographic composition of the nation, civil rights, and physical boundaries. Organization and scope in such a regime is composed of decisions about constitutional structure, governmental organization, and rules of political representation. International relations divide into the triad of defense, geopolitics, and international political economy, while domestic affairs (even from the outset of the Republic) divide into policy judgments about agriculture, planning and resources, political economy, and social policy. By elaborating this second tier of issues to be found at every time period, it becomes possible to assess the consistency and diversity of ideologies and coalitions within and across tier 1 categories at any specific temporal moment, but also to pick up the dynamics of change across periods.

These distinctions still are not fine-grained enough to surmount the problems of aggregation we have seen in other coding schemes. Utilizing our detailed review of congressional committee responsibilities, budget categories, and the classifications of existing coding approaches, we subdivided each second-tier category from 13 into 69 tier 3 substantive classifications intended to be mutually exclusive and comprehensive.[7] Over time, the relative weight of these sites of policy alters quite a lot. But by not making any assumptions about how they will, we let the data sing to us, allowing for the discovery of patterns of change to substantive agendas, roll calls, and actual statutes.

In sum, our classification is designed to code congressional roll calls and public statutes by policy area guided by visible criteria for the assemblage of categories, combining the strong deductive, institutionally and state-oriented approach to the first two tiers with a more inductive approach to filling out the third. The approach is detailed enough to discriminate clusters of policy, avoiding problems of overaggregation, yet not so lengthy as to cease to be based on clear categorizations. The coding scheme thus provides policy classifications that can be applied and combined at different levels of aggregation, thus avoiding the pitfalls of approaches that either are too broad or too detailed and unwieldy.

WHY AND HOW POLICY SUBSTANCE MATTERS

Classification schemes and coding exercises, of course, are mere make-work unless the content of policy actually affects or differentially shapes behavior that is policy-specific. Further, the power of studying policy content and legislative behavior is not simply a matter of inductive exercises demonstrating that such relationships exist but is tied closely to possibilities for the development both of theory accounting for these variations and of analytical accounts of policy history. Though our discussion here is merely illustrative, our confidence in the significance of this enterprise rests on four pillars, each of which we should like to comment on.

The first is the legacy of scholarship produced by students of policy substance before that style of work went out of fashion. Mayhew's consideration of agricultural, urban, labor, and western regional issues (1966), for example, discovered important patterns of difference in the ways postwar Republicans and Democrats managed issue-specific constituency ties to produce different patterns of legislative compromise in each party. Each issue area resonated in a distinct way depending on the type of constituency. Outside the South, he observed, "two congressmen of opposite parties from the same set of 'interested' districts were more likely to agree on issues of district relevance than were two congressmen of opposite parties from districts 'indifferent' on those issues" (163). Given the small number of roll calls in each policy area, these differences, depending on the exact number of roll call votes, are likely to wash out in highly aggregated roll call studies. But the aggregation of these patterns, Mayhew further found, varied by party. "In voting on each of the four sets of issues, Democrats from 'interested' districts maintained higher cohesion than Democrats from "indifferent" districts. In the Republican party, the reverse was true; members from 'indifferent' districts demonstrated greater unity than members from 'interested' districts" (149). This dissimilarity, too, could not have been discovered without policy splitting rather than lumping. The same is true of Mayhew's important finding that "inclusive" compromise is the hallmark of a *dominant* party rather than a welfarist one. Democratic majorities after the Second World War, he observed, had a conservative tilt because the substantive policy terms of exchange between regions was uneven. "Democratic congressmen from city and industrial areas kept the farm programs going, but a sizeable number of Southern Democrats did not reciprocate on housing and labor issues. . . . Postwar Congresses with normal Democratic majorities spoke dutifully in Rooseveltian language, but the welfare state they helped to construct was a conservative one indeed" (168).

Mayhew's suggestive work was hardly alone in establishing the potential importance of a policy domain approach to congressional studies. Clausen and his collaborators, as leading exemplars, not only demonstrated to a fair degree of plausibility the truth of their proposition that different policy areas tended to evoke distinct dimensional patterns of voting by members, and that such policy-distinct clusterings tended to hold up over the medium term and were more powerful than differences in degrees of structure in House and Senate voting. They also proposed a coherent, highly plausible, cognitive specification of mechanisms motivating and shaping policy-specific member behavior. In a summary, Clausen and Van Horn wrote (1977, 678–79):

> The policy dimension theory is a statement of the process of decision followed by individual members when confronted with policy proposals. The extremely important primary consideration in the decision process is the member's cognition, or understanding, of the policy content of a legislative motion. The member attaches policy content to a motion by referring its policy attributes to a set of policy categories, or policy concepts, and determining which of the policy concepts appears to be involved in the legislative motion. . . . Having identified the general policy concept to which the specific legislative motion relates, the MC then casts a vote according to her or his position with regard to the general policy concept. The more supportive the MC is of the policy concept, for example, social welfare, the higher is the *probability* that on any single motion the MC will choose the voting position that supports the greater federal responsibility. . . . The policy position of the member of Congress is not simply a personal policy attitude. It is, rather, the policy position taken by the individual *when functioning in the role of MC*, which includes a responsibility to a number of policy clients—constituency, party, campaign backers, the President . . . —whose demands must be reconciled with a personal policy position in the formation of an MC policy position.

This orientation is at least as mechanism-rich as other extant models of member behavior, and remains vastly underexploited in congressional research. Indeed, the substantive work performed by leading scholars of Congress three and four decades back, in short, is sufficiently rich empirically and theoretically to motivate efforts to return to their agendas while transcending the limitations imposed by their coding schemes.

The second source of support is James Heckman and James Snyder's probe (1997) regarding the importance of issue-specific attributes in shaping the behavior of members based on an application of their linear probability model used to estimate the preferences of MCs expressed in their roll call behavior. Contrasting with the conclusion of Poole and Rosenthal that such voting largely has been one-dimensional, they find that "in all of the postwar congresses, there are at least five statistically significant factors, and that these factors are also important substantively" (165). The additional factors, which they find to be stable over time, reflect specific issue dimensions of the kind that "are easily missed when classification success is used to decide how many factors to retain" since these dimensions only arise on a small number of votes in each session (172). Further, they observe, high scores on one of the higher dimensions often can go hand in hand with high scores on the first dimension, signifying the specific effects of particular sets of substantive policy issues. Digging deeper into the Ninetieth House to examine the characteristics of roll calls with high scores on factors 2–7, they demonstrate the particularity of behavior in specific, and quite fine-grained, policy domains that is sufficiently diverse to invite further and more inclusive systematic work on policy substance, overcoming the limits of aggregative median voter models of congressional behavior.

The third pillar is our own work dealing with the substance of policy. We have begun to apply our three-tier coding scheme to hunt for the effects of policy substance in order to be able to cluster like policies and empirically observe when it is that nonsimilar policies cluster together; and we are especially interested in similarities and differences in such patterns during periods of political inflection and turmoil as compared to more settled times. To date, we have applied our approach to 11,405 individual roll call votes in the House between 1800 and 1860, and to 20,771 House votes and 25,699 Senate roll calls between 1877 and 1988, aiming to discover how best to uncover and measure the preferences of legislators over a variety of policy types (total N-57,875). Our first forays have shown that different types of issues indeed cluster with each other and that these clusters vary across time. Take, for example, the issue space in the extended New Deal period we have begun to analyze.[8] During this time, the preferences of legislators proved quite stable from one Congress to the next.[9] Alongside the findings of Poole and Rosenthal, this consistency might suggest that a one-dimensional policy space and the subsequent use of first-dimension NOMINATE scores as a measurement device across all policy issue areas is not justified. These results, moreover, are consistent with other studies that also discover that members tend not to change the basis of their vote choice over the course of their congressional careers (Poole 1998).

As it turns out, though, this pattern of short-term stability also is consistent with important considerable shifts in the composition of legislator ideal points over time either because new members change the overall pattern (a point made by Poole and Rosenthal and nicely documented for the New Deal era) or because the ideal positions of individual members may change within the voting space across time as the result of a number of mechanisms. These may include shifts in district composition as the result of redistricting, changing party strategies, or, most important, transformations to the policy agenda. It is the latter, in any event, that interests us most here. As an example, consider the issue of civil rights that Poole and Rosenthal rightly identify as crucial to the emergence of southern Democrats as a semiautonomous voting bloc. During the 1930s, the Democratic Party managed its strange-bedfellows coalition of northern immigrant, ethnic, urban, and labor supporters linked to southern, native, Protestant, and rural voters in an age of Jim Crow and exclusion of blacks from the franchise by keeping civil rights legislation off the agenda and by excluding farmworkers and maids, key categories of black workers, from every major piece of New Deal legislation, including the Wagner Act, Social Security, and the Fair Labor Standards Act. During the Second World War, this equilibrium was disturbed by demographic shifts that began to make African-Americans a significant voting bloc outside the South for the first time, by successful labor organizing conducted by both the AFL and the CIO in the South, often on a multiracial basis, by the earliest victories on behalf of fair employment in war production achieved by a nascent civil rights movement, by the extension of absentee voting rights to soldiers of all races fighting overseas in what still was a segregated military, and by the *Smith v. Allwright* Supreme Court decision in 1944 to outlaw the white primary. As the racial status quo began to be dislodged with the coming to the fore of civil rights issues, southern members, unwilling to adjust their ideal points, increasingly came to be at odds with fellow Democrats. The result of this shift was the emergence effectively of a three-party Congress composed of southern Democrats, nonsouthern Democrats, and Republicans who did not align exclusively in a one-dimensional voting space.

At the start of this period until the end of Roosevelt's first term, the Democrats can be seen to cluster together on the left side of the voting space, while the Republicans occupy the right. By the 75th (1937–38), 76th (1939–40), and 77th (1941–42) Houses, elected in the last three elections before American participation in the Second World War, southern Democrats clearly are partially removed from their nonsouthern colleagues, now concentrated at the top of the second dimension (a period when labor votes were second-, not first-dimension issues, since for southern members they concerned the heart of the political economy of segregation). Still, southern and northern members remained aligned on the first dimension, clearly distinct from Republicans. Subsequently, however, southern members not only moved away from nonsouthern Democrats on the second dimension, but they noticeably came to be in motion along the first dimension in the conservative direction. By the 82nd House, the last during the presidency of Harry Truman, the three groupings had become distinct partylike clusters, forming a triangle of preferences.

Southern Democrats now were at odds with both nonsouthern Democrats and Republicans on the second dimension. At the same time, while nonsouthern Democrats and Republicans were aligned on the second dimension, they were divided on the first.[10]

This transformation to dimensionality and partisanship under the impact of changes to the policy universe thus was more extended temporally and substantively than Poole and Rosenthal lead us to expect. More generally, the development of what, in effect, was a three-party system makes it clear that congressional voting space cannot be represented as if the first dimension is always regnant or without close investigation of the second, or higher, dimensions in a manner closely in tune with an understanding of historical developments. Poole and Rosenthal are fully aware of this issue; hence our point is less a critique than a call for a more fine-grained analysis of roll call voting by specific policy areas to discern the weight associated with party and regional factors across time. It also is a call for historians to make their objects of analysis more substantively, temporally, and institutionally precise.

We find a fourth support in what a more substantive approach can bring to the most prominent existing theory of macropolitics, Keith Krehbiel's pivotal politics. This theory essentially is a formalization of the policy process within a separation-of-powers political system, incorporating the president and Congress into the "game" of policymaking. Specifically, Krehbiel's theoretical account leads us to the conclusion that policy gridlock intervals, defined by the Senate filibuster,[11] presidential veto, and the status quo point, are unique for each bill deliberated by Congress and considered by the president once it achieves legislative approval. The gridlock interval is a function of the preferences held by legislators and the president regarding the policy space for each piece of individual legislation.

This focus on the micro-level process of passing legislation thus highlights the significance of policy content, but, curiously, this inherent feature of the theory is vastly underrealized. Indeed, the three features of U.S. lawmaking Krehbiel underscores in attempting to determine "who is pivotal"—the separation of powers, heterogeneous preferences, and multistage collective choice (1998, 20)[12] both shape, and are shaped, by specific policy content at particular historical moments. Without a further specification and probe of policy substance, the theory remains incomplete.[13]

To be sure, Krehbiel provides a host of rich empirical tests of his theory, but as we read his work it is more sophisticated than these investigations. One instance central to the theory is the issue that several scholars, including Krehbiel, have probed, regarding whether the gridlock interval predicts the production of important legislation (Binder 1999; Young and Heitshusen 2002). This body of research relies on the creation of a given "Congress" gridlock interval (that is, a single score for each Congress across time) with the dependent variable being the amount of significant legislation passed (or a first difference of important legislation across time). Clearly, in the study of macropolitics, the causal linkage of legislative production with gridlock intervals requires a measure that accurately captures gridlock intervals. But as these intervals vary by policy type, especially when policy space is not well captured by a single dimension, particularly at times of robust political and policy change (Brady 1988), accurate measurements of appropriate gridlock intervals become empirical matters closely tied to policy specification. Krehbiel observes that his theory needs additional empirical testing and proposes, as a first step to assess his "basic theory" of lawmaking, that the researcher "for a given lawmaking situation, . . . identify a single, primary dimension of conflict" (Krehbiel 1988, 235). By contrast, instead of assuming that a single dimension of conflict fits all instances, we would prefer to determine empirically whether and how the dimension varies by policy issue area, whether there is stability in this respect over time in a given policy domain, and how, at times, policy voting is characterized by two or more dimensions.[14] The theory of pivotal politics, in short, can best be adumbrated by exploring the dimensions of conflict that characterize policy space disaggregated by the kind of theoretically motivated coding scheme we have designed.

CONCLUSION

The study of macropolitics is a fresh enterprise full of possibilities whose potential will best be realized if policy content is placed front and center. To this end, we have developed a new approach to policy classification as an essential step for such a research program. Grounded in understandings of political representation, this coding scheme and tandem empirical efforts are oriented to persuade colleagues that (*a*) it makes sense to replace extant approaches to coding with this new, multitiered and theoretically grounded orientation; (*b*) this tool can help advance a richer portrait of American politics across time when deployed as an instrument for studies of Congress and history; and (*c*) it can open doors to more systematic comparative studies of legislatures and the substance of representation.

Though only illustrative, the considerations and examples we have offered above suggest a return, on a reconstituted and more empirically systematic basis, to a set of questions that once motivated a good many Americanists concerning how the content of policy makes politics. Lowi's articles (1964, 1970, 1972) taking up the theme of discerning the determination of politics by policy hit political science like a bolt of lightning, but in the absence of proper means for moving beyond its lumpy policy classifications they could not illuminate its core policy-makes-politics question over a longer term, but it remains compelling and insufficiently addressed. Lowi had aimed too high, as it were, by advancing a very parsimonious and abstract classification of policy arenas (first characterized famously as distributive, regulatory, and redistributive) capable of defining "arenas of power" and placing a vast array of case studies across American politics in time. Hampered in part by the level of aggregation, this approach proved very difficult to put into practice, but the basic ideas remain compelling. Each type of issue, he hypothesized, elicits different definitions of interest, different relations among interests, and different relations between interests and government. On this basis, he generated deductive claims, projecting outcomes from types of policy with respect to units of action (individuals, groups, associations), types of relations among units (logrolling, coalitions, peak associations and social classes), structures of power (nonconflictual, pluralistic, and conflictual), as well as relative stability, loci of decision, and patterns of implementation.

These challenges still stand as important to a realistic understanding of political behavior. They also are pivotal for democratic theory. Politics in liberal democracies, especially in legislatures grappling with particular enactments, never is politics in general. It always concerns distinct subjects that bear on relationships defining ties between the modern state, the economy, society, and the international arena and that determine the content and boundaries of stateness itself. At stake in each area of policy is whether, and how, governments will govern, with what instruments, and which degrees and implements of inducement, regulation, and coercion. Although we understand a good deal about how voting, opinion, lobbying, and other forms of participation shape outcomes with determinate contours and content, we curiously know rather less, despite some notable efforts, about reciprocal causation. Thus our first goal has been to revivify the somewhat aborted lineage of inquiry that asks whether and how the substance of policy issues shapes behavior by representatives by developing a better approach to coding public policy.

In turn, the policy-makes-politics question opens fresh opportunities to probe long-standing historical issues about the content and character of the political regime in the United States. The hypothesis of one-dimensional politics associated with Poole and Rosenthal and the complementary account of the hegemony of Lockean liberalism proposed by Louis Hartz demand systematic historical investigation via studies, over time, of congressional macropolitics. Can this vision of ideational continuity, behavioral persistence, and single-vector politics be sustained when policy is taken into account in a fine-grained manner via the application of a systematic approach to the substantive content of legislative debates and votes?

One approach to these regime issues would be the development of a better— that is, more substantively oriented—theory of macropolitics theory across time. At the moment, our theoretical understanding of the policy process is better than our empirical knowledge. Krehbiel's theory of pivotal politics, as noted, remains to be adequately tested across time and across the variety of policy issue areas. We know, for example, that legislation often passes through the Senate with less than three-fifths of its members voting in the affirmative. Why does this happen? Of course, the answer most certainly is related to the intensity of preferences, and these, it is not implausible to believe, vary across both time and policy areas. Moreover, for almost every other big claim in the congressional literature about information, parties, and polarization, among other leading subjects, we know rather little about whether and how shifts in substance affect these dynamics and processes that intervene between policy agendas and legislative productivity. Our approach to policy classification, in short, does not compete with extant theories, but provides an instrument for their extension and testing.

While developed initially as a tool to study both macropolitics and the policy process in the United States, our coding scheme's orientation to the substance of politics is germane to politics and policymaking under conditions of political representation more generally. Although some of its categories are particular to the United States, its basic structure and almost all its divisions can be transported to studies of legislative behavior and policy outputs in other liberal democracies, ands it lends itself to easy modification that can facilitate systematic comparative studies. Since our classification has been developed on the basis of attention to literature on political representation, it rests on explicit assumptions about how such governments operate. Thus we hope that this approach can become a focal point not only for scholars of American politics, but for colleagues interested in studying the policy process comparatively.

NOTES

1. Writing six decades later, Lawrence Chamberlain mounted a similar argument. "It does not detract from the importance of the President," he wrote, "to point out that this tendency to magnify his participation to the exclusion or neglect of Congress distorts the facts and creates impressions that are not only false but dangerous" (1946, 15).

2. Now Vice President Cheney, then a young, aspiring political scientist.

3. This is not to say that much important work within individual policy areas has not taken place (e.g., Lieberman and Lapinski 2001; Hacker 2002).

4. Important exceptions are by Bensel (1984) and Sanders (1999).

5. Sam Peltzman has also created a specialized, highly aggregated coding scheme that focuses on budget and regulation policies (Peltzman 1984).

6. Clausen extended his coding to cover the years of 1969–70 to remove "doubt [of] the validity of projecting behavior patterns observed in the past onto the present" (1973, 5).

7. A potential problem for our coding scheme deals with the rise of omnibus bills in the U.S. Congress. Omnibus legislation dates back at least to the 1940s, but we see a tremendous rise of such legislation in the 1980s (see Krutz 2001 for detailed history of omnibus bills). Appropriation bills all receive a double tier-3 coding, as each is identified as appropriation along with a substantive policy coding. If an appropriation bill is omnibus, its second tier-3 coding is "omnibus." Of course, omnibus bills are not limited to appropriations. Consequently, all omnibus legislation is identified as such; however, we attempt to determine the primary policy content of each bill and give it a substantive coding when possible. Technically, this maneuver violates our mutually

exclusive coding rule. However, we believe that omnibus legislation must be identified even though we do attempt to give such legislation substantive codes when possible.

8. This work is a collaborative project with Rose Razaghian (Yale University).

9. First-dimension scores, estimated through the technique outlined by Heckman and Snyder (1997), correlate at the .93 level. Our second dimension scores correlate at the .74 level.

10. Interestingly, with the results of the 1952 election, southern Democrats temporarily moved back toward the left side of the first dimension while remaining in a distinct position on the second.

11. Cloture rules in the Senate have often been a contentious issue. Several major reforms over the last century have been adopted, including the formal introduction of cloture in 1917 with a two-thirds present and voting rule, a reform in 1949 to change the two-thirds rule to consider only those senators "duly chosen and sworn," and the 1975 modification that allowed for cloture with a three-fifths present and voting, except when considering Senate rules, which required a two-thirds vote.

12. In making a trademark maneuver, Krehbiel leaves out political parties as an important feature of U.S. lawmaking.

13. Krehbiel assumes a unidimensional policy space. The assumption, we have already seen, though reasonable as a theoretical heuristic, both begs the question of whether preferences associated with this single dimension are consistent across time with regard to policy content and flies in the face of our findings and those of Heckman and Snyder regarding multidimensionality. It might be noted that a multidimensional issue space need not be chaotic, as certain institutions, especially congressional committees, work to constrain the issues that come to the floor. Still, even the internal organization of Congress and the political parties are not always able to limit and structure the issue dimension space.

14. In what we might refer to as step 1 in testing Krehbiel's basic model of lawmaking, after identifying the primary dimension of conflict, he instructs researchers to then identify "which and how lawmakers (including the president) want to change policy, and in which direction" (1998, 235). This is a very important point as it relates to the idea of intensity of preferences (a point discussed nicely by Hall 1996).

REFERENCES

Baumgartner, Frank R., and Bryan D. Jones. 1993. *Agendas and Instability in American Politics*. Chicago: University of Chicago Press.

Baumgartner, Frank R., Bryan D. Jones, and Michael C. MacLeod. 1998. "Lessons from the Trenches: Ensuring Quality, Reliability, and Usability in the Creation of a New Data Source." *Political Methodologist* 8 (2): 1–10.

Bensel, Richard. 1984. *Sectionalism and American Political Development, 1880–1980*. Madison: University of Wisconsin Press.

Binder, Sarah A. 1999. "The Dynamics of Legislative Gridlock, 1947–96." *American Political Science Review* 93:519–33.

Brady, David. 1978. "Critical Elections, Congressional Parties and Clusters of Policy Changes." *British Journal of Political Science* 8:79–99.

————. 1985. "A Reevaluation of Realignments in American Politics: Evidence from the House of Representatives." *American Political Science Review* 79:28–49.

————. 1988. *Critical Elections and Congressional Policy Making.* Palo Alto: Stanford University Press.

Brady, David, and Charles S. Bullock III. 1980. "Is There a Conservative Coalition in the House?" *Journal of Politics* 42:549–59.

Brady, David, and Barbara Sinclair. 1984. "Building Majorities for Policy Change in the House of Representatives." *Journal of Politics* 46:1033–60.

Brady, David, and Joseph Stewart. 1982. "Congressional Party Realignment and Transformations of Public Policy in Three Realignment Eras." *American Journal of Political Science* 26:333–60.

Burnham, W. Dean. 1970. *Critical Elections and the Mainsprings of American Politics.* New York: Norton.

Cameron, Charles M. 2000. *Veto Bargaining: Presidents and the Politics of Negative Power.* New York: Cambridge University Press.

Cameron, Charles M. John S. Lapinski, and Charles Riemann. 2000a. "Testing Formal Theories of Political Rhetoric." *Journal of Politics* 62:187–205.

————. 2000b. "Veto Threats." In *Veto Bargaining: Presidents and the Politics of Negative Power.* New York: Cambridge University Press.

Chamberlain, Lawrence H. 1946. *The President, Congress, and Legislation.* New York: Columbia University Press.

Clausen, Aage R. 1967. "Measurement Identity in the Longitudinal Analysis of Legislative Voting." *American Political Science Review* 61:1020–35.

————. 1973. *How Congressmen Decide: A Policy Focus.* New York: St. Martin's Press.

Clausen, Aage R., and Richard B. Cheney. 1970. "A Comparative Analysis of Senate and House Voting on Economic and Welfare Policy, 1953–1964." *American Political Science Review* 64:138–52.

Clausen, Aage R., and Carl E. Van Horn. 1977. "The Congressional Response to a Decade of Change: 1963–1972." *Journal of Politics* 39:624–66.

Clinton, Joshua, and John S. Lapinski. Forthcoming. "Measuring Significant Legislation, 1877–1948." In *Process, Party, and Policymaking: Further New Perspectives on the History of Congress*, ed. David W. Brady and Mathew D. McCubbins, Palo Alto: Stanford University Press.

Coleman, John J. 1999. "Unified Government, Divided Government, and Party Responsiveness." *American Political Science Review* 93:821–35.

Cooper, Joseph, and David W. Brady. 1981a. "Institutional Context and Leadership Style: The House from Cannon to Rayburn." *American Political Science Review* 75:411–25.

————. 1981b. "Toward a Diachronic Analysis of Congress." *American Political Science Review* 75:988–1006.

DiMaggio, Paul, Bethany Bryson, and John Evans. "Have Americans' Social Attitudes Become More Polarized?" *American Journal of Sociology* 102:690–755.

Elster, Jon. 1999. "Accountability in Athenian Politics." In *Democracy, Accountability, and Representation*, ed. Adam Przeworski, Susan C. Stokes, and Bernard Manin. New York: Cambridge University Press.

Erikson, Robert S., Michael B. MacKuen, and James Stimson. 2002. *The Macro Polity.* New York: Cambridge University Press.

Hacker, Jacob. 2002. *The Divided Welfare State: The Battle over Public and Private Social Benefits in the United States.* New York: Cambridge University Press.

Hall, Richard L. 1996. *Participation in Congress.* New Haven: Yale University Press.

Hartz, Louis. 1955. *The Liberal Tradition in America: An Interpretation of American Political Thought since the Revolution.* New York: Harcourt Brace.

Heckman, James J., and James M. Snyder Jr. 1997. "Linear Probability Models of the Demand for Attributes with an Empirical Application to Estimating the Preferences of Legislators." *Rand Journal of Economics* 28 (0): 142–89.

Howell, William, E. Scott Adler, Charles M. Cameron, and Charles Riemann. 2000. "Divided Government and the Legislative Productivity of Congress, 1945–1994." *Legislative Studies Quarterly:*25:285–312.

Katznelson, Ira, Kim Geiger, and Daniel Kryder. 1993. "Limiting Liberalism: The Southern Veto in Congress, 1933–1950." *Political Science Quarterly* 108:283–306.

Katznelson, Ira, and John S. Lapinski. "At the Crossroads: Congress and American Political Development." Yale University, typescript.

Katznelson, Ira, John S. Lapinski, and Rose Razaghian. 2001a. "Does Policy Make Politics? Congressional Agendas, Lawmaking, and Sectionalism, 1930–1952." Paper presented at the Annual Meeting of the Midwest Political Science Association, Chicago.

———. 2001b. "Policy Space and Voting Coalitions in Congress: The Bearing of Policy on Politics, 1930–1954." ISERP Working Paper 01-02.

Katznelson, Ira, and Barry Weingast. 2005. *Preferences and Situations: Points of Intersection between Historical and Rational Choice Institutionalism.* New York: Russel Sage Foundation.

Key, V. O., Jr. 1955. "A Theory of Critical Elections." *Journal of Politics* 17:3–18.

Krehbiel, Keith. 1998. *Pivotal Politics: A Theory of U.S. Lawmaking.* Chicago: University of Chicago Press.

Krutz, Glen S. 2001. *Hitching a Ride: Omnibus Legislating in the U.S. Congress.* Columbus: Ohio State University Press.

Lapinski, John S. 2000a. "Representation and Reform: A Congress Centered Approach to American Political Development." Ph.D. diss., Columbia University.

———. 2000b. "Congress, Legislative Performance, and American Political Development." Paper presented at the Annual Meeting of the American Political Science Association, Legislative Politics Division, Washington, D.C.

Lieberman, Robert, and John S. Lapinski. 2001. "American Federalism, Race, and the Administration of Welfare." *British Journal of Political Science* 31:303–29.

Lijphart, Arend. 1999. *Patterns of Democracy: Government Forms and Performance in Thirty-six Countries.* New Haven: Yale University Press.

Lowi, Theodore J. 1964. "American Business, Public Policy, Case-Studies, and Political Theory." *World Politics* 16:677–715.

———. 1970. "Decision Making vs. Policy Making: Toward an Antidote for Technocracy." *Public Administration Review* 30:314–25.

———. 1972. "Four Systems of Policy, Politics, and Choice." *Public Administration Review* 32:298–310.

Manin, Bernard. 1997. *The Principles of Representative Government*. New York: Cambridge University Press.

Mayhew, David R. 1966. *Party Loyalty among Congressmen: The Difference between Democrats and Republicans, 1947–1962*. Cambridge: Harvard University Press.

———. 1974. *Congress: The Electoral Connection*. New Haven: Yale University Press.

———. 1991. *Divided We Govern: Party Control, Lawmaking, and Investigations, 1946–1990*. New Haven: Yale University Press.

———. 2002. *Electoral Realignments: A Critique of an American Genre*. New Haven: Yale University Press.

McCarty, Nolan, Keith T. Poole, and Howard Rosenthal. 1997. *Income Redistribution and the Realignment of American Politics*. Washington, D.C.: AEI Press.

Peltzman, Sam. 1984. "Constituent Interests and Congressional Voting." *Journal of Law and Economics* 27:181–210.

Pitkin, Hanna F. 1967. *The Concept of Representation*. Berkeley and Los Angeles: University of California Press.

Poole, Keith T. 1998. "Changing Minds? Not in Congress!" University of Houston. Typescript.

Poole, Keith T., and Howard Rosenthal. 1984. "The Polarization of American Politics." *Journal of Politics* 46:1061–79.

———. 1997. *Congress: A Political-Economic History of Roll Call Voting*. New York: Oxford University Press.

Przeworski, Adam, Susan C. Stokes, and Bernard Manin, eds. 1999. *Democracy, Accountability, and Representation*. New York: Cambridge University Press.

Sanders, Elizabeth. 1999. *Roots of Reform: Farmers, Workers, and the American State*. Chicago: University of Chicago Press.

Shugart, Matthew S., and John Carey. 1992. *Presidents and Assemblies: Constitutional Design and Electoral Dynamics*. New York: Cambridge University Press.

Sinclair, Barbara. 1978. "From Party Voting to Regional Fragmentation: The House of Representatives." *American Politics Quarterly* 6:125–46.

———. 1982. *Congressional Realignment, 1925–1978*. Austin: University of Texas Press.

Skowronek, Stephen. 1982. *Building a New American State: The Expansion of National Administrative Capacities, 1877–1920*. New York: Cambridge University Press.

Smith, Rogers M. 1997. *Civic Ideals: Conflicting Visions of Citizenship in US History*. New Haven: Yale University Press.

Turner, Julius. 1970. *Party and Constituency: Pressures on Congress*. Revised by Edward V. Scheiner Jr. Baltimore: Johns Hopkins University Press.

Weingast, Barry R., and William J. Marshall. 1988. "The Industrial Organization of Congress; or, Why Legislatures, Like Firms, Are Not Organized as Markets." *Journal of Political Economy* 96:132–63.

Wilson, Woodrow. 1885. *Congressional Government*. New York: Houghton Mifflin.

Young, Gary, and Valerie Heitshusen. 2002. "Testing Competing Theories of Policy Production, 1874–1946." University of Missouri. Typescript.

PART III: *Testing Theories of Macropolitics across Time*

5

Macropolitics and Changes in the U.S. Code: Testing Competing Theories of Policy Production, 1874–1946

Valerie Heitshusen and Garry Young

In recent years, there has been a surge of work examining the trends in legislative production over time. Mayhew (1991) reevaluated the conventional wisdom that divided government contributes to gridlock by examining the legislative production of major policy since World War II. Other scholars followed, attempting to explain changes in productivity in more theoretical and empirical detail, by elaborating a new theoretical structure (e.g., Krehbiel 1998), by using alternate measures of legislative productivity (e.g., Howell, et al. 2000), and by testing for other factors, including the influences of key legislative features (such as supermajority rules like the filibuster) and changing ideological patterns in Congress (e.g., Brady and Volden 1998; Binder 1999; Coleman 1999). Each of these studies has significantly advanced our understanding of legislative productivity and major policy change during the last half-century.

However, the focus on the postwar period potentially limits our understanding of policy change in the United States. While the postwar period provides fertile ground for examining the influence of divided government, for example, the period is not so useful for examining the importance of critical elections. A large literature on partisan realignments suggests that these electoral upheavals play a key role (at least in the short to medium term) in producing major policy shifts. While some scholars maintain that large partisan shifts (perhaps even realignments) have occurred during this recent period, there is no agreed-upon critical election to examine.

Furthermore, sole focus on the postwar period invites the development of theoretical and empirical results that are in some fashion historically time-bound. In our view the discipline should strive for theories that span historical eras. Divided government in the modern era may or may not have the same meaning and impact as during the latter half of the nineteenth century, a period that saw a frequency of divided government comparable to the post–

World War II period (Brady 1993). Likewise, prior to World War II the fili-buster was a very different procedural device, both formally and informally, than it is today (Wawro and Schickler 2004). Finally, of course, the nature of the American state and the level of activism taken by the national government is very different today than earlier in history. A notion such as "public mood" (e.g., Schlesinger 1986; Huntington 1981; Stimson, MacKuen, and Erickson 1995), a staple of the current literature, does not necessarily translate well to prior periods.

In addition, the measures used in these studies are generally problematic for extension back in time. The main type of data, inspired by Mayhew, relies on journalistic sources for measuring policy significance (but see Clinton and Lapinski Forthcoming). These types of sources simply do not exist, in any meaningful, reasonably systematic way, prior to the rise of the modern media. The data are thus time-bound, and the sheer lack of alternative data sources undermines claims about robustness. We need alternative measures of policy change for the modern era, and, ideally, we need alternative measures that go back further in time.

In this chapter we take some steps towards addressing these problems. We introduce a new data source, one that we believe offers great promise in pro-viding measures of policy change over much longer historical periods than has been attempted previously. In particular, we track changes in the United States Code, which can be extended as far back as 1874 (and perhaps as far back as 1789) and might also be consistently extended forward in time so that stud-ies of legislative productivity could include virtually the entire period of U.S. history. In this first effort we utilize one of our Code measures—a measure of overall policy production in the United States—for the period 1874–1946, a span of years that offers a number of notable periods in U.S. history, including two realignments, the growth of the modern American state, and two world wars. Along the way we evaluate the existing body of theory from the perspec-tive of these earlier historical periods.

MEASURING POLICY CHANGE: THE UNITED STATES CODE

Though not without flaws as a source of data (Lynch 1997),[1] the United States Code provides a comprehensive and convenient source for tracking federal statutory authority. Significantly for our purposes, the Code also provides a detailed accounting of each public law's impact on the Code since 1874. This accounting provides the basis for our examination of relative legislative pro-duction.

The Code took on its current structure with the 1926 publication of the *Code of the Laws of the United States of America*. This work represented the culmination of years of largely unsuccessful earlier efforts at comprehensive codification (United States 1926, v). A much-corrected 1934 edition followed, and new editions have been published every six years since.

As listed in table 5.1, the Code is segmented into fifty titles. This same title structure remains in use today with the exception of minor name changes and two title deletions.[2] As table 5.1 demonstrates, the titles alone provide a fairly comprehensive, albeit broad, topical description of federal policy. Topics become far more precise as we move to the various structural levels within each title, such as chapters and sections.

Since our main concern is with policy change, we need to track changes in the Code from statute to statute and Congress to Congress. The Code provides the basis for this in tabular form. In the 1994 version of the Code this table is table 3, "Statutes at Large." Earlier versions of the Code use different naming, numbering, and organization conventions for the same information. For example, in the 1934 edition the information is contained in "Parallel Reference Table II—Statutes at Large" and "Table of Statutes Repealed Prior to January 3, 1935." These tables reconcile what is found in specific titles and sections of the Code with what is found in the actual *Statutes at Large*.[3] Since this information is provided back to 1874, we can track the specific Code impact of every public law passed for all Congresses back to the forty-third and forward to the present.

Consider the Civil Service Act of 1883 (better known as the Pendleton Act). Under January 16, 1883, the relevant tables in the 1934 Code show the chapter number where the act can be found in the *Statutes at Large*. It also shows how specific sections and page numbers of the chapter affect specific titles and sections within the Code. (The Pendleton Act changed seven sections of Title 5, five sections of Title 18, and one section of Title 40.) Thus we can measure the nature and amount of Code changes down to the bill level and aggregating upward to days, months, years, Congresses, decades, and so on. Ultimately we can determine the relative depth of change within a given policy area—down to an exceptional degree of specificity—and we can measure breadth of change across a wide range of policy.

Our concern here is with measuring the amount of overall policy production produced by each Congress over the 1874–1946 period. We are not concerned with landmark legislation per se as much as we are concerned with overall production.[4] How much did a Congress, with the support or opposition of the president, change overall statutory law in the United States? The most obvious measure of policy production is simply a count of the number of bills passed into public law for a given Congress. The problem with this measure is that a mere count of bills passed says little about the overall significance of the bills themselves. In their analysis of post–World War II production, Howell et al. (2000) use counts of public laws passed, but overcome the significance problem

TABLE 5.1 U.S. Code Titles as of 1946

Title	Title Name	Topics Included (selected)
1	General Provisions	Organization & definitions in the U.S. Code; explanation of congressional acts, resolutions, and repeals
2	The Congress	Member election & compensation, congressional organization, Library of Congress, corruption
3	The President	Presidential elections & compensation, White House Police
4	Flag & Seal, Seat of Government & the States	Regulations on use of flag & seal, administration of oath to government officials
5	Executive Depts & Government Officers & Employees	General provisions, various cabinet departments (e.g. State, War, Treasury, Justice), Civil Service Commission
6	Official and Penal Bonds	Treasury bonds: custody, liability, delinquency, rates, jurisdiction of suits
7	Agriculture	Regulation of agriculture products, production statistics, agricultural pests, packers & stockyards
8	Aliens & Nationality	Citizenship, civil rights, freedmen, immigration, naturalization
9	Arbitration	Procedures & regulations of arbitration (chiefly in the area of maritime transactions & contracts)
10	Army	Organization, personnel, ranks & advancement, army property & equip, air corps, military posts
11	Bankruptcy	Courts of bankruptcy & jurisdictions, estates, debtor relief, creditors
12	Banks & Banking	National banks, Federal Reserve, taxation, Farm Credit Administration, federal home loans, credit unions
13	Census	Bureau of the Census, collection of U.S. statistics, decennial census

TABLE 5.1 (*continued*)

Title	Title Name	Topics Included (selected)
14	Coast Guard	Organization, personnel, ranks, officer offenses, medals & honors
15	Commerce & Trade	Monopolies, FTC, securities, trade-marks, Bureau of Standards, federal emergency relief, industrial recovery
16	Conservation	National parks & forests, Forest Service, protection of timber & wildlife, Bureau of Fisheries, TVA
17	Copyrights	Copyright records, authors' rights, infringement of copyright, procedures for challenging copyrights
18	Criminal Code & Criminal Procedures	Criminal offenses, criminal procedure (arrest, warrants, bail, extradition), prisons & prisoner treatment
19	Customs Duties	Collection ports & officers, foreign trade zones, Tariff Act & other tariff provisions
20	Education	Office of Education, vocational education, Smithsonian, National Zoo & Arboretum, government research collections
21	Food & Drugs	Regulation of meats, dairy, animals, serums, narcotics, and adulterated foods & drugs
22	Foreign Relations & Intercourse	Diplomatic & Consular Service, consular courts & officers, passports, foreign relations generally
23	Highways	Federal Highway Act (aid to states, construction & maintenance), miscellaneous provisions (freight, motor vehicles)
24	Hospitals, Asylums, & Cemeteries	Military & other federal hospitals, Soldiers' Home, national cemeteries
25	Indians	BIA, agreements with (and protection of) Indians, government of Indian reservations, ceded Indian lands, Indian education

TABLE 5.1 (*continued*)

Title	Title Name	Topics Included (selected)
26	Internal Revenue	Detailed tax provisions, tax officers, organization of joint taxation committees
27	Intoxicating Liquors	General regulations, Prohibition & repeal, interstate transport of liquor
28	Judicial Code & Judiciary	Organization & jurisdiction of courts, court officers, U.S. Supreme Court, juries, evidence & procedure
29	Labor	BLS, labor disputes (including mediation & court jurisdictions), employment stabilization
30	Mineral Lands & Mining	Bureau of Mines, regulations & leases of lands with minerals, oil or gas
31	Money & Finance	Treasury, U.S. Mint & general coinage provisions, legal tender, public debt, currency expansion
32	National Guard	Organization, armament & equipment, pay & training, ranks & offenses
33	Navigation & Navigable Waters	Sea navigation, inland navigation (rivers, harbors, Great Lakes), protection & improvement of navigable waters
34	Navy	Organization, personnel, ranks & advancement, naval property & equipment, Naval Academy
35	Patents	Patent Office (restrictions on officers & employees), procedures for granting & protecting patents
36	Patriotic Societies & Observances	Red Cross, BSA, American Legion, American War Mothers, commission on battle monuments
37	Pay & Allowances	Pay in the army, navy, marine corps, coast guard, Coast & Geodetic Survey, & Public Health Service
38	Pensions, Bonuses, & Veterans' Relief	Commissioner of pensions, disability pensions, veterans' pensions & relief programs

TABLE 5.1 (*continued*)

Title	Title Name	Topics Included (selected)
39	The Postal Service	Post offices & postmasters, postage, franking, stamps, mail regulations
40	Public Buildings, Property, & Works	Public buildings & grounds in DC, National Archives, Capitol buildings & grounds
41	Public Contracts	Procedures for public bids & contracts, regulations on public expenditures & accounting, public supplies, GAO
42	The Public Health & Welfare	Public Health Service, sanitation & quarantine, viruses, maternity & infancy welfare, Children's Bureau
43	Public Lands	Geological survey, land districts, homesteads, irrigation, federal lands, reclamation, timber & grazing
44	Public Printing & Documents	GPO, congressional & executive printing, distribution of public documents
45	Railroads	Adjustment boards, labor regulations, mediation & arbitration, safety regulations
46	Shipping	Vessel regulation, fisheries regulation, intercoastal shipping, merchant marine, tonnage duties
47	Telegraphs, Telephones, & Radio-Telegraphs	Telegraphs, submarine cables, radio & wire communication and regulation
48	Territories & Insular Possessions	BIA, Alaska, Hawaii, Puerto Rico, Philippines, Canal Zone, Guam, other territories
49	Transportation	Interstate commerce, air commerce, interstate rail transport, inland waterway transport
50	War	Espionage, Board of Ordnance, arsenals & arms, explosives, insurrection, land for national defense purposes

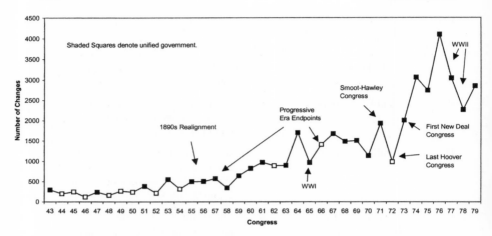

Figure 5.1: Number of U.S. Code Section Changes, 1874–1946

through a careful typology of bills into four categories of declining importance. Performing such a categorization for earlier periods is difficult since the
consistent authoritative sources necessary—such as publications by *Congressional Quarterly*—do not exist prior to World War II (but see Lapinski 2002).

Our U.S. Code–based measure of overall policy production is simply a
count of the number of sections within each title that were changed by each
public law created in a given Congress, summed across the entire Congress.
Thus we rely on a basic assumption. We assume that a statute's importance is
directly related to the substantive impact the statute had on the U.S. Code. The
more parts of the Code a bill changes, the greater a new law's importance.
Furthermore, the amount of cumulative change in the Code over a full Congress is presumed to indicate the overall productivity of that Congress. This
measure enjoys face validity. For example, elsewhere (Young and Heitshusen
2002) we found that statutes that changed the Code the most during this period
tend to be exactly those laws that historians identify as being landmarks. Further, as we see in figure 5.1, the overall trends and the most productive Congresses largely comport with expectations. Figure 5.1 presents the number of
section changes per Congress for the 43rd through 79th Congresses. The overall series exhibits a clear upward trend, mirroring the rise of the modern American state during the last years of the nineteenth century and, especially, during the New Deal years. Along the way there are notable spikes upward: the
Wilson 64th Congress (1915–17) saw passage of bills such as the Federal
Farm Loan Act and the Workmen's Compensation Act; the Hoover 70th Congress (1927–29), which passed Smoot-Hawley, most notably; and the New
Deal Congresses, starting with the 72nd (1931–33). Likewise there are spikes

downward such as the world war Congresses (65th, 77th, 78th) and Hoover's last Congress, the divided 72nd (1931–33), the least productive Congress since World War I.

ANALYSIS AND RESULTS

Clearly, our policy production measure enjoys some face validity as a measure of legislative activity, as major peaks seem to coincide with periods conventionally associated with governmental energy, while clear valleys appear in more passive times. However, a significant amount of variation remains. This presents an opportunity to examine the factors that may be driving the trends— be they associated with interinstitutional partisan control and ideological heterogeneity, electoral upheavals, the balance of power in Congress, or the political context more generally. Thus we now discuss the potential explanatory mechanisms examined in the literature on the post–World War II period and discuss their relevance (and operationalization issues) for the earlier time period.

Divided government. The U.S. system of shared separated powers highlights the potential for divided government to affect legislative production. Conventionally scholars argue that divided government decreases legislative productivity (e.g., Sundquist 1988). Mayhew's (1991) revision of the conventional wisdom spawned a still ongoing debate over the production effects of divided government (e.g., Krehbiel 1998; Binder 1999; Coleman 1999; Howell et al. 2000; see also Cameron 2000 and Groseclose and McCarty 2001). The empirical portion of this debate focuses on the post–World War II period. Divided government, however, is hardly a new phenomenon in American political history. Within the time period of our study, at least one chamber majority differed from the president's party in 11 of the 37 Congresses. Most of these occurred prior to the 55th Congress, which came in the wake of the 1896 critical election. As figure 5.1 demonstrates, the big increases in policy production occur after the period of substantial divided government; levels then drop notably for the divided 72nd Congress before rising again in the unified New Deal Congresses. To test for the effect of divided government, we score a dummy variable equal to 1 in Congresses where the president's party differs from the majority party of at least one of the two congressional chambers.[5]

Critical elections. The impact of critical elections on policy is most closely associated with Brady (1988). In brief, he argues that the locally oriented attention of legislators interacts with the myriad of obstacles facing legislation to prevent frequent occurrence of major policy change. Occasionally, an issue reaches such national salience that the normally locally oriented congressional elections nationalize in such a way as to create a new congressional majority, combined with a president of the same party. Unlike conventional unitary governments, unitary governments in the wake of these "critical elections" can pass major new policies because the normal localized tendencies of Congress have been briefly overwhelmed by factors such as heightened partisanship and committee turnover.

As noted earlier, most of the literature focuses on the post–World War II era, a period lacking in (conventionally accepted) critical elections. Our study includes two critical election periods: 1894–96 and 1932–36 (Brady 1988). While in future work we plan to more fully evaluate the critical elections literature by including, for example, data on elections, partisanship changes, and related institutional changes, for now we accommodate the possible critical elections effect as a simple dummy variable. We code a 1 for the post-critical-election Congresses: the 54th and 55th (1890s) and the 73rd–75th (New Deal).

Gridlock interval. Krehbiel (1998) develops a lawmaking theory based on a simple spatial model incorporating the two extreme points that must be overcome for legislative production to occur: the president's veto and the Senate's filibuster. In Krehbiel's theory, as the interval between the "pivot" points widens, the chances of policy change decreases since more status quo points are likely within the interval. Thus the name: gridlock interval. As Adler and Lapinski point out in this volume, Krehbiel's theory offers a highly parsimonious explanation for policy change (or the lack thereof) and offers a counter-explanation (or at least a more precise one) for potential divided government effects. Indeed, the effects of critical elections may also be accounted for by pivotal politics since, presumably, critical elections radically narrow the gridlock interval.

Pushing "pivotal politics" back to the era before World War II poses practical and theoretical problems. Most notably, the U.S. Senate did not adopt cloture until 1917. In general, terminating pre-1917 filibusters required unanimous consent (Binder and Smith 1997). Thus, strictly speaking, the pre-1917 Senate pivots were the endpoints of the Senate's ideological spectrum, that is, the chamber's most conservative and most liberal senators. In practice, a single extremist senator threatening a filibuster likely stood little chance against a determined supermajority. Presumably successful filibusters in such conditions required at least "a little group of willful men."[6]

Defining the necessary size of such a little group, and thus defining pivots interior to the Senate's endpoints, would be difficult and ad hoc. We take a mixed approach by using two different types of measures for gridlock. The first uses NOMINATE scores and treats the Senate endpoints as the gridlock interval for the pre-1917 period. The other is based on Krehbiel's (1998) inter-election swing measure of gridlock interval change.

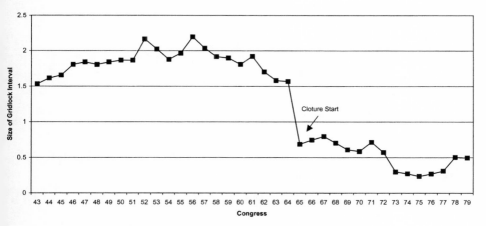

Figure 5.2: NOMINATE-based Gridlock Interval, 1874–1946

Since no cloture device existed prior to 1917, we define the gridlock interval for the pre-1917 Congresses (43rd–64th) as the distance between the most liberal and most conservative senators on the D-NOMINATE first dimension (Poole and Rosenthal 1997).[7] By doing this we assume that the president and the veto override points in the House are interior to this space. (We do not see this as a particularly heroic assumption given the wide breadth of the interval we use.) The postcloture period presents a new problem, however. Ideally, we need measures that are comparable across institutions—House, Senate, and the president—and across time. Such data does not exist for the full period of our study. Thus, our postcloture gridlock interval measure is the distance between the senators who lie at the one-third points from the Senate's two endpoints.[8] This approach is subject to two complaints. First, if the president's ideal point is interior to the one-third to one-third interval, then our gridlock interval is too large. Second, if the House pivot points, that is, veto override points, are exterior to the Senate one-third to one-third interval, then our gridlock interval is too small.

Figure 5.2 presents our gridlock interval measure for the time period. Not surprisingly, the size of the interval drops dramatically with the adoption of cloture. This drop is an artifact of our measure, but we believe it also reflects the institutional importance of cloture adoption. It is of course true that filibusters during the nineteenth century were less frequent than in the twentieth century (Binder and Smith 1997). One can argue that this is evidence that filibusters posed a lesser threat in the nineteenth century and thus our precloture measure overaccounts for the filibuster. (The obvious counterfactual problem here is that the lack of cloture made filibuster threats more credible—and probably more successful—thus reducing filibusters.) As a control, when we

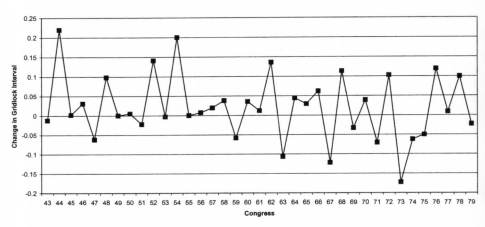

Figure 5.3: Krehbiel's Change in Gridlock Interval Variable, 1874–1946

use this gridlock variable, we also include a dummy variable for the precloture and cloture periods (scored as 1 beginning with the 65th Congress).

As an alternative to our NOMINATE-based measure we also use Krehbiel's (1998) gridlock interval change variable. Krehbiel's measure was meant to capture the logic of pivotal politics, with cloture being a key component. However, Krehbiel's measure does not directly assess the location of the pivot points; rather it taps into the interelection swings that occur every two years by tracking the party of the president in conjunction with the inflow and outflow of Democrats and Republicans in the two chambers. The basic logic of this measure should hold before and after cloture.

Creating this variable involves several steps: (1) calculating net Democratic gains/losses in each congressional chamber; (2) averaging the two scores across the chambers; (3) determining whether or not the gridlock interval expanded or contracted based on (a) which party won the presidential election and which party gained net seats in Congress or (b) whether the president's party gained or lost seats in the midterm elections. Based on whether or not the interval expanded or contracted, the average turnover score (calculated in step 2) is coded as negative (for contraction) or positive (for expansion). For cases that Krehbiel terms "indeterminate," the coding is 0. (See Krehbiel 1998, 58–62, for spatial diagrams illustrating the logic and to see how these coding rules work for the 80th–104th Congresses.) Figure 5.3 presents the Krehbiel measure for our period of study.[9] The mean is 0.02 (indicating a small expansion of the interval, on average); the largest expansions occur after the 1874 and 1894 midterm elections, and the largest contraction of the interval occurs after the 1932 contest, in which preferences become homogenized with the election of FDR and an influx of his partisans in Congress.[10]

The role of party. While measures of the gridlock interval are designed to account for the extent of ideological room within which elected officials have to maneuver (theoretically, vis-à-vis the policy status quo), such measures are, in theory, strictly apartisan. Thus if party—in some combination with preferences—affects production, the gridlock measure falls short. There is no need here to delve into the well-worn party-versus-preferences debate, but we find it prudent to provide some competing party-based explanation for production.

The presence or absence of divided government is also intended to capture the ideological interinstitutional context, and unlike the gridlock interval it does so in an inherently partisan way. Yet the way the literature treats divided government is exceptionally blunt—divided government exists, or it does not exist. Some distinguish between full divided government and partial divided government, based on whether the president's party is a minority in both chambers. Such treatment cannot account for a simple fact: all divided governments (and all unified governments) are not created equal. Consider a familiar modern example. Richard Nixon and Gerald Ford both served during divided governments. In general, Nixon faced a heterogeneous, relatively small, Democratic majority, especially in the House; indeed the Nixon Congresses largely featured the cross-partisan Conservative Coalition. In contrast, the 1974 Watergate election dramatically increased both the margin and the homogeneity of the Democratic majority, and Ford was forced to resort to the veto.[11]

Statistically, scholars treat these two very different divided governments identically. Both are coded as a 1 or 0 dummy variable, depending on the coding scheme. A key strength of Krehbiel's work on gridlock is that he subsumes these issues into a more powerful explanatory and elegant framework that captures the institutional structure of our separation-of-powers system. Yet in doing so, his model has no need for a party component, as party, in his words, is not outcome-consequential to lawmaking. Other scholars have argued that more nuanced measures of congressional coalitional dynamics are necessary to accurately model policy production. Scholars such as Binder (1999) and Coleman (1999) have included measures of bicameral ideological difference, the presence of a chamber supermajority, and the percentage of congressional moderates as indications of the balance of power within Congress.

Each of these measures has its strengths, though none addresses the separation-of-powers dynamic that the gridlock interval or a divided/unified government dummy variable provides. Our approach is to take into account two salient issues in divided and unified governments, and then consider their relation to the president. Namely, as in the Nixon/Ford example, the impact of divided government depends on the cohesion of the majority party, and on the majority party's size. An incohesive majority party lies prey to the president's ability to construct bipartisan or cross-partisan coalitions. A small majority party, even one that is relatively cohesive, finds it difficult to muster a majority

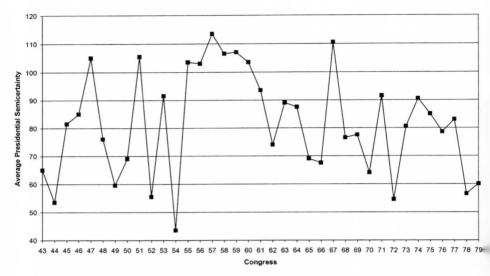

Figure 5.4: Semicertainty Score of the President's Party Averaged across Both Chambers, 1874–1946

against the president's party. To incorporate both unity and size we adapt the semicertainty scores developed by Cooper and Young (1997). Cooper and Young's semicertainty score identifies all the members of the majority party who supported the party on at least 80 percent of all party votes (where at least 50 percent of one party opposed at least 50 percent of the other party). The score is created by dividing the number of these "semicertain" party supporters by the number of members needed for a majority (multiplied by 100). So if the Senate's majority party had fifty-one 80 percent-plus supporters, the score is 100. If they had sixty 80 percent-plus supporters, the score is 118.

For our purposes we need to account for both chambers and the president. We do this by identifying the semicertainty score of the *president's* party in each chamber. We then take the average across the two chambers. Figure 5.4 shows the semicertainty variation.

Public mood. Thus far, the determinants of policy production we have discussed tend to focus on the direct policymaking constraints (or lack thereof) on public officials, rather than the broader political context of the day. Divided government, the gridlock interval, and the semicertainty scores all tap into the ideological and partisan landscape in Congress and in relation to the president in various ways. The occurrence of a critical election is arguably more related to the larger context since it indicates a sea change in the political cleavages among voters, and thus taps voter policy demand. However, this notion also relates to constraints on officials; specifically, scholars argue that the importance of election-induced legislative turnover lies as much in its effect on the power-making structure within Congress as in the influx of legislators with new preferences (Brady 1988). Thus, we are left with only this (very blunt) measure of citizen demand for legislative production.

Many scholars, some of whom are not specifically interested in legislative production, have argued that we can identify changes in the general political climate among the populace, and that public demand for legislative action can be thought of in terms of proclivities towards (or against) government activism. The terms used for public sentiment are varied—for example, *public mood* (Stimson 1991), *public purpose* (Schlesinger 1986), *creedal passion* (Huntington 1981), *national mood* (Kingdon 1984)—but each implies that there is some sort of public demand for policy action or inaction. Some scholars who examine policy production (e.g., Stimson, Mackuen, and Erikson 1995; Taylor 1998; Binder 1999) have used public opinion data to measure public mood. Survey data does not exist for the period of our study.

Other scholars (e.g., Mayhew 1991) code dummy variables for eras during which there is scholarly agreement that an activist mood did, in fact, exist. For example, Mayhew (1991) codes the years in the 1960s and early 1970s as "activist" years. For our earlier period, one might argue for variables that indicate activist periods such as the Progressive Era, the New Deal period, and so on. However, as we will discuss again later, the inclusion of such variables is open to theoretical debate. Public demands for policy change ought to be at least indirectly accounted for in electoral, partisan, and ideological shifts that are at some level already measured by indicators of divided government, critical elections, the gridlock interval, and the semicertainty scores. Including variables for certain periods allows for debate over which eras to include, as well as concern that they simply are retrospective alternative measures of the dependent variable. Thus, we do not include such measures here, in the hopes that our more parsimonious and theoretically defensible models will suffice for present purposes.

Budgetary situation. Perhaps more policy production is possible or attractive when budgets are in surplus (Mayhew 1991). The New Deal, however, featured a period of deficit spending coupled with high policy production, suggesting that the opposite relationship may hold. Indeed, governments that (consciously or not) follow Keynesian-like fiscal policies probably will produce more policy while also producing greater deficits. We control for budgetary conditions by using deficits (surpluses) as a percentage of budgetary outlays. Thus a positive relationship between budgetary situations and policy production would suggest that production increases with surpluses.

War. Finally, it is possible that policy production is affected by war. To control for this we scored a dummy variable accounting for the Spanish-American War, World War I, and World War II.

RESULTS

Table 5.2 reports ARIMA estimates for policy production levels (first differenced) from 1847 to 1946.[12] In the third column, we present results using the NOMINATE-based measure of the gridlock interval size (model 1); the right-hand column (model 2) instead uses Krehbiel's interelection swing measure of change in the gridlock interval. Each model performs well, with some support for most of the theoretically expected relationships, with one notable exception.

TABLE 5.2 Overall Policy Production (1874–1946)

| | | Model 1 | | Model 2 | |
| | | Estimate | | Estimate | |
Variable	Expectation	(SE)	p	(SE)	p
Divided Government	−	42.57 (101.80)	.68	15.18 (106.68)	.89
Average Semicertainty Score of the President's Party	+	4.45 (2.47)	.07	1.25 (2.76)	.65
Critical Election	+	317.58 (73.65)	.00	285.52 (77.53)	.00
Gridlock Interval (NOMINATE)	−	−305.97 (134.11)	.02		
Gridlock Interval (Krehbiel)	−			−1348.11 (669.56)	.04
Cloture	?	−330.12 (179.42)	.07		
War	−	−544.79 (125.04)	.00	−527.59 (132.12)	.00
Budgetary Situation	?	−2.16 (1.18)	.07	−3.22 (1.10)	.00
Constant		244.05 (327.95)	.46	13.41 (285.96)	.96
Wald χ^2 $n = 36$		158.22	.00	147.81	.00

Note: ARIMA (AR2) models, estimated in Stata 6.0. The dependent variable is the number of section changes (first-differenced).

In particular—and consistent with Mayhew—we find that the Divided Government estimate is not statistically significant; indeed, the coefficients are positive. The "culprit" here is our use of the semicertainty score. As we argued, we believe the semicertainty score more adequately accounts for not just the overall effects of divided or unified government, but also for the large variation not captured by a simple divided/unified government dummy variable. Indeed, what happens in the estimates is that the semicertainty score drives out the effect of the divided government variable. Removing the semicertainty score and reestimating the models yields a negative and statistically significant effect for divided government.

The semicertainty score itself does have the expected effects, though it reaches significance only in model 1. The independent effect of this variable suggest that interinstitutional legislative bargaining and productivity is about more than just ideological distance as measured by the gridlock interval. Increasing this score from its mean (81.5) to one standard deviation above the mean (100.2) yields a predicted 39 percent increase in the production measure (model 1).

The estimates provide some evidence that the electoral upheaval that accompanies a partisan realignment does have strong and expected (positive) effects in both models. Using the estimates in model 1, the independent effect of a critical election is a 149 percent predicted increase in the production measure. Furthermore, the effect is not just from the New Deal realignment. From figure 5.1 it appears that the effects of the 1890s realignment were modest at best. However, if we rerun the estimates from models 1 and 2, but with separate dummy variables for the 1890s and New Deal realignments, we obtain positive coefficients for each variable in both models. The New Deal is statistically significant in both models; the 1890s realignment, while smaller in effect than the New Deal, is statistically significant in model 1, and just short of significance in model 2. We thus conclude that the effect we report in table 5.2 for the Critical Elections variable is not simply an artifact of the New Deal.

Both gridlock interval measures seem robust; a large or increasing gridlock interval—however measured—dampens overall legislative productivity. For example, again using model 1, the effect of increasing the gridlock score from its mean (1.3) to one standard deviation above its mean (1.99) is a 98 percent predicted decrease in the dependent variable (from 213 to 4, when all other variables are set at their mean, or at 0 for the dummy variables).

The control variables measuring the incidence of war and the budgetary situation are also statistically significant. Wartime apparently diverts significant attention from policy production.[13] In addition, a budgetary surplus somewhat decreases production. Finally, the coefficient on the cloture variable (model 1 only) is negative and significant.

DISCUSSION AND CONCLUSION

In this chapter, we have really only begun to scratch the surface of how our data can be used to study macropolitics. With the level of programmatic detail in the data, we will eventually be able to not only extend studies of legislative production forward in time, but also provide a more detailed and nuanced set of measures that identify different types and importance of policy change. For example, we can divide U.S. Code titles by sublevels (e.g., chapter) to more carefully distinguish among more specific policy categories. Factors that produce policy change should arguably differ across these categories. Perhaps more importantly, we will produce measures of various dimensions of policy change. For example, we can measure Code changes along *breadth* measures. That is, we can look at periods in which Congress produces a wide variety of policy change that is broad in scope. On the other hand, we will also be able to measure the *depth* of policy change. Specifically, legislative production and major policy change may be alternatively viewed in terms of the importance of Code changes. For example, enactments that make wholesale changes to virtually every section of a Code title tap into a different type of policy change than a similar number of enactments with broad (but "shallow") consequences for policy. In future cuts at these data, we will be able to measure both of these dimensions of policy change and examine the extent to which the explanatory factors for each dimension may differ.

As far as explaining the variation in legislative production—as measured by U.S. Code changes—the results presented here are very encouraging. Scholars have been engaging in a lively debate over the implications of divided government for legislative productivity—with mixed results that have spurred a reevaluation of the presumed theoretical importance of this variable. Our analysis yields null results for divided government, once the size and unity of the president's party in Congress are taken into account. In addition, critical elections have been presented as watershed moments in U.S. political development and linked in various ways to the introduction of policy changes. Based on our evidence, critical elections affect policy production, ceteris paribus. This finding deserves closer inspection as well, with better measures on both sides of the equation. As Brady (1988) and others have pointed out, the 1890s critical elections differed significantly from the New Deal critical elections. The regional orientation of the 1890s realignment may exhibit policy production in a more narrow fashion than is seen in the New Deal case. Regardless, from a macro perspective both gridlock measures (figures 5.2 and 5.3) show an *increase* in the gridlock interval in the wake of the 1894 and 1896 elections, while the New Deal elections yielded a *dramatic* decrease in the interval for both measures.

In comparison to the post–World War II–centered work of other scholars, our models' chief omissions are measures of contextual demands for governmental action—as measured either through survey data (i.e., public mood) or using scholarly identified eras of demands for policy change (e.g., Progressive Era). As noted, using survey data is not feasible for this earlier period. It is perhaps tempting to include variables to indicate activist eras in our tests. However, whether such variables are warranted is an open question. They are arguably just measures of the dependent variables rather than external causes of change in it. Since our models seem fairly robust, it seems hard to justify the inclusion of "era" variables that have fairly weak theoretical bases.[14]

Finally, in future work we hope to incorporate a more central role for the internal dynamics of Congress. The existing body of "macropolitics" studies boasts several important achievements. They are parsimonious and perform well empirically. Quite importantly, for a field too long obsessed with not just Congress but a single chamber of Congress, these studies incorporate salient features of bicameralism and incorporate the president. Ironically, though, most of this work distills out much of what congressional scholars often view as crucial to understanding national politics: the internal dynamics of Congress, most notably its committee organizations.[15]

NOTES

Grant support for data collection provided by a 1999–2000 Dirksen Congressional Center Congressional Research Award and the University of Missouri Research Board (RB96-030). We thank Brandon Bartels, Mikael Pelz, Su-Mi Lee, Jaechul Lee, and Moxi Upadhyaya for valuable research assistance.

1. Lynch (1997) notes the gradual and incomplete transition of the Code from "prima facie evidence of the law" to positive law, discrepancies between the Code and the *Statutes at Large*, and various questionable omissions from the Code. For a history of the Code and earlier attempts at codification, see Surrency 1990.

2. For example, Title 5 in the 1926 publication was named "Executive Departments and Government Officers and Employees," while in the 1994 Code it is "Government Organization and Employees." Titles 6 (Surety Bonds) and 34 (Navy) were eventually repealed, with their substance folded into other titles. This occurred after 1946 and thus does not affect the results in this chapter.

3. *Statutes at Large* is published after each Congress and, among other things, details each public law passed in that Congress.

4. With a few exceptions, the literature spawned by Mayhew's (1991) book examines the overall amount of landmark legislation produced by post–world war Congresses, rather than the overall amount of policy production. The most notable exception is Howell et al. 2000, which we discuss further in the text. Young and Heitshusen (2002) and Lapinski (2002) attempt to develop a measure of landmark legislation for the pre–World War II period.

5. Tests of the two different varieties of divided government—pure and partial— yielded results similar to those reported.

6. Woodrow Wilson (as quoted in *Congressional Quarterly* 1976, 220) responding to the 1917 Armed Neutrality filibuster. Rule 22 (cloture) was adopted soon after.

7. D-NOMINATE scores are temporally comparable and thus superior to W-NOMINATE scores for our purposes.

8. See Krehbiel 1998, figure 2.2, for the basic logic used here, but with the important condition that his figure addresses the modern era, when cloture requires a three-fifths vote. During our period cloture required a two-thirds vote. Veto overrides also require two-thirds; thus the pivot placements are at the opposite one-third marks.

9. We use Martis 1989 as the source for party turnover and party affiliation of legislators over our time period.

10. There are some complications in adapting Krehbiel's measure to this earlier time period. Since the size of the House and Senate are changing during our series, Krehbiel's method of using the Democratic gain/loss figures (in percentage terms) runs into problems in some early Congresses in the series, in which both parties had net gains or losses (as small parties gained or lost seats simultaneous to changes in the number of congressional seats). In these cases, we used the turnover for the Democrats. However, we also constructed the measure using a slightly different method—calculating each party's net gain or loss in relation to the number of seats needed for a chamber majority. While this produced slightly different gridlock calculations, this method did not produce a very different measure; the two measures are highly correlated ($r = .98$) and perform very similarly in model estimations. Perhaps the larger problem with this variable in this time period is the underlying assumption in the measure that enough ideological homogeneity exists within each major party to use electoral turnover as a surrogate for preference changes.

11. Compare the 91st (1969–71) and 94th (1975–77) Houses. Nixon faced a 243–192 majority, while Ford faced a 291–144 majority. In addition, intraparty unity and interparty conflict was notably higher in the latter House. See Cooper 2001 for a related attempt to distinguish among divided governments.

12. As can be seen in figure 5.1, as confirmed by a series of tests, the series is not stationary. We address this by using first differences.

13. The relationship between production and war is interesting and worth further exploration. Indeed, this finding takes on added significance given the apparent decrease of congressional focus on domestic policy in the wake of September 11, 2001, and the buildup to war with Iraq. This diversion of attention is consistent with what we found with the two world wars.

14. As a test, we ran the models with a dummy variable for the Progressive Era Congresses (57th–66th). The effect was positive and statistically significant and had little impact on the other estimates in the model.

15. An obvious exception here is Brady 1988, which is very much about the role of committees in affecting major policy change.

REFERENCES

Binder, Sarah. 1999. "The Dynamics of Legislative Gridlock." *American Political Science Review* 93:519–33.

Binder, Sarah, and Steven S. Smith. 1997. *Politics or Principle? Filibustering in the United States Senate*. Washington, D.C.: Brookings Institution Press.

Brady, David. 1988. *Critical Elections and Congressional Policy Making*. Stanford: Stanford University Press.

————. 1993. "The Causes and Consequences of Divided Government: Toward a New Theory of American Politics?" *American Political Science Review* 87:189–94.

Brady, David, and Craig Volden. 1998. *Revolving Gridlock: Politics and Policy from Carter to Clinton*. Boulder, Colo.: Westview Press.

Cameron, Charles M. 2000. *Veto Bargaining: Presidents and the Politics of Negative Power*. London: Cambridge University Press.

Clinton, Joshua, and John S. Lapinski. Forthcoming. "Measuring Significant Legislation, 1877–1948." In *Process, Party, and Policymaking: Further New Perspectives on the History of Congress*. Stanford: Stanford University Press.

Coleman, John. 1999. "Unified Government, Divided Government, and Party Responsiveness." *American Political Science Review* 93:821–35.

Cooper, Joseph. 2001. "The Twentieth-Century Congress." In *Congress Reconsidered*, ed. Lawrence C. Dodd and Bruce I. Oppenheimer. 7th ed. Washington, D.C.: CQ Press.

Cooper, Joseph, and Garry Young. 1997. "Partisanship, Bipartisanship, and Crosspartisanship in Congress since the New Deal." In *Congress Reconsidered*, ed. Lawrence C. Dodd and Bruce I. Oppenheimer. 6th ed.Washington, D.C.: CQ Press.

Congressional Quarterly. 1976. *Origins and Development of Congress*. Washington, D.C.: CQ Press.

Groseclose, Timothy, and Nolan McCarty. 2001. "The Politics of Blame: Bargaining before an Audience." *American Journal of Political Science* 45:100–119.

Howell, William, E. Scott Adler, Charles M. Cameron, and Charles Riemann. 2000. "Divided Government and the Legislative Productivity of Congress: 1945–94." *Legislative Studies Quarterly* 25:285–312.

Huntington, Samuel. 1981. *American Politics: The Promise of Disharmony*. Cambridge: Harvard University Press.

Kingdon, John. 1984. *Agendas, Alternatives, and Public Policies*. Boston: Little, Brown.

Krehbiel, Keith. 1998. *Pivotal Politics*. Chicago: University of Chicago Press.

Lapinski, John S. 2002. "Legislative Performance and American Political Development: A Research Note." Paper presented at the Meetings of the Midwest Political Science Association, Chicago.

Lynch, Michael J. 1997. "The U.S. Code, the Statutes at Large, and Some Peculiarities of Codification." *Legal References Services Quarterly* 16:69–84.

Martis, Kenneth. 1989. *The Historical Atlas of Political Parties in the United States Congress, 1789–1989*. New York: Macmillan.

Mayhew, David R. 1991. *Divided We Govern*. New Haven: Yale University Press.

Poole, Keith. 1999. "Recovering a Basic Space from a Set of Issue Scales." *American Journal of Political Science* 42:954–93.

Poole, Keith, and Howard Rosenthal. 1997. *Congress: A Political-Economic History of Roll Call Voting*. Oxford: Oxford University Press.

Schlesinger, Arthur, Jr. 1986. "The Cycles of American Politics." In *The Cycles of American History*. Boston: Houghton Mifflin.

Stimson, James. 1991. *Public Opinion in America: Moods, Cycles, and Swings.* Boulder, Colo.: Westview.

Stimson, James, Michael B. MacKuen, and Robert S. Erikson. 1995. "Dynamic Representation." *American Political Science Review* 89:543–65.

Sundquist, James. 1988. "Needed: A Political Theory for the New Era of Coalition Government in the United States." *Political Science Quarterly* 103:613–35.

Surrency, Erwin. 1990. *A History of American Law Publishing.* New York: Oceana Publications.

Taylor, Andrew. 1998. "Explaining Government Productivity." *American Politics Quarterly* 26:439–58.

United States. Various years. *Statutes at Large.* Washington, D.C.: GPO.

———. 1926. *The Code of the Laws of the United States of America of a General and Permanent Character in Force December 7, 1925.* Washington, D.C.: GPO.

———. 1935. *The Code of the Laws of the United States of America of a General and Permanent Character in Force January 3, 1935.* 1934 ed. Washington, D.C.: GPO.

Wawro, Gregory, and Eric Schickler, 2004. "Where's the Pivot? Obstruction and Lawmaking in the Pre-cloture Senate." *American Journal of Political Science* 48: 758–74.

Young, Garry, and Valerie Heitshusen. 2002. "Testing Competing Theories of Policy Production, 1874–1946." Paper presented to the Meetings of the Midwest Political Science Association, Chicago.

6

Does Divided Government Increase the Size of the Legislative Agenda?

Charles R. Shipan

Divided government has become one of the defining features of the political landscape in the United States. This represents a dramatic change from the first half of the twentieth century, when divided government was an infrequent phenomenon. From 1900 through the end of World War II, the president's party controlled both chambers of Congress in all but the last two years of Taft's term, the last two years of Wilson's second term, and the last two years of Hoover's term.[1] In the post–World War II era, on the other hand, 17 of 28 elections produced divided government. Furthermore, this increase in divided government is not purely a national-level phenomenon. As Fiorina (1996) has documented and analyzed, divided government at the state level also increased markedly in the postwar era.

Given the increasing presence of divided government in American politics, it is no surprise that scholars have turned their attention to explaining both the causes and the consequences of this type of government. With respect to consequences, much of the work that has been done so far has focused on the *outcome* of the legislative process. To this end, scholars have sought to learn whether (and how) the presence of divided government affects the production of significant legislation, the incidence of failed legislation, and the probability of bills being passed into law.

In this chapter, I examine a different sort of consequence of divided government. Instead of focusing on the relationship between divided government and the success or failure of issues on the agenda, I examine whether divided government influences the *number* of issues on the agenda. Given that the size of the legislative agenda varies over time, a focus on the number of issues on the agenda is inherently interesting to students of American politics and public policy. But even more importantly, learning about causes of the size of the agenda will give us a better context for understanding the production of legislation and policy.

Issues must first be on the agenda in order to become law, which, while obvious, has some important implications. Most importantly, we need to know which factors influence this earlier stage of the legislative process in order to gain a better handle on the ultimate success or failure of bills. From an analytical point of view, if we want to have a better understanding of the causes and consequences of gridlock, we first need to understand what causes the legislative agenda to expand or contract. This means that studies that attempt to predict the percentage of bills that pass or fail need to take into account the size of the agenda, since the size may be systematically related to successes or failures. From a policy perspective, policy change can occur only after an issue appears on the agenda. At a maximum, more issues on the agenda means more potential new policies, either in current or in future Congresses. And at a minimum, since the conditions that increase the size of the agenda may also decrease the likelihood that a bill will become law, the size of the agenda may increase the odds that certain types of policies, and not others, will become law.

The chapter proceeds as follows. I begin by reviewing research on the relationship between divided government and legislative outcomes. Next I argue that divided government provides a systematic explanation for the variation over time in the size of the agenda. After testing this argument, I conclude by suggesting future paths of study regarding divided government and the size of the agenda.

THE CONSEQUENCES OF DIVIDED GOVERNMENT

Prior to 1991, journalists and scholars shared a conventional wisdom about the consequences of divided government. When the president's party controls only one, or perhaps neither, chamber of Congress, the legislative process is crippled, leaving our government unable to pass needed policies. Simply put, divided government produces gridlock.[2]

This view began to change when Mayhew (1991) observed that no one had actually systematically and empirically *examined* whether there was a link between divided government and gridlock. To address this gap, Mayhew compiled and analyzed a novel dataset consisting of all postwar legislation deemed major either at the time or in retrospect. To the surprise of almost everyone, Mayhew did not find any significant difference between divided and unified government in terms of the amount of important legislation produced. That is, contrary to conventional wisdom, Mayhew concluded that divided government does *not* produce less major legislation than does unified government, and therefore is not a significant cause of gridlock.

As the introductory chapter to this volume points out, studies have reassessed Mayhew's findings from a variety of perspectives (e.g., Kelly 1993; Howell et al. 2000; Edwards, Barrett, and Peake 1997; Binder 1999; Coleman 1999; Jones 2000). While these studies have reached a variety of conclusions about the consequences of divided government, they have a common focus on *outcomes* in the legislative process.[3] Each of these studies, however, has implicitly taken the *size* of the agenda as exogenous without considering whether the very factors that might (or might not) affect the passage of legislation also might affect whether bills appear on the agenda in the first place. Is it possible that divided government influences not only what eventually happens to issues on the legislative agenda, but also influences which issues are on this agenda—in other words, that divided government influences the size the agenda? It is to this question that I now turn.

DIVIDED GOVERNMENT AND THE SIZE
OF THE LEGISLATIVE AGENDA

A number of theoretical perspectives suggest that divided government should increase the number of issues on the legislative agenda. To begin with, we can draw on a theoretical explanation of the causes of divided government—Petrocik's (1991, 1996) *issue ownership* theory—to provide insight into the potential consequences of divided government. While Petrocik's empirical evidence is about presidential candidates, the logic of his argument is equally applicable to Congress. Public opinion polls regularly demonstrate that the public believes that Republicans deal better with some issues, while Democrats deal better with others. Because the public tends to favor one party over the other on specific issues, reelection-minded politicians emphasize issues on which their party has a stronger reputation. Democrats, for example, tend to emphasize issues related to social welfare, whereas Republicans emphasize foreign policy issues. When one party dominates the government, we would expect to see a more limited number of issues arise. Conversely, when control over government is divided, we would expect to see the size of the agenda increase, as each party places its favored issues on the agenda.

Obviously issues can appear on the agenda for reasons having nothing to do with which party controls which branch of government—domestic or international crises can force issues onto the agenda, for example. However, to the extent that elected politicians, especially the president and members of the majority party in Congress, promote some issues instead of others, the issue ownership argument suggests that more issues will arise when control of government is divided than when it is unified. When the president and majority party leaders come from different parties, each will attempt to place a different set of issues on the legislative agenda. Thus, the issue ownership theory suggests that electoral incentives will lead each of the two parties to emphasize different issues, and that when parties share control of government, a broader set of issues will be on the agenda than when one party controls both houses of Congress and the presidency.[4]

A perspective on presidential-congressional relations lends further support to this view by suggesting that the minority party will be able to put more issues on the agenda during divided government than during unified government. Many scholars assert that the president is often (if not always) able to draw attention to issues he favors and to force Congress to deal with these issues (e.g., Huntington 1965; Spitzer 1993). Thus, when the president's party is in the minority, he is able to give effective voice to the sorts of issues that his party wants to address and to force these issues onto the legislative agenda. In a sense, then, this perspective complements and builds on the issue ownership explanation. The minority party will always want to put its issues—the issues that it "owns"—on the agenda, regardless of whether government is unified or divided. But when the minority in Congress belongs to the same party as the president, it will be more able to do so. Insofar as the president is able to influence the legislative agenda, we should see a larger agenda under divided government and a smaller one under unified government.[5]

The idea that divided government will produce more issues is consistent with a number of other theoretical and empirical studies. Groseclose and McCarty (2001), for example, theorize that because voters are not fully informed, Congress will have an incentive to propose legislation that it knows the president will veto. In other words, Congress will be playing "blame game" politics. It will propose a bill that it knows will lose, because such a proposal may benefit Congress by reducing the president's approval ratings.

The blame game model helps explain the empirical regularity, documented by Rohde and Simon (1985) and Woolley (1991), that vetoes tend to increase under conditions of divided government. Congress can send issues to the president to force a veto when it believes such a veto will hurt him politically.[6] Since issues that Congress sends to the president in order to force a veto are less likely to be raised when government is unified, it follows that divided government will lead to a larger legislative agenda.

Thus, these different perspectives suggest that divided government should produce an increase in the size of the legislative agenda. Parties will each emphasize issues that they own. When control of government is divided, the majority party in one or both houses of Congress will emphasize one set of issues, while the president and his allies will emphasize a different set of issues. The total number of issues, under such circumstances, should exceed the number of issues when there is unified control of government. Furthermore, the party that opposes the president will have an incentive to propose issues that the president will veto, issues that would not be on the agenda under unified government. All of these perspectives suggest that the legislative agenda will be larger under divided government than under unified government.

MEASURING THE SIZE OF THE LEGISLATIVE AGENDA

In order to determine whether divided government influences the number of issues on the agenda, we need to have a measure of the size of the agenda. To

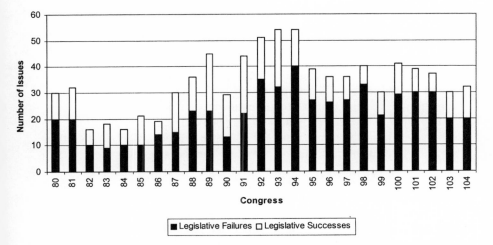

Figure 6.1: The Number of Issues on the Legislative Agenda (80th to 104th Congresses)

obtain this measure, I draw on two of the most well known and accepted measures of legislative output—Mayhew's (1991) list of legislative successes and Edwards, Barrett, and Peake's (1997) list of the number of legislative failures. In doing so, I follow the lead of other authors (e.g., Coleman 1999; Krutz 2000; and Edwards, Barrett, and Peake 1997) who have combined these measures, in part to examine the effects of divided government on legislative success or failure.

The logic behind combining these measures is straightforward. One of these studies identifies all of the major issues that Congress considered and passed into law. The second identifies all of the major issues that Congress considered seriously but did not pass into law. Taken together, these two measures—the number of successes and the number of failures—can be considered as the complete set of issues that were on the agenda. Figure 6.1 shows the number of successes and failures for each Congress, as well as the total number of issues, which is represented by the combined successes and failures.

Because I am combining two separate measures into one, it is worth discussing each of these measures individually. First, Mayhew (1991) identifies the number of important laws enacted by each Congress. He identifies those laws that were considered to be "both innovative and consequential" (1991, 37) either by contemporary observers or by retrospective judgments. By these criteria, he identifies 274 pieces of legislation that the president and Congress made into law between 1947 and 1992.

Second, Edwards, Barrett, and Peake (1997) identified all bills that were seriously considered by Congress and that failed to become law. Using *Congres-*

sional Quarterly Almanac, they first identified over two thousand bills that were mentioned in the period between 1947 and 1992. A bill was included in their final count if Congress took any formal action on the proposal (e.g., at least one congressional committee or subcommittee held hearings on the issue) and the president took an identifiable position on the bill; or if no formal action was taken, but the absence of a formal action was due to policy disagreement. Using this method, they identified a total of 519 failed bills.

Two other scholars recently have constructed different measures of the size of the agenda in the postwar era (Taylor 1998a; Binder 1999). While their studies offer valuable insights into different aspects of the policy process, both of their measures of the size of the agenda have limitations that make them less appropriate for use in this study. Taylor (1998a), in his thoughtful study of the role that different political actors play in setting the agenda, uses *Congressional Quarterly Almanac* to determine which significant issues were on the agenda in each Congress. While his approach provides a useful baseline for his study of which actors place items on the agenda, it is less useful for an investigation of the size of the agenda. First, as Taylor notes (1998a, 375), several times over the past few decades *Congressional Quarterly* varied the way in which it identified major legislation. Second, and more importantly, more than two-thirds of the items on his list of agenda items became law, indicating that the list is heavily skewed toward bills that are likely to pass.

Binder (1999) also compiled a list of the number of issues on the agenda in each Congress, using *New York Times* editorials to determine the set of issues. While this is a tremendous data collection effort that will likely yield numerous additional dividends regarding policymaking in the second half of the twentieth century, it, too, is less appropriate for determining whether divided government influences the size of the agenda. To begin with, as Binder acknowledges, not every issue identified by the *Times* maps neatly onto a specific piece of legislation. In addition, although *New York Times* editorials certainly capture much of the legislative agenda, it also seems very likely that the *Times* editorializes about issues that are not yet officially on the legislative agenda—in other words, issues that might be on the broader political agenda but have not yet made it to the legislative agenda. Indeed, recent evidence seems to indicate that not only does the press report the agenda, the press influences it (Edwards and Wood 1999). Overall, Binder's measure is probably a better measure of the broader political agenda, or what she labels the *systemic agenda,* than of the specific legislative agenda. The arguments I made in the previous section about the influence of divided government on the agenda pertain specifically to the size of the legislative agenda.[7]

Combining the Mayhew list of successes with the Edwards, Barrett, and Peake list of failures works well—and is more appropriate than other measures—for several reasons. First, Edwards, Barrett, and Peake explicitly made their list of bills comparable to those identified by Mayhew. It is likely that if any of the bills they identified had passed rather than failed, they would have been included in Mayhew's list.[8] Second, as noted above, adding together the number of successes and the number of failures produces the total number of significant bills that Congress seriously considered. Importantly, it does so without overemphasizing successes at the expense of failures. Third, because the list includes all bills that were considered seriously by Congress and that either failed or passed, it gives us a measure of the size of the legislative agenda, as opposed to the more general political or systemic agenda. From the perspective of the arguments made above about the influence of divided government, it is more important to identify bills that appear on the legislative agenda—in other words, that are raised and dealt with in a serious way by members of Congress and the president—than to identify the broader set of issues of concern to the Washington, D.C., policy community. Combining legislative successes and failures gives us such a measure.

DIVIDED GOVERNMENT AND THE LEGISLATIVE AGENDA

Figure 6.1 demonstrates that the overall size of the legislative agenda, as determined by combining successes and failures, has varied markedly over time. Over the course of the time period examined, the mean number of issues on the agenda is 34.5. The number of issues in the post–World War II era starts out near this mean, then drops dramatically during the 1950s. Beginning in the mid-1960s, there is an increase in the number of issues on the agenda. The five years with the greatest number of issues on the agenda all occur between 1965 and 1976. Following this period, the number of issues drops off somewhat for the remaining part of the time period.

Based on the theoretical arguments discussed earlier, we should expect divided government to have a systematic influence on the size of the agenda. A preliminary look at the data demonstrates that, on average, more issues appear when government is divided than when government is unified. However, although an average of 36.6 issues appear on the agenda under divided government and 31.2 appear under unified government, this difference, while in the predicted direction, does not attain standard levels of significance ($p = .13$, assuming unequal variances). What we need to do is to control for other factors that might influence the size of the agenda, since failure to include them would result in misspecification and biased estimates of the effect of divided government.

ADDITIONAL EXPLANATORY VARIABLES

First, increases (or decreases) in the size of the agenda may be due to the public's demand for more (or less) legislation. In their study of the effects of divided government during the Bush administration, for example, Quirk and

158

CHAPTER SIX

Nesmith argue that "the most general, fundamental, and significant source of deadlock was the influence of mass opinion" (1994, 207). To tap the influence of public opinion on the size of the legislative agenda, I rely on Stimson's (1999) "Public Mood." This measure, which is based on surveys of the public's attitude toward a variety of policies, is available from 1952 to 1996.[9] If the public favors a more activist government, it receives a higher rating on this scale and thus favors a more active role for the government in dealing with issues. An increase in this variable should be associated with an increase in the size of the agenda.

Second, the beginning of a presidential administration is a period in which more legislation gets considered and put on the legislative agenda. To control for this effect, which might either be considered a "honeymoon" effect (e.g., McCarty 1997) or a disruption of the previous equilibrium (Krehbiel 1998), I include a dummy variable for the start of a presidential administration. This variable should have a positive coefficient, indicating that more issues appear on the agenda at the start of a presidential administration.

Third, the congressional reforms of the 1970s provide another potential explanation for changes in the size of the agenda in recent years, although the effect of these reforms is somewhat unclear. As many authors have noted (e.g., Loomis 1996; Rohde 1991; Davidson 1992), in the mid-1970s the House in particular underwent a number of institutional changes. On the one hand, these changes devolved power from a handful of committee chairs to subcommittees and to individual members, which potentially could cause an increase in the number of issues on the agenda. The changes also centralized power in the hands of party leaders, however, and it is these leaders who play a major role in setting the agenda (Taylor 1998a). Having power centralized in the hands of a few party leaders, rather than a greater number of committee chairs, should lead to a decrease in the number of items on the agenda.

One way in which party leaders were able to develop more control over the agenda was by using omnibus legislation, in which disparate issues are bundled together into a single bill (Davidson 1992; Taylor 1998b; and Krutz 2000). Studies differ in the way they identify omnibus legislation and in their findings of the effects that such legislation has on legislative productivity. Krutz, for example, who defines omnibus legislation as "any piece of major legislation that: (1) spans three or more major-topic areas OR ten or more subtopic policy areas, AND (2) is greater than the mean plus one standard deviation of major bills in size" (2000, 539), finds that the increase in omnibus activity is associated with an increase in legislative productivity. Using a different definition—"all items that were referred to multiple committees in the House or Senate and that contained provisions that touched on multiple issue areas" (1998b, 454 n. 5)— Taylor finds that an increase in the use of omnibus legislation results in a decrease in legislative productivity. Yet while these studies attribute different effects to the trend toward omnibus legislation, they identify the mid-1970s as the period in which the use of omnibus legislation increased markedly.

TABLE 6.1 Independent Variables

	Predicted Effect on Agenda Size	Mean	SD	Minimum	Maximum
Primary independent variables					
Divided Government	+	0.6	0.5	0	1
Public Mood	+	60.4	4.9	50.7	69.7
New Presidential Administration	+	0.4	0.5	0	1
Post-Reform Era	–	0.4	0.5	0	1
Failed Bills (used in lagged form)	+	22.6	8.9	9	40
Additional independent variables					
Mayhew dummy	–	0.13	0.34	0	1
Budget	–	–8.4	10.5	–24.5	21.1
Unified Government (Republican)	–	0.04	0.2	0	1
Unified Government (Democratic)	–	0.36	.049	0	1

To the extent that omnibus legislation is used more frequently starting in this time period, we would expect to see a decrease in the number of bills on the agenda. Two bills that might have passed, or failed, as separate bills prior to the mid-1970s might now be combined into one bill. Because both the centralization of power in the hands of party leaders and the increased use of omnibus legislation occurred in the mid-1970s, I need to include a dummy variable for the postreform Congress. This variable takes on a value of 0 from 1947 to 1974 and a value of 1 beginning in 1975. The expectation is that this variable will be negative.

Finally, I include a variable representing the number of failed bills in each of the previous two congresses. As countless scholars (e.g., Jones 1994) have observed, passing major legislation is an arduous and iterative process that often takes years. Because of the difficulty inherent in passing policy, in any given year the vast majority of issues on the agenda fail to become law. If we assume that at least some portion of these issues remains on the agenda, then we need to control for the number of issues that appeared on the agenda in the previous session of Congress.[10] These control variables should both be positive. In addition, both should take on values less than 1, and the value of the two-year lag should be less than the value of the one-year lag.

Table 6.1 summarizes the discussion above by presenting the predicted effects of each of these variables. The most important prediction is that the existence of divided government will lead to an increase in the number of issues on the agenda. The size of the agenda also should increase as the Public Mood becomes more liberal, at the start of a new presidential administration, and as there are more issues left on the agenda from previous Congresses. On the other hand, the number of issues should decrease in the wake of changes in congressional rules and practices in the mid-1970s.

EMPIRICAL RESULTS

To test whether divided government increases the number of issues on the agenda, I use as my dependent variable the total number of issues on the legislative agenda in each Congress. This measure, as discussed earlier, is created by combining the number of legislative successes identified by Mayhew (1991) with the number of legislative failures identified by Edwards, Barrett, and Peake (1997). Because the data is time series, I use Prais-Winsten regression, a generalized least squares autoregressive procedure that corrects for first-order serial correlation, to analyze the data.[11] The Prais-Winsten results presented in the tables are very similar to those obtained using standard OLS. Given that the regressions include the lagged number of failed bills, which already helps to control for any problems that might be created by autocorrelation, this similarity between OLS and Prais-Winsten results is not surprising.

The empirical results are presented in table 6.2. Column 1 of this table shows that each of the variables is significant and in the predicted direction. Most importantly, the theoretical argument about the effect of divided government is borne out—the dummy variable for divided government is significant and positive. It also has a substantively large influence on the size of the agenda. Controlling for other factors, divided government by itself causes an additional eight issues to appear on the agenda.

The other variables also have the effects predicted by the preceding discussion. As the public's mood becomes more liberal, more issues appear on the agenda. Similarly, we find more issues on the agenda at the start of a new presidential administration. There is a drop in the number of bills produced in the postreform era. And the existence of failed bills from previous congresses increases the number of bills on the current agenda.[12]

These results are robust to a wide range of other specifications and operationalizations, as columns 2, 3, and 4 demonstrate.[13] Column 2 repeats the regression found in column 1, but adds two other potentially important variables. The first is a dummy variable designed to capture the fact that in the last years of his analysis, Mayhew was able only to rely on contemporary judgments to identify significant bills. Thus, we might expect fewer pieces of significant legislation to be coded in the last few years of Mayhew's dataset, not because of a drop in the number of bills, but because of the method used to identify the bills. This variable takes on the value of 1 beginning in 1987, with

TABLE 6.2 Determinants of the Number of Issues on the Legislative Agenda

	1	2	3	4
Constant	−54.03*	−72.91**	−39.89	−71.73***
	(27.35)	(33.61)	(30.41)	(25.89)
Divided Government	7.94**	8.80**		66.12**
	(3.95)	(4.27)		(33.64)
Republican Unified Government			−16.48*** (4.80)	
Democratic Unified Government			−7.66** (4.27)	
Public Mood	0.86**	1.12**	0.76*	1.16***
	(0.40)	(0.51)	(0.43)	(0.43)
Divided Government × Public Mood				−0.97* (0.57)
New Presidential Administration	5.91* (3.49)	6.69** (3.64)	7.58** (3.52)	6.18* (3.76)
Post-Reform Era	−15.72***	−14.56**	−16.70***	−14.43**
	(4.10)	(6.85)	(3.87)	(4.53)
Failed Bills $(t-1)$	0.86***	0.95***	0.86***	0.97***
	(0.24)	(0.24)	(0.25)	(0.24)
Failed Bills $(t-2)$	0.77**	0.84**	0.78**	0.66**
	(0.34)	(0.39)	(0.33)	(0.34)
Mayhew dummy		−5.14 (6.78)		
Budgetary Situation		0.07 (0.36)		
N	21	21	21	21
Rho	0.04	−0.11	−0.10	−0.22
Durbin-Watson (original)	1.88	2.03	1.99	2.13
Durbin-Watson (transformed)	1.90	2.04	1.96	2.12
R^2	.64	.74	.74	.79

Note: Estimated using Prais-Winsten regression. Numbers in parentheses are semirobust standard errors.
*$p < 10$.   **$p < .05$.   ***$p < .01$. All significance tests (except for the constant) are one-tailed.

the expectation that it will have a negative coefficient. The second variable is the Budgetary Situation, which is calculated as the budget surplus or deficit as a percentage of federal governmental outlays and is designed to capture the notion that when there is a budget deficit, the enactment and production of significant legislation will be constrained. Although some analyses find no support for the influence of this measure of legislative productivity (e.g., Mayhew 1991; Binder 1999), others do (Coleman 1999; Krutz 2000; and, with a different operationalization, Taylor 1998b).

When these two variables are added to the equation presented in column 1, all of the other variables perform at least as well, with one variable (New Presidential Administration) performing better. In addition, all coefficients stay at roughly the same levels. Somewhat surprisingly, although the Mayhew dummy variable achieves the expected negative sign, it is not significant.[14] Less surprisingly, given the results of other studies, the variable representing the budgetary situation is also not significant. More importantly, though, the divided government variable remains strong.

Column 3 presents a regression similar to that found in column 1, but from a different perspective. In this regression I look at unified government instead of divided government, and I distinguish between Republican unified government and Democratic unified government. The expectation is that both forms of unified government will produce fewer items on the agenda than will divided government. Furthermore, because Republicans have traditionally favored a more limited role for government, we would expect to see even fewer issues produced by Republican unified government than by Democratic unified government.

The results bear out these hypotheses. Both forms of unified government are statistically significant. In addition, the size of the Republican variable is more than twice that of the Democratic variable. Unified government in general produces fewer issues than divided government; but unified government under Republicans produces even fewer issues than unified government under Democrats.[15]

Throughout this chapter I have hypothesized that the existence of divided government should be associated with an increase in the size of the agenda, as should an increase in Public Mood. However, it is possible that the influence of Public Mood should be dependent on whether or not control of government is divided (Coleman 1999). When activism is low, we might expect large differences between unified and divided government, but when activism is high, the difference should decrease, since all elected officials will have the incentive to produce more legislation. Thus, an increase in the public's level of activism should minimize differences between unified and divided government.

In column 4 I interact Public Mood with Divided Government. Once again, all variables, including divided government, are significant. To determine the magnitude of the difference between divided government and unified government, however, we need to take into account the interacted term and the size of the Public Mood. When the Public Mood takes on its mean value (60.4), and holding all other values constant, divided government produces an additional 7.5 issues per year, which is consistent with the results produced in columns 1 and 2. When Public Mood takes on its maximum value (69.66), divided government and unified government produce roughly the same number of issues (79 and 80, respectively). And when Public Mood takes on its minimum value (50.73), nearly 17 more issues appear under divided government than under unified government. These results imply that when the public is in a very activist mood, the difference between unified and divided government all but disappears, with officials serving in unified government feeling the pressure to produce a substantial amount of legislation. When, on the other hand, the public is less activist, the difference between unified and divided government is great.[16]

Finally, it is worth examining whether the results are dependent on the way in which the dependent variable—the size of the legislative agenda—is operationalized. When I use Binder's measure of the size of the agenda, I find no relationship between divided government and the size of the agenda. On the other hand, when I use Taylor's (1998a) count of the number of issues on the agenda, the results generally support the argument that divided government increases the size of the agenda.[17] Furthermore, when I create an index that combines the measure I have been using with the number of issues identified by Binder and by Taylor and use this index as the dependent variable, I find strong support for the influence of divided government and the other independent variables.

DISCUSSION

The analysis in this chapter demonstrates that divided government produces a larger legislative agenda than does unified government. Even when a variety of other factors is taken into account, this relationship remains strong. Congress faces a smaller agenda when the same party that controls both chambers also controls the presidency and a larger agenda otherwise, a finding that is consistent with the expectations set out at the beginning of this chapter. When the president's party controls both houses, it will be less likely to introduce and consider bills that will embarrass the president. Furthermore, under divided government each party will want to introduce the issues that it owns; and having the president act as a spokesman for these issues will help the minority party get these issues on the agenda.

In addition to providing strong evidence in support of the link between divided government and the size of the agenda, this analysis also raises a number of other points and questions that, while beyond the scope of this study, should attract the attention of scholars. First, and most importantly, the argument and findings in this chapter suggests that scholars who are interested in the link between divided government and legislative outcomes or performance need to take into account the link between divided government and the size of the agenda. Indeed, this link might help to explain the difference between studies that find that divided government does not cause fewer pieces of significant legislation to pass (e.g., Mayhew) and those that find that divided government does cause more bills to fail and also causes a lower proportion of bills to pass (Edwards, Barrett, and Peake 1997; Binder 1999; Coleman 1999). The results also can be seen as providing support for the argument that presidents are able to help the minority party in Congress place items on the agenda.

Moreover, the evidence of a link between divided government and the size of the agenda also indicates that scholars who examine the influence of divided government on legislative output need to be aware of the strong potential for selection bias. The passage or success of legislation, after all, is the second step of a two-step process—legislation first must get on the agenda in order to pass or fail. Insofar as the variables that influence the agenda also influence the likelihood that any given issue passes or fails (and insofar as the error terms in the two stages are correlated), excluding how the agenda is determined from analyses of passage or failure effectively "selects" issues that get on the agenda, ignoring the ones that do not. This amounts to sample selection that, as Achen (1986) and others have shown, can produce biased parameter estimates and inefficient standard errors.

Future work thus should consider the theoretical linkage between these two previously separate questions: how items get on the agenda, and whether or not these items succeed. Analyses of legislative outputs might seek to link these causally related questions via the growing class of selection models (e.g., Reed and Clark 2000). Importantly, this selection bias could work in two separate ways. The majority party might be more likely to introduce bills that it thinks will pass, and repress those it thinks will fail, under unified government. Yet it might do the opposite under divided government, and introduce bills that it thinks will fail.

Second, although the results show a strong link between divided government and the number of issues on the agenda, they do depend to some extent on how the dependent variable is measured. As I pointed out earlier, there are a number of reasons to prefer the measure I have constructed to Taylor's measure, which is biased toward successful bills, and Binder's, which is a more systemic measure. Still, it is clear that using different methods to measure the size of the agenda can produce very different outcomes. At a minimum, this should spur researchers to examine in more detail the question of how to measure the size of the legislative agenda, and how to compare the legislative agenda with the systemic agenda. The size of the agenda as computed by

Binder (1999, table 1) is correlated with the measure constructed in this chapter ($r = .68$), but there are differences over time especially in recent years. Which issues should be included in a study of the size of the agenda? What explains the differences between the sizes as computed by various methods? How can the difference between the specific legislative agenda and the more general political agenda be identified? In the opening chapter of this volume Adler and Lapinski demonstrate the importance of variable measurement in macropolitics research. Accordingly questions about measuring the size of the agenda are all worthwhile topics of study.

Third, this study suggests additional avenues of research for scholars interested in determining the relationship between divided government and legislative outcomes. To begin with, this analysis suggests that we should move to an individual level of analysis. That is, scholars need to begin to disaggregate data in order to see whether there are specific patterns that underlie those found at the aggregate level. In particular, it would be useful to focus on specific policy areas. Are certain *types* of policy issues more likely to arise under divided government than under unified government (Talbert and Potoski 2002)? This is what Petrocik's (1991, 1996) argument, as well as Jacobson's (1990), would seem to indicate. Similarly, an implicit assumption throughout this chapter is that the size of the agenda increases under divided government because there are more issues, and not just more versions of the same issue. An individual-level focus would allow us to know whether this is true. Scholars also should investigate whether specific issues that appear and fail under divided government are then passed into law when government becomes unified (see also Coleman 1999). If this happens, does it happen more often than the reverse (i.e., bills that fail under unified government become law under divided government)?

Finally, it would be worthwhile to focus on the states in order to examine the consequences of divided government. Because states provide cross-sectional as well as across-time variation on factors such as divided government, they provide an ideal opportunity for comparative testing of institutional effects (Huber and Shipan 2000, 2002). Scholars can address aggregate patterns in the passage of laws, or look at specific issue areas in more detail, to determine whether divided government produces legislation or gridlock—or a larger agenda—at the state level.

NOTES

I would like to thank Scott Adler, Sarah Binder, Kelly Chang, Dave Clark, John Coleman, Cary Covington, Doug Dion, John Lapinski, Mike Lewis-Beck, Bill Lowry, Nolan McCarty, and Matt Potoski for helpful discussions and suggestions. I would also like to thank Sarah Binder, Glen Krutz, George Edwards, and Andrew Barrett for sharing their data with me. Finally, I would like to acknowledge the support received from the Obermann Center for Advanced Studies at the University of Iowa.

1. In the election of 1930, Republicans actually won more House seats than Democrats, but because of Republican deaths between the time of the election and the beginning of the congressional session, Democrats were able to organize and control the House. On the other hand, Wilson could have faced divided government following the 1916 election, in which Republicans won more House seats than Democrats; but Democrats combined with minor party candidates to control the House.

2. See, among others, Mayhew 1991; Fiorina 1996; and Coleman 1999 for more detailed discussions of this conventional wisdom. As Krehbiel nicely summarizes, "the consensus view of practitioners and pundits of American national government seems to be that divided government is associated with some or all of the following: bitter partisanship, poor governmental performance, policy incoherence, nondecisions, showdowns, standoffs, checkmate, stalemate, deadlock and . . . gridlock" (1996, 9).

3. I do not mean to suggest that scholars studying the effects of divided government have looked at only the success or failure of bills. See Fiorina 1996, chap. 11, for a discussion of studies that have looked at a number of other consequences. Since Fiorina's summary, studies have appeared that empirically examine the influence of divided government on a wide range of topics, including budgetary conflict (Clarke 1998), the partisanship of laws (Thorson 1998), delegation to bureaucracies (Epstein and O'Halloran 1999; Huber, Shipan, and Pfahler 2001; Huber and Shipan 2002), changes in the ideological content of bills (Covington and Bargen 2002), presidential vetoes (Cameron 2000), and presidential job approval (Groseclose and McCarty 2001).

4. A number of studies in recent years, including Rohde 1991 and Sinclair 1995, have emphasized the strong and increasing ability of the majority party leadership to place issues on the agenda, often in the face of presidential opposition. Furthermore, Taylor, in his analysis of domestic agenda-setting, concludes that "during divided government, increasingly more domestic agenda items are being proposed by the congressional majority party leadership" (1998a, 390). Taylor also finds that when there is divided government, the majority party in Congress puts a higher percentage of issues on the agenda, which buttresses the argument made above.

5. The empirical evidence on the extent to which the president can do this is both scant and mixed, and most studies have looked at the president's success on such bills. Classic studies that disagree with the notion of presidential dominance over Congress include Chamberlain 1946; Moe and Teel 1970; and Jones 1994; those that agree include Goldsmith 1983 and Huntington, who wrote that the president "now determines the legislative agenda of Congress almost as thoroughly as the British Cabinet sets the legislative agenda of Parliament" (1965, 23). See also O'Neill 1987, in which the former Speaker argued that the president had earned the right to get his items on the agenda.

6. Jones (1995, 244), for example, notes that during the Bush administration the Democratic Congress passed laws that members knew would be vetoed by the president.

7. The distinction between the legislative agenda and broader political agenda— that is, between the items specifically discussed in Congress and those being discussed more generally by the Washington, D.C., community—draws on Kingdon (1984). See

also Taylor 1998a. While I have strong reasons for not using these alternative measures, in the conclusion I discuss how using them affects the empirical results.

8. As Edwards, Barrett, and Peake observe, they made their decision rules for coding the legislation as close to Mayhew's as possible. Further, they write, "Although our concern is less to make exact comparisons with Mayhew than to determine what potentially important legislation failed to pass, we nevertheless employed Mayhew's list of important legislation that *did* pass as a guide to the potential importance of legislation" (1997, 551).

9. Stimson's data, updated through 1996, is available at http://www.unc.edu/~jstimson/time.html. For each Congress, I used the average of the policy mood scores for each session.

10. Failure to include a lagged version of the dependent variable ignores problems of autocorrelation and, even more importantly, can result in biased coefficients. Thus, including something like a lagged version of the dependent variable is a statistical necessity. In this case, however, lagging the dependent variable does not make sense—if an issue passed in the previous Congress, it is not likely to come up again in the current Congress. However, including a lagged version of the number of failures performs the same statistical function.

11. Although somewhat less well known than the Cochrane-Orcutt method, Prais-Winsten is more appropriate in cases with a small number of observations (Greene 1990).

12. Results for the equations in table 6.2 remain substantially the same when I remove the two-Congress lagged version of Failed Bills from the equation. However, since the two-Congress lag is significant and adds to the overall fit of the model, and since there is no theoretical reason to expect issues to remain on the agenda for only one session after they fail, I leave this variable in the model. In addition, the coefficients have the expected magnitudes—both are less than 1, and the coefficient for the two-Congress lag is smaller than the coefficient for the one-Congress lag.

13. In addition to the results reported in table 6.2, other unreported tests also demonstrate robustness. For example, results remain strong when I set the Post-Reform variable equal to 1 starting in 1975 and when the Policy Mood variable is lagged. In addition, when dummy variables for the Vietnam War and the Great Society era are added to the equation in column 1, Divided Government, the lagged versions of Failed Bills, and the dummy for the Post-Reform era all remain significant at $p < .05$ or better. Only the Public Mood variable loses significance.

14. The insignificance of this variable indicates that the small drop in the number of issues due to the lack of sweep 2 at the end of the time series is not a serious problem. An alternative way to address this is to use only those bills identified by Mayhew in his sweep 1. When using this alternative measure to compute the dependent variable, divided government remains significant, although in some specifications at the somewhat less impressive level of $p < .10$. Because bills identified by sweep 2 would have been designated as important by Edwards, Barrett, and Peake (1997) had they failed, it is more appropriate to use the full dataset. See Mayhew 1993 for a more general defense of combining these two sweeps.

15. The results are just as strong when the additional variables used in column 2 are included in the equation. While these results are consistent with expectations, we

should avoid making too much of them, as there were only two years during this period in which the government was unified under Republican control.

16. I also interacted divided government with the level of party polarization, using the difference between adjusted ADA scores for Democrats and Republicans in the House as the measure of polarization. When this variable is included, both it and divided government are insignificant, almost certainly because the two variables are so highly correlated ($r = .92$). When I include the interaction term, but not the main effect of divided government, the interaction is significant, generally at the level of $p < .10$. Including polarization on its own does not affect the other results, and the coefficient for this variable is not significant.

17. Divided government, in different specifications, remains significant at either $p < .05$ or $p < .10$. Some of the other variables, however, especially the variable representing a new presidential administration, lose significance.

REFERENCES

Achen, Christopher. 1986. *The Statistical Analysis of Quasi-Experiments.* Berkeley and Los Angeles: University of California Press.

Binder, Sarah A. 1999. "The Determinants of Legislative Gridlock, 1947–1996." *American Political Science Review* 93:519–33.

Cameron, Charles M. 2000. *Veto Bargaining: Presidents and the Politics of Negative Power.* Cambridge: Cambridge University Press.

Chamberlain, Lawrence. 1946. *The President, Congress, and Legislation.* New York: Columbia University Press.

Clarke, Wes. 1998. "Divided Government and Budgetary Conflict." *Legislative Studies Quarterly* 23:5–23.

Coleman, John J. 1999. "Unified Government, Divided Government, and Party Responsiveness." *American Political Science Review* 93:821–35.

Covington, Cary R., and Andrew Bargen. 2002. "The Effect of Divided Government on the Partisan Impact and Coherence of Bills Enacted by the House of Representatives, 1955–1994." Paper presented to the Annual Meeting of the Midwest Political Science Association, Chicago.

Davidson, Roger H. 1992. "The Emergence of the Postreform Congress." In *The Postreform Congress,* ed. Roger H. Davidson. New York: St. Martin's Press.

Edwards, George C., III, Andrew Barrett, and Jeffrey Peake. 1997. "The Legislative Impact of Divided Government." *American Journal of Political Science* 41:545–63.

Edwards, George C., III, and B. Dan Wood. 1999. "Who Influences Whom? The President and the Public Agenda." *American Political Science Review* 93:327–44.

Epstein, David, and Sharyn O'Halloran. 1999. *Delegating Powers.* Cambridge: Cambridge University Press.

Fiorina, Morris P. 1996. *Divided Government,* 2nd ed. Boston: Allyn and Bacon.

Goldsmith, William. 1983. *The Growth of Presidential Power.* New York: Chelsea House.

Greene, William H. 1990. *Econometric Analysis.* 2nd ed. Englewood Cliffs, N.J.: Prentice-Hall.

Groseclose, Timothy, and Nolan McCarty. 2001. "The Politics of Blame: Bargaining before an Audience." *American Journal of Political Science* 45:100–119.

Howell, William, E. Scott Adler, Charles M. Cameron, and Charles Riemann. 2000. "Divided Government and the Legislative Productivity of Congress, 1945–1994." *Legislative Studies Quarterly* 25:285–312.

Huber, John D., and Charles R. Shipan. 2000. "The Costs of Control: Legislators, Agencies, and Transaction Costs." *Legislative Studies Quarterly* 25:25–52.

———. 2002. *Deliberate Discretion? The Institutional Foundations of Bureaucratic Autonomy*. New York: Cambridge University Press.

Huber, John D., Charles R. Shipan, and Madelaine Pfahler. 2001. "Legislatures and Statutory Control of Bureaucracy." *American Journal of Political Science* 45: 330–45.

Huntington, Samuel. 1965. "Congressional Responses to the Twentieth Century." In *The Congress and America's Future*, ed. by David B. Truman. Englewood Cliffs, N.J.: Prentice-Hall.

Jacobson, Gary. 1990. *The Electoral Origins of Divided Government*. Boulder, Colo.: Westview Press.

Jones, Charles O. 1994. *The Presidency in a Separated System*. Washington, D.C.: Brookings Institution Press.

———. 1995. *Separate but Equal Branches*. Chatham, N.J.: Chatham House.

Jones, David. 2000. "Party Polarization and Legislative Gridlock." *Political Research Quarterly* 53:125–414.

Kelly, Sean Q. 1993. "Divided We Govern: A Reassessment." *Polity* 25:475–84.

Kingdon, John. 1984. *Agenda, Alternatives, and Public Policies*. Boston: Little, Brown.

Krehbiel, Keith. 1996. "Institutional and Partisan Sources of Gridlock: A Theory of Divided and Unified Government." *Journal of Theoretical Politics* 8:7–40.

———. 1998. *Pivotal Politics: A Theory of U.S. Lawmaking*. Chicago: University of Chicago Press.

Krutz, Glen S. 2000. "Getting around Gridlock: The Effect of Omnibus Utilization on Legislative Productivity." *Legislative Studies Quarterly* 25:533–49.

Loomis, Burdett A. 1996. *The Contemporary Congress*. New York: St. Martin's Press.

Mayhew, David R. 1974. *Congress: The Electoral Connection*. New Haven: Yale University Press.

———. 1991. *Divided We Govern: Party Control, Lawmaking, and Investigations, 1946–1990*. New Haven: Yale University Press.

———. 1993. "Reply: Let's Stick with the Longer List." *Polity* 25:485–88.

McCarty, Nolan. 1997. "Presidential Reputation and the Veto." *Economics and Politics* 9(1): 1–26.

Moe, Ronald C., and Steven C. Teel. 1970. "Congress as Policy-Maker: A Necessary Reappraisal." *Political Science Quarterly* 85:443–70.

O'Neill, Tip. 1987. *Man of the House: The Life and Political Memoirs of Speaker Tip O'Neill*. New York: Random House.

Petrocik, John R. 1991. "Divided Government: Is It All in the Campaigns?" In *The Politics of Divided Government*, ed. Gary W. Cox and Samuel Kernell. Boulder, Colo.: Westview Press.

———. 1996. "Issue Ownership in Presidential Elections, with a 1980 Case Study."
    American Journal of Political Science 40:825–50.
Quirk, Paul J., and Bruce Nesmith. 1994. "Explaining Deadlock: Domestic Policymak-
    ing in the Bush Presidency." In *New Perspectives on American Politics*, ed. Lawrence
    C. Dodd and Calvin Jillson. Washington, D.C.: CQ Press.
Reed, William, and David H. Clark. 2000. "War Initiators and War Winners: The Con-
    sequences of Linking Theories of Democratic War Success." *Journal of Conflict
    Resolution* 44:378–95.
Rohde, David W. 1991. *Parties and Leaders in the Postreform House*. Chicago: Uni-
    versity of Chicago Press.
Rohde, David W., and Dennis M. Simon. 1985. "Presidential Vetoes and Congressional
    Response: A Study of Institutional Conflict." *American Journal of Political Science*
    29:397–427.
Sinclair, Barbara. 1995. *Legislators, Leaders, and Lawmaking: The U.S. House of Rep-
    resentatives in the Postreform Era*. Baltimore: Johns Hopkins University Press.
Spitzer, Robert J., ed. 1993. *Media and Public Policy*. Westport, Conn.: Praegar.
Stimson, James A. 1999. *Public Opinion in America: Moods, Cycles, and Swings*. 2nd
    ed. Boulder, Colo.: Westview Press.
Talbert, Jeffrey, and Matthew Potoski. 2002. "The Changing Public Agenda over the
    Post-war Period." In *Policy Dynamics*, ed. Frank R. Baumgartner and Bryan D.
    Jones. Chicago: University of Chicago Press.
Taylor, Andrew J. 1998a. "Domestic Agenda Setting, 1947–1994." *Legislative Studies
    Quarterly* 23:373–98.
———. 1998b. "Explaining Government Productivity." *American Politics Quarterly*
    26:439–58.
Thorson, Gregory R. 1998. "Divided Government and the Passage of Partisan Legisla-
    tion, 1947–1990." *Political Research Quarterly* 51:751–64.
Woolley, John T. 1991. "Institutions, the Election Cycle, and the Presidential Veto."
    American Journal of Political Science 35:279–304.

PART IV: *Macropolitics and Public Policy*

7

The Macropolitics of Telecommunications Policy, 1899–1998: Lawmaking, Policy Windows, and Agency Control

Grace R. Freedman and Charles M. Cameron

In this chapter, we use a macropolitics approach to study a century of congressional policymaking for telecommunications. What we attempt to explain is the production of major laws—their timing and volume—in the area of telecommunications policy. Our real subject, however, is the creation and operation of regulatory regimes. Therefore, we view the chapter not only as an experiment in macropolitics but also as one in policy history or "American Political Development" (APD). We show that simple and largely intuitive notions from rational choice institutionalism afford at least some purchase on the historical data.

Let us stake out more clearly the terrain over which we maneuver. Why is the production of major laws interesting? From a substantive viewpoint, Congress's enactments of the Radio Act of 1912, the Communications Act of 1934, and the Telecommunications and Deregulation Act of 1995, along with many lesser statutes, *were* the creation of the American state in this policy arena—though hardly the whole story, of course. And, Congress's willingness or reluctance to allow its creations, especially the Federal Communications Commission (FCC), to make decisions ranging from the mundane to the momentous, has been a central feature of the *operation* of this regulatory regime. In our view, understanding when and why Congress creates regulatory regimes, and how it manages them, is crucial for understanding the history of the American state.

Theoretically, and in practice, Congress creates a regulatory agency in order to delegate policymaking functions to it. If the agent is a trusted and effective regulator, Congress members will mostly leave the agency to its tasks and devote its own energies to other issues. Stated another way, there must be a positive reason for Congress to involve itself in a technically difficult area such as telecommunications, rather than rely on agents in the executive to manage affairs. Ideological estrangement between the executive agent and the congressional overseers creates such an impetus. We argue that a necessary condition for lawmaking, then, is the degree of ideological distance among the key oversight committees in the House and Senate and the delegated agency. Since House and Senate political ideology can also be a barrier or incentive for legislative action, the spatial position of the median floor member is also taken into account. As we show, these arrangements are predictive of lawmaking activity in telecommunications policy from 1899 to 1998.

The chapter is organized in the following way. The following section sets the stage by presenting a highly schematic history of federal telecommunications policy. We present this abridged history in terms of "regimes," focusing on key changes in the relationships among Congress and its agents in telecommunications policy over time. The third section presents the theoretical framework and discusses its plausibility in this policy arena. The next section explains how we measure key variables and presents some basic information about them. The fifth section undertakes an empirical analysis of the data. The sixth section concludes.

HISTORY OF TELECOMMUNICATIONS POLICY

TABLE 7.1 Theorized Regimes in Telecommunications Policymaking

Regime	Date	Characteristics
1	pre-1934	Early regulatory structures, weak and ineffective
2	1934–late 1950s	Creation of FCC as single regulatory authority, Congress defers powers to agency
3	1960s–1982	Technological pressures and eroding political support of existing regime; FCC, Department of Justice, and Congress active
4	1982, 1996	Regulatory framework switch to favor competition; tension among Congress, Department of Justice, and FCC over regulatory powers; FCC strengthened in 1996

Regime 1: Early Attempts at a Regulatory Regime (before 1934)

Though historical accounts of the regulation of telecommunications often begin with the 1934 Communications Act, which established the Federal Communications Commission (FCC), state and federal regulation of telephone, telegraphy, and radio preceded this historic enactment. As early as 1910, the first federal, executive agencies in telecommunications were established. The Mann-Elkins Act of 1901 placed telephone regulation under the Interstate Commerce Commission (ICC) and the Radio Acts of 1910 and1912 placed radio licensing and registration under the secretary of commerce.[1]

Despite the established regulatory regime, the ICC did not aggressively implement the Mann-Elkins mandate and rarely invoked its given powers.[2] The agency concentrated more on its original charge to oversee railroad and transportation-related commerce cases. Only a handful of telephone regulation cases were brought before the ICC during its tenure over the area, begging the need for continued congressional oversight (Cohen 1991; Robinson 1989).

Radio regulation was similarly flawed. The permission of unlimited radio licenses under the Radio Acts of 1910 and 1912 created broadcasting jamming by the early 1920s. Since there was more demand than capacity, a great influx of radio stations began transmitting over open airwaves, sometimes in a haphazard and uncontrolled fashion. An estimated seven hundred licensed stations were operating only 90 available radio channels in 1924 (Wollenberg 1989, 66). Herbert Hoover, then the secretary of commerce, tried to reduce radio license awards, but he was barred by the Supreme Court in the *Zenith* decision. The Court upheld the Radio Act of 1912, reasoning that the executive branch office could not regulate without further legislative action.

In response to these political and technological pressures, Congress created the Federal Radio Commission (FRC), empowering it as regulatory agent in the provision of licenses and other oversight of the new industry. Enacted as a temporary measure with only a one-year life span, this law (Radio Act of 1927) was not meant to be a comprehensive solution to the regulation of the radio industry. The arrangement set down in 1927 proved permanent.

Regime 2: New Deal, New Regime (1934–1960)

The Communications Act of 1934

Seven years later, with considerably more political support and attention, the Communications Act of 1934 established the FCC as the federal agency with sole authority to regulate telecommunications and the broadcast industry with a vague mandate "to protect the public interest, convenience, and necessity." The essential structure and powers of the FRC were adopted and expanded over a more broad terrain of telephony and broadcasting. Some legal historians, though, deride the creation of the FCC from the FRC as little more than a one-letter name change (Robinson 1989).

Yet the timing of its creation cannot be dismissed. Franklin D. Roosevelt, newly in office, made a specific request of Congress to organize a new body to control both broadcasting and telephony, although technically there is little reason to do so. There was no prevailing economic or technological rationale for creating this body in 1934. Neither did the Communications Act add new regulatory powers, although a provision to expand the oversight of mergers was considered by Congress. (Vigorous AT&T opposition blocked it [Robinson 1989].) In retrospect, experts have ascribed the primary motive for establishing the FCC to the claim that the previous structures, oversight by the ICC and the FRC, were not sufficient. The ICC, in short, was too busy with railroad and other transportation-related commerce to pay much attention to telecommunications, and the FRC was too slow in adopting a new licensing system. The status quo regulatory powers were not considered deficient, only unused.

The explanation is somewhat unsatisfying given the broad delegation of authority in the Communications Act and does not account for the timing of the enactment. Could sheer politics—namely that Franklin D. Roosevelt wished to remove Hoover appointees and replace them with his own—provide a better explanation? A comparison of the ideological standpoints of the regulatory agents and key committees should shed light on this question.

Regime Status Quo

Even though the new agency claimed no new federal powers, the establishment of the FCC itself did prove to be a significant change. There was now an attentive expert panel, if not exactly a watchdog, which took seriously the role of regulating these industries in the name of the public interest. Over the next half-century, the ebb and flow of FCC control would be related to court challenges and decisions, antitrust proceedings of the Department of Justice (Cantor and Cantor 1986), technological and economic changes in the industry. It is also related to the ideological and legislative inclinations of Congress and key oversight committees, which is our focus here.

World War II, and the economic expansion that followed, represented an important time in the development of the telecommunications industry. There was extensive public support for private research and development of telecommunications tools, including microwave communications, computer systems, and satellite technologies (Cantor and Cantor 1986). In terms of congressional activity, though, the status quo was unchallenged; there was a long lull in congressional lawmaking on telecommunications in the 1940s and 1950s. This was due, at least in part, to the broad support enjoyed by AT&T and the pro-business stance of President Eisenhower, who on several occasions called the AT&T monopoly a "national resource" (Rosenstiehl 1997).

Regime 3: Pushing the Envelope—Technological and Political Shifts (late 1950s–1960s)

Still, technological advances pushed the status quo points even if political concerns did not. New technologies of microwave and satellite communications, as well as cable television and the broad acceptance of network television, were developed in the late 1950s.[3] The FCC claimed jurisdiction over these new industries and was largely unquestioned in doing so, even though the 1934 act did not expressly support it (Robinson 1989). Another development was the waning of the previously monolithic support for market leader industries in telephone and traditional broadcasting, both in the FCC and Congress.

Though AT&T and national network broadcasters still had great regulatory advantages, several policy decisions from the FCC, Congress, and the Department of Justice signaled changes in political support. Among these was the *Above 890 Decision*,[4] a 1959 FCC ruling that allowed private licensing of microwave telephone technology and mandated free interconnection with the existing telephone system (Zarkin 1998). The decision allowed MCI, the first major competitor to AT&T in over three decades, to offer enhanced telephone services, ushering in the potential for competition.[5] Another change was the consent decree of 1956, by which the Justice Department broke up AT&T's monopoly over the manufacture of telephone equipment (Rosenstiehl 1997). The regulatory regime of the 1940s and 1950s that featured FCC rule-making, monopolistic industry dominance, and little congressional lawmaking was pushed on both technological and political fronts.

In the midst of the Cold War, still broader political concerns influenced support of the regulatory regime. Soon after the landmark FCC microwave decision, Congress enacted the Communications Satellite Bill of 1962 (COMSAT), which represented a congressional mandate to open and promote private market investment in satellite-based communications. The push for this bill, one of the first noteworthy telecommunications laws since the 1934 Communications Act, took place when Congress and the American people were concerned about the nation's ability to maintain technological superiority over the Soviet Union, a concern fueled by the launch of *Sputnik* in 1957.[6] These events arguably spurred members of Congress to reconsider how well the federal government was supporting technological advancements and to possibly rethink how well the old alliances and state-supported monopoly of AT&T served the public interest.

Regime 4: Regulatory Framework in Flux—Breakdown of Support for Existing Regulatory Structures (1970s–1982)

In the 1970s, there was a renewed interest in reforming telecommunications policy more broadly. Reacting in part to the technological advances of the 1960s, policy experts,[7] regulators, and legislators no longer unanimously held state-sanctioned monopolies in telecommunications to be in the public interest. Demands for regulatory change came from consumer advocates, who were concerned about telephone rates in a time of rising inflation (Crandall and Waverman 1995), start-up industries that wanted to enter markets untapped but controlled by AT&T, and the FCC, which instituted reforms to increase competition. Within Congress, committee reforms of 1974 had created specific House and Senate subcommittees for communications policy and increased the number of research staff available to legislators in this policy area (Rosenstiehl 1997). To many legislators (the chair of the House subcommittee, in particular) competition and deregulation were now more in the public interest than the preservation of the AT&T monopoly, in contrast to the policies of previous decades.

The Department of Justice and the federal courts were the most aggressive in their efforts to open telephone markets to competition. The centerpiece of the judicial branch approach was the antitrust case brought against AT&T, which after eight years resulted in the breakup of AT&T in 1982. This settlement was a radical departure from existing policy, prompting some in Congress to challenge the authority of the Justice Department (Rosenstiehl 1997). Public opinion about the breakup was decidedly mixed, and policy historians agree that there was never a public outcry against AT&T's monopoly status to prompt the drastic action (Hudson 1997; Crandall and Waverman 1995). The aftermath of the AT&T breakup undoubtedly left Congress and the FCC in new regulatory terrain. Increased congressional lawmaking in the late 1980s and 1990s may be an indicator of these new demands.

A New Regime? The Telecommunications Competition and Deregulation Act of 1996

The Telecommunications Competition and Deregulation Act of 1996 (referred to as the Telecommunications Act of 1996) represents a comprehensive reworking of the regulatory regime in telecommunications. The legislation represents a trend, several years in the making, where congressional committees leaders, the courts, FCC regulators, and the states were all moving towards removing and reducing regulatory barriers to competition in the telecommunications arena ("Congress Puts Finishing Touches" 1995, 4). Enacted by a Republican Congress and supported by the Clinton administration, the Telecommunications Act of 1996 affects every segment of the telecommunications industry: telephone, cable TV, broadcasting, and computer communications. The primary mechanism of deregulation in this act was to reverse the long-standing policy of placing regulatory barriers between each of the niches in the telecommunications industry.[8]

Rather than reducing the need for the FCC, the new legislation has provided a new charter and a raft of regulatory questions to address. The FCC is still the primary federal interpreter of telecommunications regulations and the chief agency in charge of the law's smooth and consistent implementation. The FCC, for instance, has to "grant permission" in order for a previous monopolist to enter a new field. In addition, the agency was given new roles in order to assure that competition would not adversely affect the public interest.

Historically, federal telecommunications regulation has always supported private sector control of the industry. The aim of regulation was to create safeguards to assure that the private, profit-motivated companies would also serve "the public interest" in providing fair, equitable, and affordable access. The regulatory regime that is thought to best serve these goals changed over the course of the twentieth century. Competition is now seen as better than the protection of a "natural monopoly," as a way to advance technological improvement, improve service, and lower costs.

Experts, industry leaders, and legislators continue to debate how effective the new regulatory regime of the Telecommunications Act of 1996 has been in ensuring "public interest" goals. Indeed, the policy environment has greatly changed since the law was enacted. Since 1996, wholly new markets for telecommunications services have been created, as seen in the rise of Internet and cable/DSL services and the explosion of the market for cell phones and other wireless communication devices. Competition within the industry may be more connected to technological innovation and market forces than to regulatory changes, as industry price standards are tied more to premium services than basic access.

THE POLITICS OF TELECOMMUNICATIONS POLICY

A Theoretical Framework

The theoretical ideas we employ have become common currency among rational choice institutionalists, though no one has implemented them exactly this way before (at least to the best of our knowledge). In essence, we combine standard ideas from the spatial theory of policy bargaining with standard ideas from the theory of political delegation, to explain surges and slumps in legislative productivity.

In simplest form, the spatial theory of bargaining can be illustrated as ideal points along a line.[9] The line is a one-dimensional policy space, and is a convenient way to represent the array of policy choices. The points can be marked *H* and *S* to represent the "ideal points" of two actors, for examples, the chairmen of the House and Senate Commerce committees. These points indicate the most preferred policies of the two chairmen. We assume that the value to a chair of other policies declines proportionately with distance from her ideal point.

The interval between the two ideal points is known as the *Pareto set*, and it plays an important role in the analysis. Note that, for any given point outside the Pareto set, one can find a point within the Pareto set that *both* chairs prefer. On the other hand, given a point within the Pareto set, it is impossible to find a point that both prefer. Suppose the two chairs bargain about changing policies, with either free to propose any change she wishes. But suppose further that both chairs must agree on the change if it is to occur (as the rules of Congress assure). Then it seems reasonable to believe that, over time, the two chairs will replace policies outside the Pareto set with ones inside them. But once a point has entered the Pareto set, it will be invulnerable to further change.

This exceedingly simple setup affords one way to think about "policy windows." For policies outside the Pareto set, the policy window is open. For policies inside the Pareto set, it is closed. Suppose that new "policies" arrive randomly throughout the policy space, as new problems arise within a dynamic, industrial society. If the ideal points of the two players are close, then the Pareto set is small and the policy window for the new problems is apt to be open. But if the ideal points of the two players are far apart, then the new policy may well lie within the Pareto set—the policy window is apt to be closed. Thus, simple notions of bargaining suggest that ideological agreement between the House and Senate chairmen of relevant committees is apt to be necessary for much legislative action.

In the modern administrative state, Congress directly manages few areas. More typically, it delegates authority to an agent in the executive. In the last few years, political scientists have devoted a great deal of thought to the dynamics of delegation.[10] Again, we will employ only a sketch of these interesting ideas. Thinking of the one-dimensional line described above, suppose that an agency has an ideal point outside the Pareto set. It would seem that the agency must set policy within the Pareto set to avoid triggering congressional reversal of its policy. However, information costs or other transaction costs for the chairmen may give the agency a degree of "wriggle room." If so, the chairmen may be reluctant to delegate to an agency whose ideal point lies far outside the Pareto set, as this agency will face strong incentive to exploit the "wriggle room" and bend policy in its favor. Thus, when the agency is ideologically distant, the chairs may find it more attractive to direct policy themselves. Hence, more legislation. Somewhat similarly, if an agency lies outside the Pareto set, attempts to "cheat" on policy, but is found out by the chairs, then the two chairs will be able to agree on remedial legislation altering the policy of the agency. Both arguments suggest that legislation is apt to be more frequent as the agency lies further outside the Pareto set. And both arguments suggest that the key distance is from the agency's ideal point to the *nearer* of the two committees, since it is the willingness to act of the "more friendly" of the two chairs that is the real constraint on legislating.

Where is the president in this picture? At one level, the president is another veto player. But perhaps even more crucially, he is an administrative one as well. If the president shares the ideology of the key congressional actors, then his appointments to the agency will bring it closer to the preferred ideological stance of the congressional overseers. In addition, if the president has any direct administrative authority, he may use it to eliminate the agency's ideological "cheating" or "wriggling," if he shares the ideology of the chairs. In either case, ideological conformity between the chief executive officer of the administrative state and key legislative actors is apt to decrease direct legislative intervention in policymaking, at least in areas where Congress prefers to delegate rather than legislate directly.[11] Epstein and O'Halloran (1999) provide evidence that this is apt to be more likely in technologically difficult areas, like telecommunications.[12]

In sum, these simple ideas suggest that legislative action is more likely to be *possible* if the two chairs are ideological soul mates. But even so, action will actually *happen* only if the two chairs have reason to act. In an area in which Congress prefers to delegate policymaking, an impetus to action is more likely if the relevant agency is ideologically estranged from the chairs, and if the president is ideologically untrustworthy as well.

Congress and the FCC

Are these ideas at all plausible in this policy arena? The history of the relationship between the FCC and Congress strongly supports a principal-agent dynamic. Case studies suggest that Congress has often held the FCC on a "short lease" (Emery 1971; Krasnow and Longley 1973). During its 65-year history, the FCC has most often been headed by a chairman from the same party as the president, with a majority advantage (though usually by one vote only) of that party among the FCC commissioners. In times of divided government, this often puts the agency at odds with congressional leadership.

Detailing several ways in which Congress influences the FCC, Krasnow and Longley (1973) conclude that the most obvious, control by statue, is the least employed. More often nonstatutory control is used, such as investigations, oversight and review of all agency budgetary expenditures, and the watchfulness of the House and Senate Commerce committees, other committees with vested interests, and individual members of Congress and staff. Over the time of Krasnow and Longley's study, congressional involvement in directing and overseeing broadcast regulatory policies took place on an "almost daily" basis, even in times of relatively little legislative production. Former chairman Newton Minow is quoted as saying, "When I was Chairman, I heard from

Congress about as frequently as television commercials flash across the screen" (Krasnow and Longley 1973, 53).

Within Congress, the most important touch points for the FCC are the House and Senate Commerce committees, particularly their chairmen. The authors cite a highly placed FCC staff member who explained that "the word of Senator Warren Magnuson, Chairman of the Senate Commerce Committee, is practically law to the FCC" (Krasnow and Longley 1973, 53). Legislators also use inaction in policy debates that are politically contentious. In these cases, the administrative decisions fall to the FCC, which bears the brunt of the criticism should the agency's policy interpretations prove unsatisfactory to Congress or other stakeholders.

Furthermore, Krasnow and Longley suggest that the National Association of Broadcasters concentrates its lobbying efforts on Congress, not the FCC directly. Former vice president and general counsel of the National Association of Broadcasters Paul B. Comstock notes,

> Most of our work is done with congressional committees. We concentrate on Congress. We firmly believe that the FCC will do whatever Congress tells it to do, and will not do anything Congress tells it not to do. (Krasnow and Longley 1973, 56)

This is not to say that organizations, especially large firms and industry organizations, do not lobby the FCC directly. They do. Indeed, a study by de Figueiredo and Tiller (2000) analyzed over nine hundred lobbying contacts between industry and the FCC, covering over one hundred issues, and occurring in just the early portion of 1998.[13] The evidence suggests that industry lobbyists seek to influence policy decisions at both ends, the FCC and Congress.

Caveats aside, the FCC has substantive policymaking authority and makes many of the rules and regulations that affect the telecommunications field.[14] Its jurisdiction and administrative capacity far exceed the original mandate of the Communications Act of 1934 (Paglin 1989). Nonetheless, the commission fulfills its mandate to gather information for Congress and to deliberate on broad policy matters related to serving the public interest of telecommunications. Over its history, the FCC has sometimes taken a far-reaching and activist role, but it remains, ultimately, tethered to Congress and the executive.

Measurement

Our background knowledge of telecommunications policy, then, supports a more systematic investigation of ideological leadership in the FCC and Congress and its relationship to policymaking. The challenge is how to capture this interaction, keeping in mind the other influences to policymaking. In this section, we discuss how we measure key variables associated with these relationships.

The central difficulty in measuring legislative productivity is how to count and calibrate lawmaking to create a dependent variable across long periods of time. Counting actual laws is a starting point, but a major challenge is how to count the relative importance of laws enacted in each congressional session. Clearly some laws are more important than others, but this truism must be accounted for systematically. A problem in constructing such a measure is that many of the sources typically used to construct post–World War II measures of significance are not available for the entire time series. *Congressional Quarterly Almanac*, for instance, was first published in 1945, and no comparable sources exist for the period prior to 1945.

Our approach is to rate the historical significance of each telecommunications policy enactment from 1899 to 1998 on a five-point scale from historic to very minor. Then we "weight" each law with a computed value and sum the weights to calculate the legislative productivity in each congressional session. The "weight" (Wdtlaws2) used was equivalent to the average number of pages of *CQ* coverage for laws in each significance category enacted from 1945 to 1998. This value was used retroactively by attempting to match earlier laws of similar historical significance to those passed after 1945.

For example, there were only two telecommunications laws in the set deemed historic: the Federal Communications Act of 1934 and the Telecommunications Deregulation and Competition Act of 1996. Given the time frame, only the latter had coverage in *Congressional Quarterly*, 27 pages to be exact. This value became the "weight" for historic laws, and the 1934 act was weighted as 27 as well. For all other significance levels, the average number of *CQ* pages from 1945 to 1998 was substituted for the corresponding level from 1899 to 1944.

The Laws and Legislative Productivity

We use a broad definition of telecommunications policy and include legislation related to broadcasting (radio, television, cable television) and communication devices (telegraph, telephone, wireless and Internet/computer) that have been widely used. The set of telecommunications laws ($N = 162$) was identified by reading through lists of laws in the *Statutes at Large* (1900–44, table of contents) and *Congressional Quarterly* (1945–98, lists of laws) and by cross-checking the lists via the index for keywords related to telecommunications. Expert sources[15] were also used to verify that no major laws were omitted and to rank laws by historical significance. All telecommunications legislation was coded to identify historic laws, major laws, ordinary laws, and minor ones. Major laws were identified in two ways: (1) by consensus of expert opinion, including Mayhew's (1991) list; (2) by coverage in *Congressional Quarterly* after 1945 (number of pages written about final passage of law). Prior to 1945, historical expert sources necessarily took on greater weight; also the length of

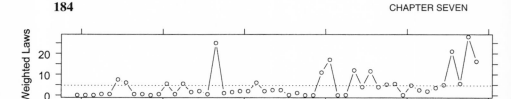

1. Early Regime (1900-1930): low level attention
2. FCC Regime: (1934 (peak) to1956) Boom in creation (1934), than status quo of low level
3. Challenged Regime: (1958-1970) Increased activity
4. Changing Regime: (after 1970s) regulatory framework of moves toward competition: low
   activity, (1970-1982) then Increased activity after AT&T break-up (1990s)

Figure 7.1: Congress Makes Telecom Policy, 1899–1998

Notes:

1. Early regime (1900–1930): low-level attention.
2. FCC Regime: [1934 (peak) to 1956] boom in creation (1934), then status quo of low level.
3. Challenged regime: (1958–70) increased activity.
4. Changing regime: (after 1970s) regulatory framework of moves toward competition: low activity (1970–82), then increased activity after AT&T breakup (1990s).

the law (number of pages in the *Statues at Large*) was considered, since more important laws tended to be of longer length.

Figure 7.1 shows the dependent variable, Weighted Laws, over time. The circles indicate each data point. The dotted line indicates the mean of the data (4.8 per Congress). In general, the amount of congressional lawmaking in the telecommunications area is rather low, reflecting a high degree of delegation to the FCC after 1934. However, there have been three bursts of policymaking activity: 1934, 1959–71, and 1991–97.

Agency-Committee Proximity

Our theory suggests that the ideological distance between the agency and the nearest relevant committee in the House or Senate affects the volume of significant enactments. We capture ideology of key players using the first dimension of Poole's common space NOMINATE scores. NOMINATE scores, based on a scaling of roll call votes on the floors of each chamber, are one of the most frequently used measures of congressmen's political ideology (Poole and Rosenthal 1997). Roughly speaking, the scores are bounded by −1 and 1, with negative scores being "liberal" and positive scores being "conservative." The common space scores use the movement of House members to the Senate to standardize the scaling across the two chambers, so that scores for House members and Senators are comparable. In this analysis, we used the NOMI-

Location of Median FCC Commissioner

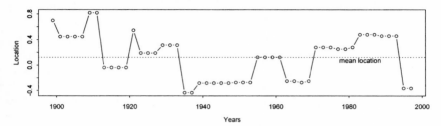

Agency's Distance from Nearer Committee

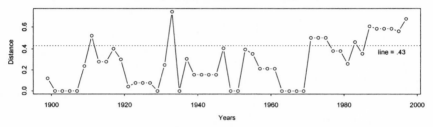

Figure 7.2: Agency-Committee Distance, 1899–1998

NATE scores for the chairmen of the House and Senate Commerce committees as well as the floor medians in the House and the Senate.

To determine the agency's ideal points at each congressional session, we
first identified all the commissioners of the Federal Radio Commission
(1927–34) and the FCC (post-1934) and the presidents who appointed them.
As a proxy for the commissioners' own ideology, we used McCarty's pseudo-
NOMINATE scores for the appointing president.[16] Then we identified the ideology of the median commissioner. For the period before 1927, we proceeded
in a similar way, but used the score imputed to the secretary of commerce (that
is, McCarty's pseudo-NOMINATE score for the sitting president).[17]

To estimate the proper distances among these actors, we first created spatial
arrays for each Congress, marking the ideal points (by NOMINATE scores)
for the agency, the chairmen of the House and Senate Commerce committees,
and the median voter in the House and Senate. If the median commissioner lay
outside the interval on the NOMINATE scale bounded by the House and Senate chairs, we calculated the distance between the median commissioner and
the most proximate of the two committee chairs. In this case, the (absolute)
distance became the variable. However, if the median commissioner lay within
the interval, we scored the variable as 0.

Figure 7.2 displays agency-committee distances. The top panel shows the
location of the median FCC commissioner per congressional session. The bottom panel displays the distance from relevant committees. Rather obviously,

the likelihood of measurement error means that this variable needs to be taken with a grain of salt—or perhaps a whole fistful! Nonetheless, we hope that large scores for the variable indicate that the preferred policies at the FCC are likely to be rather discordant with those favored by both committee chairs. Conversely, we hope that low scores indicate that the preferred policies at the FCC are not likely to be very discordant with those supported by both committee chairs.

As shown in figure 7.2, the variable for agency-committee distance takes large values at several interesting junctures in the time series. Relatively high distance values occur in the 61st and 62nd Congresses, when the first Radio Acts of 1910 and 1912 were enacted, in the 73rd Congress which enacted the legislation to create the FCC in 1934, and in the early 1970s (the 92nd–94th Congresses), when several laws on the Public Broadcasting Corporation were enacted. The distances remain high in the 1990s (the 100th–105th Congresses), when Congress turned its lawmaking attention to changing technological and economic conditions following the breakup of AT&T.

THE PRODUCTION OF TELECOMMUNICATIONS LAWS

In building a predictive model for legislative production, we theorized that agency distance would operate under a "threshold" effect. In other words, if the agency was close enough to one of the committee's ideal points, the nearer chairman would be satisfied to delegate telecommunications policy to the agency. However, if the distance between them became too great, exceeding a certain threshold of tolerance, the nearer chairman would be motivated to act, resulting in a greater likelihood for lawmaking. Figure 7.3 displays legislative productivity in relation to agency-committee distance. As both the top and lower panels show, the amount of legislative activity and the probability of enacting a major law increase as agency-committee distance increases. Both figures support the idea of a break-point threshold near the 0.4 distance.

To capture this effect, we used the median agency distance ($x = .43$) as the threshold level and computed a variable that represented law production above that level interacted with production below that level. We used this model to predict both total production of telecommunication laws (Weighted Laws) and the probability of enacting a major law (historic and major significance levels). Table 7.2 reports results from these regression models.[18]

Both models perform surprisingly well considering they represent only one explanatory variable. Over 40 percent of the lawmaking performance, measured by the R^2 value, can be accounted for with this simple story. Substantially more telecommunications laws (weighted value 61.76) are enacted when agency distance from the relevant committees is greater than the threshold mark. The probability of enacting a major law is also increased during these periods. These findings indicate that Congress is willing to act when its

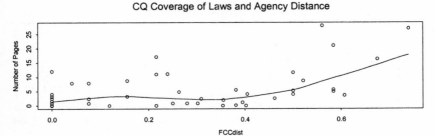

Figure 7.3: Legislative Productivity and Agency-Committee Distance

agent diverges from the committee's ideological preferences. When the agency is estranged from the committee in terms of ideology, committee members seem to reverse their tendency to delegate and take on a more active role in policymaking.

Clearly there are other important factors at work to explain legislative

TABLE 7.2 Regression Models Predicting Legislative Activity, 1899–1998

	Production of Laws (weight)	Probability of Major Law
Agency distance above threshold		
Coefficient	61.76	11.74
S.E.	10.37	5.09
t-value	5.96	2.3
Intercept		
Coefficient	3.21	−1.29
S.E.	0.80	0.38
t-value	3.99	−3.4
degrees of freedom	48	48
R^2	.42	
Durbin-Watson	2.26	2.23

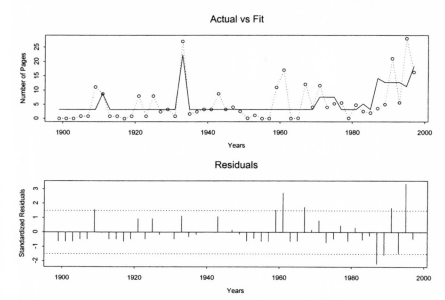

Figure 7.4: The Model's Predictions: *Congressional Quarterly* Coverage of Enactments

production in this policy area. Lawmaking, it would seem, would be sensitive to technological changes, economic stresses, and the political actions or pressures from other influential players, such as the Department of Justice, the courts, and telecommunications market leaders, like AT&T. We attempted to measure and model several of these elements, but without success.[19] More appropriate measures must be devised. In addition, we theorized that "regimes" of FCC oversight might explain different periods of legislative production. Yet the small number of data points in each time period undermined our ability to detect a clear relationship.

Figure 7.4 examines the predictions of the model against the historical record. The top panel shows actual observations (the points) and the model's predictions (the line). The lower panel shows the corresponding (standardized) residuals. Though the R^2 for this extremely simple model is surprisingly robust at .425, it is expected that one will find discrepancies between the model and the data. The bottom panel identifies a few large differences that require further explanation.

First, the model predicts high levels of legislative production from the 100th to the 105th Congresses. There are high levels of lawmaking in the 102nd and 104th (actually higher than predicted), but there are depressed levels in the 100th, the 101st and the 103rd. This could be an indication of the time needed for Congress to consider and to pass legislation in the highly technical area of telecommunications. Ideologically, Congress may have been motivated to act throughout the 1990s, but the actual laws took time to craft and be successfully enacted. There are definite bursts of legislation in the 1990s, but they were not sustained at each and every congressional session in the period. Nonetheless, the model correctly identifies this period as one of ideological tension that proceeds to "open a window" for policymaking.

Second, the model fails to predict the surges that occurred in the 86th and 87th Congresses. In these Congresses, the House and Senate Commerce committees were ideologically proximate, but the FCC was not particularly out of step with them. Factors not strictly related to ideology must be driving these surges. In the late 1950s and 1960s, the tensions caused by the appearance of new technologies and, perhaps, Cold War concerns may have held greater influence.

DISCUSSION AND CONCLUSION

The model presented here, which taps into the role of ideology and principal-agent relationships in predicting legislative productive, does a pretty good job at identifying key moments in telecommunications policymaking. But its failures suggest the need for greater attentiveness to other dynamics in the regulatory regime. That remains a difficult task for the macropolitics enterprise to tackle in the future. Nonetheless, we have shown that a simple political theory can afford real purchase on a difficult dataset.

In our view, a new kind of history of the administrative state—one that is theoretically driven yet also sensitive to the internal logic of regulatory regimes—demands to be written. This new kind of political history has yet to find its Gibbon or Namier. But when it does, the ideas we explore here may prove useful—at least, that is our hope.

NOTES

1. The very first federal involvement in telecommunications was research and development subsidies prior to the 1840s, and the first federal regulations were enacted in 1866 (the Post Roads Act).

2. The commission's regulatory inaction in telecommunications continued even as its powers were expanded to oversee mergers and acquisitions with the Willis-Graham Act of 1921.

3. Both television and microwave technologies can be used for long-distance communications and were threatening to the AT&T monopoly.

4. "Above 890" is a reference to the frequency threshold of microwaves, which can be used for telephone transmissions.

5. MCI, founded in the early 1960s, used microwave technology to provide better telephone service to business subscribers. It was not until the Telecommunications Act of 1996 that coaxial cable restrictions would be lifted to allow cable companies the ability to transmit telephone service.

6. The House Committee on Science and Astronautics was also created in 1959, although it did not sponsor the COMSAT bill.

7. Experts from right-leaning (The American Enterprise Institute) and left-leaning (The Brookings Institution) think tanks were in relative agreement in supporting deregulation (Rosenstiehl 1997).

8. At one time, technological barriers separated these industries, and natural monopoly arguments were used to establish a protectionist monopoly system. Over the years, especially with advancements in digital technology and computers, these barriers no longer existed.

9. For more carefully articulated models with relevance to this discussion, see Krehbiel 1999; Brady and Volden 1998; Cameron 2000; and Ferejohn and Shipan 1990, among many others.

10. Among the more interesting studies are Kiewiet and McCubbins 1991; McCubbins, Noll, and Weingast 1999; Snyder and Weingast 1999; de Figueiedo and Tiller 2000; Epstein and O'Halloran 1999; and Huber and Shipan 2002.

11. This argument stands the normal "veto player" argument on its head. Obviously, it applies only to areas in which Congress prefers delegated rather than direct policymaking.

12. In addition, see Price 1979, which provides evidence on committee policymaking in the telecommunications arena.

13. In one of the first large-scale empirical studies to analyze actual lobbying events (rather than by proxy via PAC contributions or by case study), they found that large firms' behavior is consistent with economic theories of transaction costs.

14. The judiciary and the Department of Justice also influence telecommunications policy. Both have been active in oversight since the early days of telephone and radio regulation, predating the Communications Act of 1934 and the FCC. It is beyond the scope of this chapter, though, to deal with those interactions.

15. Telecommunications policy sources included Compaine 1984; Kahn 1968; Paglin 1989; Brock 1981; Cohen 1991; Rosenstiehl 1997; Zarkin 1998; Cantor and Cantor 1986; and Teske 1995.

16. McCarty calculated these using each president's requests to Congress, treating the president as if he were a House member. His DW-NOMINATE data was adjusted to match the common space values needed for this analysis (McCarty 2001, private communication).

17. A plausible alternative here would be to calculate the median for the ICC.

18. Models with additional variables were tested, but none proved substantively or statistically significant. Better variables and measurement are needed to capture key factors of interest.

19. Variables we tested, unsuccessfully, included "technology stress," which was computed by the percentage of household adoption of a particular technology (televisions, radio, computer), presidential mentions of telecommunications policy in his State of the Union address, and standard variables of unified versus divided govern-

ment. We also considered using dummy variables for crisis events and Department of Justice actions, but decided that the few instances could not be properly modeled.

REFERENCES

Binder, Sarah A. 1999. "The Dynamics of Legislative Gridlock, 1947–1996." *American Political Science Review* 93:519–33.

Brady, David, and Craig Volden. 1998. *Revolving Gridlock: Politics and Policy from Carter to Clinton*. Boulder, Colo.: Westview Press.

Brock, Gerald W. 1981.*The Telecommunications Industry: The Dynamics of Market Structure*. Cambridge: Harvard University Press.

Burnham, Walter Dean. 1994. "Pattern Recognition and 'Doing' Political History: Art, Science, or Bootless Enterprise?" In *The Dynamics of American Politics: Approaches and Interpretations*, ed. Lawrence Dodd and Calvin Jillson. Boulder, Colo.: Westview Press.

Byrd, Robert C. 1988. *The Senate, 1789–1989: Historical Statistics*. Washington, D.C.: Government Printing Office.

Cameron, Charles M. 2000. *Veto Bargaining: Presidents and the Politics of Negative Power*. New York: Cambridge University Press.

Cantor, Muriel G., and Joel M. Cantor. 1986. "Regulation and Deregulation: Telecommunication Politics in the United States." In *New Communication Technologies and the Public Interest*, ed. Marjorie Ferguson. Beverly Hills: Sage.

Cass, Ronald O. 1989. "Title IV, V, and VI. Review, Enforcement, and Power under the Communications Act of 1934: Choice and Chance in Institutional Design." In *A Legislative History of the Communications Act of 1934*, ed. Max O. Paglin. New York: Oxford University Press.

Center for Information Policy Research. 1984. Project Director: Benjamin Comagine. *Chronology of Telecommunications and Cable Television Regulation in the United States*. Cambridge: Harvard University Press.

Cohen, Jeffrey E. 1991. "The Telephone Problem and the Road to Telephone Regulation in the United States, 1876–1933." *Journal of Policy History* 3 (1): 42–69.

———. 1997. *Presidential Responsiveness and Public Policy-Making*. Ann Arbor: University of Michigan Press.

Coleman, John J. 1999. "Unified Government, Divided Government, and Party Responsiveness." *American Political Science Review* 93: 821–35.

Compaine, Benjamin, ed. 1984. *Understanding New Media: Trends and Issues in Electronic Distribution of Information*. Cambridge, Mass.: Ballinger.

"Congress Puts Finishing Touches on Major Industry Overhaul." 1995. *Congressional Quarterly Weekly Report* 4:3–29.

Congressional Quarterly Almanac. (Various Years.) Washington, D.C.: Congressional Quarterly Press.

Cox, Kenneth A., and William J. Brynes. 1989. "Title II: The Common Carrier Provisions—a Product of Evolutionary Development." In *A Legislative History of the Communications Act of 1934*, ed. Max O. Paglin. New York: Oxford University Press.

Cox, Gary W., and Mathew McCubbins. 1993. *Legislative Leviathan: Party Government in the House.* Berkeley and Los Angeles: University of California Press.

Crandall, Robert W., and Leonard Waverman. 1995. *Talk Is Cheap: The Promise of Regulatory Reform in North American Telecommunications.* Washington, D.C.: Brookings Institution Press.

de Figueiredo, John M., and Emerson H. Tiller. 2000. "The Structure and Conduct of Corporate Lobbying: How Firms Lobby the Federal Communications Commission." National Bureau of Economic Research Working Paper 7726, June, www .nber.org/papers/w7726.

Edwards, George C., III, Andrew Barrett, and Jeffery Peake. 1997. "The Legislative Impact of Divided Government." *American Journal of Political Science* 41: 545–63.

Emery, Walter B. 1971. *Broadcasting and Government: Responsibilities and Regulations.* 2nd ed. East Langing: Michigan State University Press.

Epstein, David, and Sharyn O'Halloran. 1999. *Delegating Powers: A Transaction Cost Politics Approach to Policy Making under Separate Powers.* Cambridge: Cambridge University Press.

Erikson, Robert S., Michael B. MacKuen, and James A. Stimson. 2002. *The Macro Polity.* New York: Cambridge University Press.

Fenno, Richard. 1973. *Congressmen in Committees.* Boston: Little, Brown.

Ferejohn, John, and Charles R. Shipan. 1990. "Congressional Influence on Bureaucracy." *Journal of Law, Economics, and Organization* 6:1–21.

Fiorina, Morris P. 1996. *Divided Government.* Boston: Allyn and Bacon.

Freedman, Grace R. 2000. "A Cascade of Laws, a Crush of Policy: The Evolution of Federal Authority in Health and Telecommunications Policy, 1960–1996." Ph.D. diss., Columbia University.

Freitag, Peter J. 1982. "The Myth of Corporate Capture: Regulatory Commissions in the United States." *Social Problems* 30:480–91.

Howell, William, E. Scott Adler, Charles M. Cameron, and Charles Riemann. 2000. "Divided Government and the Legislative Productivity of Congress, 1945–1994." *Legislative Studies Quarterly* 25:285–312.

Huber, John D. and Charles R. Shipan. 2002. *Deliberate Discretion: Institutional Foundations of Bureaucratic Autonomy in Modern Democracies.* New York: Cambridge University Press.

Hudson, Heather. 1997. *Global Connections: International Telecommunications Infrastructure and Policy.* New York: Van Nostrand Reinhold.

Jillson, Calvin. 1994. "Patterns and Periodicity in American National Politics." In *The Dynamics of American Politics: Approaches and Interpretations*, ed. Lawrence Dodd and Calvin Jillson. Boulder, Colo.: Westview Press.

Kahn, Frank, J., ed. 1968. *Documents of American Broadcasting.* New York: Appleton-Century-Crofts, Meredith.

Kelly, Sean Q. 1993a. "Divided We Govern: A Reassessment." *Polity* 25:475–84.

———. 1993b. "Response. Let's Stick with the Larger Question." *Polity* 25:489–90.

Kiewiet, D. Roderick, and Mathew McCubbins. 1991. *The Logic of Delegation.* Chicago: University of Chicago Press.

King, Gary, and Lyn Ragsdale. 1988. *The Elusive Executive: Discovering Statistical Patterns in the Presidency.* Washington, D.C.: Congressional Quarterly Press.

Kingdon, John W. 1995. *Agendas, Alternatives, and Public Policies*. 2nd ed. New York: HarperCollins College Publishers.

Krasnow, Erwin G., and Lawrence D. Longley. 1973. *The Politics of Broadcast Regulation*. New York: St. Martin's Press.

Krehbiel, Keith. 1991. *Information and Legislative Organization*. Ann Arbor: University of Michigan Press.

———. 1993. "A Theory of Divided and Unified Government." Research Paper No. 1270, Graduate School of Business, Stanford University, September 29.

———. 1999. *Pivotal Politics: A Theory of U.S. Lawmaking*. Chicago: University of Chicago Press.

Mayhew, David R. 1974. *Congress: The Electoral Connection*. New Haven: Yale University Press.

———. 1991. *Divided We Govern: Party Control, Lawmaking, and Investigations, 1946–1990*. New Haven: Yale University Press.

———. 1993. "Reply: Let's Stick with the Longer List." *Polity* 25:489–90.

McCubbins, Mathew D., Roger G. Noll, and Barry R. Weingast. 1999. "The Political Origins of the Administrative Procedures Act." *Journal of Law, Economics, and Organization* 15:180–217.

McCubbins, Mathew D., and Thomas Schwartz. 1987. "Congressional Oversight Overlooked: Police Patrols versus Fire Alarms." In *Congress: Structure and Policy*, ed. Mathew D. McCubbins and Terry Sullivan. Cambridge: Cambridge University Press.

McCubbins, Mathew D., and Terry Sullivan, eds. 1987. *Congress: Structure and Policy*. Cambridge: Cambridge University Press.

Nelson, Garrison, ed. 1993. *Committees in Congress, 1947–1992*. Washington, D.C.: Congressional Quarterly Press.

Noll, Roger G. 1986. "The Political and Institutional Context of Communications Policy." In *Marketplace for Telecommunications*, ed. Marcellus Snow. New York: Longman.

———. 1987. "The Political Foundations of Regulatory Policy." In *Congress: Structure and Policy*, ed. Mathew D. McCubbins and Terry Sullivan. Cambridge: Cambridge University Press.

Ornstein, Norman J., Thomas E. Mann, and Michael J. Malbin, eds. 1980–. *Vital Statistics on Congress*. Washington, D.C.: Congressional Quarterly Press.

Paglin, Max O., ed. 1989. *A Legislative History of the Communications Act of 1934*. New York: Oxford University Press.

Peterson, Mark A. 1990. *Legislating Together: The White House and Capitol Hill from Eisenhower to Reagan*. Cambridge: Harvard University Press.

Petrocik, John R., and Joseph Doherty. 1996. "The Road to Divided Government: Paved without Intention." In *Divided Government: Change, Uncertainty, and the Constitutional Order*, ed. Peter F. Galderisi, R. Q. Herzberg, and P. McNamara. Lanham, Md.: Rowman and Littlefield.

Poole, Keith T., and Howard Rosenthal. 1997. *Congress: A Political-Economic History of Roll Call Voting*. New York: Oxford University Press.

Price, David E. 1979. *Policymaking in Congressional Committees: The Impact of "Environmental" Factors*. Tucson: Institute of Government Research, University of Arizona.

Robinson, Glen O. 1989. "Title I: The Federal Communications Act: An Essay on Origins and Regulatory Purpose." In *A Legislative History of the Communications Act of 1934*, ed. Max O. Paglin. New York: Oxford University Press.

————. ed. 1978. *Communications for Tomorrow: Policy Perspectives for the 1980s*. New York: Praeger.

Rosenstiehl, Michael C. 1997. "The Shared Understandings of Interests and Institutions: Cases from Telecommunication Policy." Paper prepared for the Annual Meeting of the American Political Science Association, Washington, D.C.

Shapiro, Martin. 1988. *Who Guards the Guardians?* Athens: University of Georgia Press.

Silbey, Joel H. 1996. "Divided Government in Historical Perspective, 1789–1996." In *Divided Government: Change, Uncertainty, and the Constitutional Order*, ed. Peter F. Galderisi, R.Q. Herzberg, and P. McNamara. Lanham, Md.: Rowman & Littlefield.

Snyder, Susan K., and Barry R. Weingast. 1999. "The American System of Shared Powers: The President, Congress, and the NLRB." Working paper, Hoover Institution, Stanford University.

Teske, Paul, ed. 1995. *American Regulatory Federalism and Telecommunications Infrastructure*. Hillside, N.J.: Lawrence Erlbaum Associates.

Tobias, Jeffery. 1995. "Comments—'Notwithstanding Section 2(b) . . .' Recent Legislative Initiatives Affecting the Federal-State Balance in Telecommunications Regulation." In *American Regulatory Federalism and Telecommunications Infrastructure*, ed. Paul Teske. Hillside, N.J.: Lawrence Erlbaum Associates.

Weingast, Barry, and Mark Moran. 1983. "Bureaucratic Discretion of Congressional Control? Regulatory Policymaking by the Federal Trade Commission." *Journal of Political Economy* 96:132–63.

Wollenberg, Roger. J. 1989. "Title III: The FCC as Arbiter of 'The Public Interest, Convenience, and Necessity'." In *A Legislative History of the Communications Act of 1934*, ed. Max O. Paglin. New York: Oxford University Press.

United States. 1859–1945. *Statutes at Large*. Washington, D.C.: Government Printing Office.

————. 1925–98. *U.S. Code of Law*. Washington, D.C.: Government Printing Office.

————. 1994–98. *U.S. Code Congress and Administrative News*. Washington, D.C.: Government Printing Office.

————. *Statistical Abstract*. www.fedstats.gov; www.census.gov.

————. Congress. House Committee on Interstate and Foreign Affairs. 1976. *180 Years of Service: A Brief History of the U.S. House Commerce Committee*. Washington, D.C.: Government Printing Office.

United States President. 1929–96. *Public Papers of the President*. Washington, D.C.: Government Printing Office.

Zaragoza, Richard R., Richard J. Bodorff, and Jonathan W. Emord. 1989. "The Public Interest Concept Transformed: The Trusteeship Model Gives Way to a Marketplace Approach." In *Public Interest and the Business of Broadcasting*, ed. Jon T. Powell and Wally Gair. New York: Quorum Books.

Zarkin, Michael J. 1998. "The Transformation of U.S. Telecommunications Policy: Political Learning and Policy Change, 1920–1996." Paper prepared for the Annual Meeting of the American Political Science Association, Boston.

8

The Influence of Congress and the Courts over the Bureaucracy: An Analysis of Wetlands Policy

Brandice Canes-Wrone

A major finding of research on congressional-bureaucratic relations is that members of Congress can influence administrative decisions absent explicit legislative action. For example, Arnold (1979) shows that bureaucrats allocate projects to the districts of those members with the most influence over the bureaucrats' programs. Arnold argues that the legislators do not need to command the allocation; rather, the threat of budgetary cuts or other statutory reform causes the officials to anticipate the members' likely reactions and allot the projects accordingly. Similarly, Calvert, Moran, and Weingast (1987) demonstrate that the Federal Trade Commission's decisions are correlated with change in the ideological composition of Congress, even when legislators do not seek to reform the agency.

When these studies were first published, they refuted economists' perceptions of a "runaway" bureaucracy that was free from political oversight.[1] Within political science, the work was also controversial, but not because political scientists generally believed in a bureaucracy free from political oversight. Instead, many scholars questioned whether Congress was the primary political overseer of the bureaucracy and maintained that the president, in particular, has more influence over bureaucratic decision-making (e.g., Moe 1985, 1987; Wood and Anderson 1993). Analogous to the initial findings concerning congressional influence, this later generation of work shows that the president's ideological beliefs can influence bureaucratic decisions even when the president does not overtly attempt to affect the decisions.

Within this next generation of research, only a few studies have compared the influence of Congress and the courts over the bureaucracy. This scarcity is unfortunate given that the literature on administrative behavior underscores the importance of the judiciary to policy implementation (e.g., Kagan 1995; Melnick 1983; Tiller and Spiller 1999). Moreover, the existing work that compares judicial and congressional influence generally fails to examine critical facets of the judiciary. For instance, it generally does not account for variation across appellate and district courts even though these courts are the primary venue for judicial review of agency decisions (e.g., Humphries and Songer 1999; Ringquist and Emmert 1999). In addition, the work typically does not analyze the composition of the courts independently of rulings despite the fact that the composition may affect bureaucratic decisions when litigation does not occur, just as congressional ideology can influence them absent explicit legislative activity.[2]

The only studies that account for these facets of the judiciary and examine congressional influence over the bureaucracy are Howard 2001 and Canes-Wrone 2003, which each indicate that the courts have more influence than Congress does. However, the studies fail to analyze key components of congressional oversight. Howard does not examine the impact of committees, a factor that scholars have consistently found to influence bureaucratic behavior (e.g., Scholz and Wood 1998; Weingast and Moran 1983), and neither study analyzes the effect of the chambers' floors. The literature thus does not provide a good understanding of whether Congress influences bureaucratic decisions as much as does the judiciary.

I address this issue using data that revolve around 18,331 decisions by the Army Corps of Engineers between 1988 and 1996 over whether to issue permits for the development of wetlands. An advantage of the data is that they concern individual bureaucratic decisions rather than aggregate administrative outputs, which are more easily manipulated by officials (Ringquist 1995). In the analysis, I allow that the bureaucrats' decisions may be influenced by whether they concern the districts of members who sit on the relevant oversight committees, by the ideological leanings of the chambers, and by the composition of the lower courts in which the decisions would be litigated. The results indicate that Congress has more influence over bureaucratic decision-making than does the judiciary, but that the effect of the courts is of a comparable magnitude substantively.

The remainder of this chapter is divided into four sections: a discussion of wetlands policy; a description of the data, empirical specification, and measurement; the presentation of the results; and a conclusion that discusses the relevance of the findings to the broader literature on congressional influence over the bureaucracy.

WETLANDS PERMITS

The *Code of Federal Regulations* defines wetlands as "those areas that are inundated or saturated by surface or ground water at a frequency and duration sufficient to support, and that under normal conditions do support, a prevalence of vegetation typically adapted for life in saturated soil conditions. Wetlands generally include swamps, marshes, bogs and similar areas."[3] Federal jurisdiction is established in Section 404 of the Clean Water Act (CWA) of 1977. Building upon the Rivers and Harbors Appropriation Act of 1889, which accords the Army Corps of Engineers authority over navigable waters, the act classifies wetlands as such waters and requires that a permit be obtained from the Corps for their filling, dredging, or other development. In addition, the CWA authorizes the Environmental Protection Agency (EPA) to set the guidelines for the issuance of wetlands permits and confers the agency veto power over any permit issued by the Corps.

The EPA has stipulated three major guidelines, each of which allows for substantial discretion on the part of the Army Corps official who evaluates an application for an individual permit.[4] The first requirement is that no practicable alternative to the project may exist. In other words, if officials determine that the project could be conducted without developing the wetlands, then the permit should be denied. The second guideline is that the permit cannot result in the significant destruction of waterways, such as causing an existing waterway to become impassable. The third stipulation is that proper mitigation be conducted. An applicant can be required to create or restore other wetlands to compensate for the environmental impact of the proposed project.

Applicants submit their proposals to the Corps district office with jurisdiction over the property of the wetland. The Corps has 38 U.S. district offices, each of which is supervised by one of eight regional Corps divisions. Once an application is completed, the Corps issues a notice that invites comments on the proposed project. The notice is placed in public locations such as the post office and sent to all potentially interested parties, including adjoining property owners, state and local officials, and conservation organizations. At this stage, as well as other stages of the process, conservation groups tend to be particularly active players, often offering detailed alternative plans that demand less development of the existing wetlands.[5] If the issues raised by these types of comments cannot be handled informally, then the Corps calls a public hearing to which all interested parties are specifically invited. The hearing allows for the discussion of any differences among the private parties, or between them and the Corps. Only subsequent to all of these stages does the Corps issue a decision. The entire process, from the completion of the permit application through the decision, generally takes between two and three months.

As mentioned previously, if the Corps issues a permit, the EPA can veto it. In practice, such vetoes are extraordinarily rare; since the regulations went into effect in 1979, the EPA has vetoed only 11 of the approximately 150,000 permit applications.[6] Given this infrequency, the empirical analysis does not try to predict the occurrence of EPA vetoes but instead the probability that the Corps issues a wetlands permit. In doing so, the analysis accounts for the possibility that the Corps may be influenced by the threat of an EPA veto.

The federal courts have jurisdiction over lawsuits protesting a decision by the Corps. In general, the venue is limited to the district court of the wetland or the Corps district office responsible for the decision.[7] The relevant appellate court thus hears appeals, and as Humphries and Songer (1999, 208) note, the appellate court is almost always "the final arbiter" for lawsuits over administrative decisions. My data are consistent with this claim. For these decisions of the Corps, the appellate courts heard 24 cases, while the Supreme Court did not hear any.

Lawsuits against the Corps can be divided into two categories: suits by applicants contesting the denial of a permit and suits by environmental groups or other parties challenging the issuance of one. A standard charge of an applicant is that the Corps behaved in an "arbitrary and capricious" manner, while a standard charge of a party contesting a permit is that officials failed to implement a nondiscretionary portion of the Clean Water Act. As is the case with much of the federal environmental legislation enacted in the 1970s, the Clean Water Act explicitly grants any citizen the right to sue administrative officials for not implementing a nondiscretionary component of the law.[8] Other legal grounds are possible for either type of plaintiff, such as the constitutionality of the permitting process or whether the property constitutes a wetland under federal law. However, the "arbitrary and capricious" and "failure to implement" charges are particularly attractive because they are difficult to dismiss summarily.

As this description of the administrative process has indicated, Congress is not involved in the day-to-day implementation of wetlands policy. This lack of explicit involvement does not imply, however, that bureaucrats need not be concerned about members' preferences. All of the 102nd, 103rd, 104th, and 105th Congresses held hearings on the regulatory program. The 104th House even passed legislation that would have weakened federal protection of wetlands.[9] It therefore seems reasonable to expect that Corps officials would fear legislative repercussions if the program were administered in a manner inconsistent with members' desires, and base decisions on the permits accordingly.

DATA, MODEL, AND MEASUREMENT

The data revolve around 18,331 decisions by the Army Corps between 1988 and 1996 over whether to accept an application for the development of wetlands. Canes-Wrone (2003) describes the compilation of the data on the decisions, although a few details are worth emphasizing here. First, the data include only administrative decisions for which the district court with jurisdiction over the wetland is the same as the district court with jurisdiction over the Corps office responsible for evaluating the application. Potential litigants could therefore not forum shop between these venues.[10] Second, the Corps has delegated to a few state governments the primary authority for the review of applications, and the observations concern only states in which the Corps has the primary authority.[11] Finally, even with these exclusions, the decisions have substantial regional variation. They encompass 19 different states that span the Northeast, Southeast, Midwest, Southwest, and Northwest. In addition, they concern nine of the regional appellate courts and 23 of the district courts.

To estimate relative effects of congressional and judicial ideology over these bureaucratic decisions, I adopt an econometric specification in which the dependent variable, Permit Issued, equals 1 if the Corps grants a permit to an applicant and equals 0 otherwise. The key independent variables measure the liberalism of Congress and the courts. Because the lower courts in practice have jurisdiction over litigation involving the bureaucratic decisions, these variables are the central ones regarding the judiciary. The specification also accounts for the ideology of the Supreme Court, however, as well as for additional factors such as the president and the local economy. Formally, the model is stated:

$$\Pr (\text{Permit Issued} = 1)$$

$$= \Phi \, (\alpha + \beta_1 \text{ Liberalism of District Representation on House Committees}$$

$$+ \, \beta_2 \text{ Liberalism of State Representation on Senate Committees}$$

$$+ \, \beta_3 \text{ Liberalism of Chamber Floors} \tag{1}$$

$$+ \, \beta_4 \text{ Liberalism of District Court}$$

$$+ \, \beta_5 \text{ Liberalism of Appellate Court} + \beta_6 \text{ Applicants' Legal Success}$$

$$+ \, \beta_7 \text{ Interest Groups' Legal Success} + \eta \text{ control variables}).$$

Two issues regarding the econometric analysis require particular attention. First, to the extent that applicants account for the liberalism of Congress and the courts in designing applications, the coefficients of equation 1 are biased *against* finding significant effects. Thus, the estimates I present may be considered a "lower bound" on the impact of the factors. The second issue concerns the possibility that the data selection biases the results. Canes-Wrone (2003) analyzes a Heckman selection model to assess this possibility and does not find evidence of selection bias. I therefore proceed with the simpler, probit model of equation 1.

The following describes the measurement of the factors, including each control variable.

Liberalism of district representation on House committees, liberalism of state representation on Senate committees. The variables reflect whether the wetlands are located in the district of a member who sits on the authorization committees or appropriations subcommittees that oversee the wetlands program. These committees include the House Committee on Public Works and

Transportation (1988–94), the House Committee on Transportation and Infrastructure (1995–96), the House Appropriations Subcommittee on Energy and Water Development, the Senate Committee on Environment and Public Works, and the Senate Appropriations Subcommittee on Energy and Water Development.[12] I base the variables on regional representation because research suggests that bureaucrats may target their decisions to particular districts as a function of members' committee assignments (e.g., Arnold 1979). In addition, collinearity prevents examining the effects of the median preferences of the various committees as well as the chamber floors simultaneously.

Accordingly, the variable for representation on the House committee equals the number of relevant committee assignments held by a Democratic representative of the district in which the wetland is located minus the number of relevant committee assignments held by a Republican representative of that district. Given that only one member represents each district, the variable ranges from 0 to 2 if the member representing the district of the wetland is a Democrat and −2 to 0 if the member is a Republican. If, for instance, the wetland is located in the district of a Republican representative who sits on the House Committee on Transportation and Infrastructure, the variable equals −1. Liberalism of State Representation on Senate Committees is coded analogously, equaling the number of relevant committee assignments held by Democratic senators for the state in which the wetland is located minus the number of relevant committee assignments held by Republican senators in that state. Thus if the wetland is located in a state in which both senators are Democrats who sit on the Senate Appropriations Subcommittee on Energy and Water Development, the variable equals 2.

Liberalism of chamber floors. The factor equals the annual average percentage of Democrats in each chamber of Congress. While much of the literature on congressional oversight emphasizes the role of committees, some evidence suggests that bureaucrats are also concerned about the influence of the floor (e.g., Arnold 1979). I control for the House and Senate jointly due to the collinearity of the partisan composition of the chambers during the years of my data.

Liberalism of district court, liberalism of appellate court. A range of work emphasizes the importance of presidents in determining the ideological composition of the lower courts, with Democratic presidents appointing more liberal judges than Republican presidents appoint (e.g., Carp and Stidham 1985; Goldman 1997; Rowland and Carp 1996). This finding of ideological divergence extends to the domain of environmental policy; several studies show that judges appointed by Democratic presidents are more likely to rule in favor of environmental protection than those appointed by Republicans (e.g., Kovacic 1991; Ringquist and Emmert 1999). I therefore use the party of the appointing president to measure the liberalism of the lower courts. For both the district and the appellate court, the variable is based on the fact that potential litigants do not know who will hear their case prior to filing suit. Liberalism of District Court equals the percentage of full-time judges appointed by a Democratic president, given that in district court a single judge rules on each case. A panel of three judges typically hears cases in the courts of appeals,[13] and accordingly Liberalism of Appellate Court equals the likelihood a case is heard by a panel in which the majority of the judges are Democratic appointees.[14]

Applicants' legal success, interest groups' legal success. These two variables, which account for the influence of judicial rulings, are based on published lawsuits concerning the Corps' decisions over wetlands permits.[15] The first factor equals the number of suits won by applicants minus the number lost during the previous year in the lower courts in which the bureaucratic decision would be litigated. Analogously, the second factor equals the net number of lawsuits won by parties contesting permits during the previous year in the lower courts in which the administrative decision would be litigated. In almost all of these latter challenges, an interest group participated in the litigation.[16] I separately account for the suits of applicants and interest groups because research suggests that groups may sue merely to delay a project, even if they are unlikely to win in court (Meier 1985). A delay can allow a group time to marshal other means to prevent a project from proceeding, and particularly if it is a commercial enterprise, may result in the expiration of the applicant's purpose for developing the property.

Liberalism of the Supreme Court. The probability of the Supreme Court granting certiorari to a case regarding a wetlands permit is low, but given that it is nonzero I still control for the potential effect of the ideological composition of this court. The measure analogous to the ones for the lower courts is an indicator for whether a majority of the justices was appointed by a Democratic president.[17] Including such a variable is impossible, however, given that in each year of the time series, Republican presidents had appointed a majority of the Court. I therefore employ Martin and Quinn's (2002) dynamic ideal point scores, which rank each justice on a liberal-conservative ideological spectrum. The variable equals the median Martin-Quinn score for each year.

Reagan administration, Bush administration, Clinton administration. The literature suggests that presidents as well as the individual leaders of an agency can affect policy implementation (e.g., Meier 1979). For the years of the data, the service of each president overlaps perfectly with the service of his commander of the Army Corps and administrator of the EPA.[18] (The potential influence of the EPA administrator is recognized given that the EPA can veto decisions of the Corps.) Consequently, I control simultaneously for these three factors.

Budget. Previous research shows that higher expenditures on environmental programs tend to increase bureaucrats' protection of the environment (Ringquist 1995; Wood and Waterman 1993). The variable Budget, which equals annual average of budgetary outlays to the Army Corps and the environmental programs account of the EPA, accounts for this possibility. The factor is based on outlays rather than budget authority because the latter can reflect the obligation of funds for future years while the former reflects the actual spending of a given year.

State ideology. Research suggests that local preferences may influence bureaucratic decisions (e.g., Selznick 1949; Scholz, Twombly, and Headrick 1991). Officials may desire status within the community in which they live, and moreover, successful implementation may depend upon the cooperation of the community. I account for this type of influence using Berry et al.'s (1998) measure of state government ideology.[19] The higher is the Berry et al. rating, the more liberal is the ideology of the state.

County per capita income. Grossman and Krueger (1995) find a positive correlation between economic performance and environmental outcomes in wealthy countries, such as the United States. Consistent with this finding, research suggests that bureaucratic officials are more likely to favor the interests of business when an economy is weak (e.g., Krause 1996). These results indicate that the Corps' decisions may be influenced by the local economy. To account for such influence, I control for the annual per capita income of the county in which the wetland of the application is located.

Percentage of state with wetlands. The factor accounts for the possibility that the natural environment may influence a regulator's decision over whether to issue a wetlands permit. The variable equals the percentage of surface area in the state covered by wetlands according to the National Resource Inventory (NRI), which is conducted every five years by the National Resources Conservation Service.[20] I use the 1987 NRI for the bureaucratic decisions of 1988–91 and the 1992 NRI for the later years.

Year indicators.[21] Given that several factors vary only across time (for example, the presidential administration and liberalism of the Supreme Court), a full set of year indicators cannot be included. I therefore control for two years, 1992 and 1994, in which electoral results may have been particularly likely to affect bureaucratic behavior. President Clinton's electoral success in the fall of 1992 (as well as the expectation of it in the preceding months) may have caused officials to be less likely to issue permits.[22] Likewise, the large number of congressional seats that went from being Democratic to Republican in 1994 may have caused officials to become more likely to accept an application.

Army Corps division indicators. Research suggests that the federal structure of agencies may create differences in administrative outputs among geographic units (e.g., Hunter and Waterman 1996), and I control for this cross-sectional variation to avoid overestimating the impact of regional differences in committee representation and the ideological composition of the courts. My data encompass seven of the Corps' eight supervisory divisions: the Great Lakes and Ohio River Division, the Mississippi Valley Division, the North Atlantic Division, the Northwestern Division, the South Atlantic Division, the South Pacific Division, and the Southwestern Division. I include a dummy variable for each of these divisions.

RESULTS

Table 8.1 describes the results. Because the specification consists of a probit model, the coefficients are not readily interpretable. Therefore, the table presents not only coefficients and standard errors but also the marginal effect of each factor increasing a standard deviation from its mean, holding all other variables at their means. This last statistic approximates the impact of a typical change in the factor.

The findings suggest that Congress influences bureaucratic behavior in the ways predicted. When a wetland is located in the district of a Democratic (Republican) House member who sits on the principal House authorization committee or appropriations subcommittee for the program, the Corps is significantly less (more) likely to grant a permit to develop the property. Likewise, the Corps is significantly less (more) likely to grant a permit the higher the number of Democratic (Republican) senators that represent the state in which the wetland is located and have assignments to the principal committees. In addition, the preferences of the floors are found to affect the Corps decisions: the greater the percentage of Democrats in the House and Senate, the less likely are officials to issue permits.

The estimates on the judicial variables are also largely consistent with expectations. The probability that the Corps grants a permit significantly declines the more liberal are the district and appellate courts for the bureaucratic decision. Moreover, the more successful are applicants in litigating the denial of permits, the more likely is the Corps to issue permits in the future. The Supreme Court, as predicted, does not have a significant impact,[23] and the effect of interest groups' lawsuits is also not found to be significant. As mentioned at the outset, groups may use the legal process to delay wetlands projects even when it is likely that the courts will ultimately rule in favor of the developers; thus the lawsuits lost by groups may send little or no new information about the ideology of the courts. Consistent with this explanation, when one substitutes groups' gross (rather than net) wins, the effect is in the expected direction and statistically significant.

TABLE 8.1 Congressional and Judicial Influence over Army Corps Decisions

Dependent Variable = Pr (Wetlands Permit Issued = 1)	Probit Coefficient (SE)	Marginal Effect
Liberalism of District Representation on House	−0.182 (0.030)	−0.025
Liberalism of State Representation on Senate Committees	−0.406 (0.044)	−0.075
Liberalism of Chamber Floors	−3.603 (0.435)	−0.073
Liberalism of District Court	−0.416 (0.059)	−0.033
Liberalism of Appellate Court	−0.529 (0.111)	−0.029
Applicants' Legal Success	0.093 (0.029)	0.015
Interest Groups' Legal Success	−0.028 (0.026)	−0.005
Liberalism of Supreme Court	−0.123 (0.192)	−0.006
Reagan Administration	0.161 (0.070)	0.017
Clinton Administration	0.066 (0.077)	0.013
Budget	−0.109 (0.014)	−0.153
State Ideology	−0.308 (0.077)	−0.021
County Per Capita Income	−0.163 (0.023)	−0.034
% State with Wetlands	0.012 (0.003)	0.056
1992 (Election of Clinton)	−0.193 (0.054)	−0.027
1994 (Election of 104th Congress)	0.188 (0.046)	0.026
Constant	5.996 (0.573)	
Army Corps division indicators	Included. LR test for inclusion: $\chi^2 = 1041.672$ ($p = 0.000$)	
Number of observations	18,331	
Log likelihood	−12663.770	

Note: The omitted presidential administration is that of Bush Sr. The marginal effect reported equals the impact of a standard deviation increase in the variable from its mean, holding all other variables at their means.

The marginal effects suggest that the congressional factors have a greater influence than the judicial factors. A standard deviation increase in the liberalism of the representation on the relevant House committees reduces the probability that the Corps issues a permit by 2.5 percent, and an analogous change in representation on the key Senate committees decreases the probability of a permit by 7.5 percent. An increase of a standard deviation in the liberalism of the chamber floors also decreases the probability that a permit is granted by around 7.5 percent. In comparison, an increase of a standard deviation in the liberalism of the district court lowers the likelihood that the Corps issues a permit by 3.5 percent and the analogous change in the liberalism of the appellate court reduces the probability by 3 percent. The impact of rulings is even lower: a standard deviation increase in the legal success of applicants increases the probability of a permit by only 1.5 percent. Comparing the individual congressional and judicial effects, the impact of each congressional factor is never statistically less than that of a judicial factor, and in some cases is significantly greater. The marginal effects of the congressional factors are also jointly more significant than those of the judicial factors ($\chi^2(1) = 48.61, p < .001$).

Of course, these results do not refute the claim that the judiciary has a substantial impact on bureaucratic behavior; they even suggest that the effects of Congress and the judiciary are substantively comparable in magnitude. Thus, the analysis in one sense supports research that extols the influence of the judiciary over administrative decision-making. However, contrary to previous studies that have examined the influence of congressional ideology and the composition of the courts, I find that Congress has a greater impact than the judiciary. Notably, this result accounts for geographic as well as intertemporal variation in both congressional and judicial influence.

The effect of the congressional factors also appears substantial when compared with the control variables. For example, the coefficients for the variables representing the Reagan administration, county per capita income, and state ideology are each significant and in the expected direction, but less than the estimated effects of representation on the Senate committees or the liberalism of the floors. Moreover, the control variable with the largest impact, the budget for the wetlands program, is a shared power of Congress and the president. The increase of a standard deviation in outlays is found to reduce the likelihood of the Corps granting a permit by 15.5 percent, a result consistent with previous analysis of whether expenditures affect bureaucrats' protection of the environment (Ringquist 1995; Wood and Waterman 1993).

Among the other control variables, most have the expected effects. The dummies for the elections of 1992 and 1994 are each in the predicted direction and significant, suggesting that bureaucrats adjust their behavior in anticipation of presidential and congressional turnover. Also as expected, the Army Corps division indicators are jointly significant. This result supports the argument that bureaucratic structure affects administrative behavior.

The only findings that do not comport with previous research are those regarding the Clinton administration and the percentage of the state covered by wetlands. The results indicate that the probability of a permit being issued did not significantly differ between the Clinton and Bush administrations. This result mirrors that in Canes-Wrone (2003), which argues that the effect of the administrations may be largely captured by the difference in the budgets between them. In addition, the result is consistent with Bush's claims to be an "environmental president." The coefficient on Percentage of State with Wetlands contradicts Canes-Wrone 2003 in that here I find a positive correlation between this factor and the likelihood of receiving a permit to develop wetlands. A potential explanation for these seemingly contradictory findings is that areas with a high concentration of wetlands are more likely to be represented by Democrats who serve on the committees that oversee wetlands regulation. Thus when the variables on committee representation are not included as an explanatory factor, as they are not in Canes-Wrone 2003, one observes a negative correlation between the concentration of wetlands and the likelihood of the Corps issuing a permit. My data provide some support for this explanation in that the correlation between committee representation in the Senate and the concentration of wetlands is highly positive,[24] and when the former variable is excluded from the analysis, the concentration of wetlands has a significant, negative effect. Notably, excluding either of the factors does not change the key results of the analysis.

CONCLUSION

In an effort to improve understanding of the importance of Congress in controlling bureaucratic behavior, I have compared judicial and congressional influence over a set of 18,331 decisions by the Army Corps of Engineers regarding whether to issue a permit for the development of wetlands. To assess the impact of the judiciary, I examined the effects of judicial ideology and rulings across the different levels of the federal court system. I estimated the impact of Congress by analyzing how the bureaucratic decisions were influenced by the composition of membership on the House and Senate oversight committees as well as by the ideological inclination of the chambers' floors. The analysis found that Congress has a statistically greater influence over bureaucratic behavior than does the judiciary.

In one sense, the findings support research that Moe (1987) and others have dubbed the literature on "congressional dominance," which maintains Congress is the primary political overseer of the bureaucracy (e.g., McCubbins and Schwartz 1984; Weingast and Moran 1983). The cumulative effect of the congressional factors is greater than that of the judicial ones, as well as greater than the individual effects of most other factors, including presidential administration, the local economy, and the ideology of the state. Yet to the extent that the literature on congressional dominance is meant to suggest that Congress literally dominates bureaucratic behavior, my results support the critics of this work (e.g., Moe 1987). Taken together, the various noncongressional factors have a greater influence than Congress does. Moreover, even though the impact of the judiciary is statistically less than that of Congress, the effects are of a similar magnitude substantively.

What does this analysis suggest about the macropolitics of Congress? Most obviously, the results show that Congress affects government outputs—in the form of bureaucratic behavior—even when not explicitly directing these outputs. The decisions by the Army Corps were not guided by detailed instructions in bills, or even strict administrative guidelines. Yet, as Congress became more liberal, the bureaucracy became more active in regulating economic activity.

Additionally, the chapter addresses a theme that is emphasized in the introduction to this volume and the conclusion by David Brady: namely, that understanding the macropolitics of Congress requires studying how the interaction among the different parts of the U.S. government affects macropolitical outputs. The findings show that congressional influence over such outputs must be considered within the context of other political actors. The results on the judiciary, in particular, are noteworthy. They highlight that control of the bureaucracy is a phenomenon that encompasses all three branches of American government. More broadly, the chapter indicates that understanding the macropolitics of Congress requires careful analysis of the interaction between Congress and the courts.

NOTES

I thank Chuck Cameron, John de Figueiredo, John Scholz, and Andy Whitford for valuable suggestions on previous drafts and Stephanie Ng for excellent research assistance. Seminar participants at Columbia, Northwestern, NYU, Princeton, Rice, Stanford, the 2001 "Scientific Study of the Bureaucracy" conference, and "The Macropolitics of Congress" conference provided helpful comments on related work. The research was funded in part by a Science to Achieve Results Fellowship from the Environmental Protection Agency. All remaining errors are naturally my own.

1. See also McCubbins and Schwartz 1984 and Weingast and Moran 1983.

2. Moe (1985), Wood and Anderson (1993), Wood and Waterman (1993), and Hunter and Waterman (1996) all examine the effects of judicial rulings on bureaucratic behavior. As a whole, these studies provide mixed evidence as to whether Congress or the rulings have greater influence.

3. 40 CFR (*Code of Federal Regulations*) Part 230.3(t). Much of this section is taken from Canes-Wrone 2003, which provides a more detailed description of the regulatory process for wetlands permits.

4. The following description refers to applications for individual permits, the source of my data. Individual permits must be obtained unless a general class of permit (e.g., nationwide) has been issued for a particular type of project.

5. Interview with district engineer (name withheld upon request), Jacksonville District of the Army Corps of Engineers, January 9, 2001.

6. Official EPA website on the veto authority, http://www.epa.gov/owow/wetlands/facts/fact14.html.

7. See 28 USC (United States Code) §§1391(b), 1391(e) and 1402, and 33 USC §406 and 1319(b). Also verified by a lawyer for the Sierra Club (telephone interview, January 12, 2001).

8. Clean Water Act §505; 33 USC part 1365.

9. See H.R. 961, which was never taken up on the floor of the Senate.

10. The boundaries of the district courts and Army Corps districts differ. President Herbert Hoover, who was trained as an engineer, designed Corps boundaries that depend in part on watersheds.

11. These states include Massachusetts, Michigan, and, since 1993, New Jersey.

12. Several other committees may be referred legislation concerning wetlands. For example, the House Resources Committee, which is the committee that Canes-Wrone 2003 examines, and the House Committee on Small Business deal with policy issues that pertain to wetlands regulations. Here I focus on the primary committees that oversee the Army Corps of Engineers.

13. Litigants can petition an appellate court for an en banc hearing in which the entire court reviews the case. None of the cases in my data were decided in this manner, and collinearity prevents including a variable that represents the possibility of an en banc hearing along with the other factors.

14. Studies of the appellate courts suggest alternative estimates of judicial preferences, including ones that classify judges by an ideological rating of the appointing president, by the region of appointment, and by the ideological composition of the appointing Senate (e.g., de Figueiredo 2001; Humphries and Songer 1999; Tate and Handberg 1991). I have analyzed the model with such alternative estimates and in each case found substantively similar results.

15. I constructed this variable through content analysis of all lawsuits concerning Corps' decisions over wetlands permits in the Lexis-Nexis database of federal litigation.

16. In the exceptions, of which there are three, a neighbor of the property challenged the permit.

17. All justices hear any case granted certiorari.

18. The appointees include Lieutenant General Elvin R. Heiberg III and Administrator Lee M. Thomas under Reagan, Lieutenant General Henry J. Hatch and William K. Reilly under Bush, and Lieutenant General Arthur E. Williams and Carol M. Browner under Clinton.

19. These data are from ICPSR Study No. 1208.

20. The NRI is conducted using sampling techniques that do not allow for analysis at the county level.

21. Excluding the year indicators changes only the results regarding the factors that lack cross-sectional variation. Thus the effects of committee representation and

the ideology of the lower courts are not in any way affected by excluding the year indicators. In addition, excluding them would not alter the overall conclusions of the analysis.

22. My data are only as precise in time as the year of the bureaucratic decision, so I cannot differentiate observations by whether they are pre- or postelection.

23. Although the impact of the Supreme Court is not significant in this specification, it is in alternative models that measure congressional liberalism with the ideology scores of the League of Conservation Voters.

24. The correlation between the concentration of wetlands and committee representation in the Senate equals .77.

REFERENCES

Arnold, R. Douglas. 1979. *Congress and the Bureaucracy: A Theory of Influence.* New Haven: Yale University Press.

Berry, William D., Evan J. Ringquist, Richard C. Fording, and Russell L. Hanson. 1998. "Measuring Citizen and Government Ideology in the American States, 1960–93." *American Journal of Political Science* 42:327–48.

Calvert, Randall L., Mark J. Moran, and Barry R. Weingast. 1987. "Congressional Influence over Policy Making: The Case of the FTC." In *Congress: Structure and Policy,* ed. Mathew D. McCubbins and Terry Sullivan. Cambridge: Cambridge University Press.

Canes-Wrone, Brandice. 2003. "Bureaucratic Decisions and the Composition of the Lower Courts." *American Journal of Political Science* 47:205–14.

Carp, Robert A., and Ronald Stidham. 1985. *The Federal Courts.* Washington, D.C.: Congressional Quarterly Press.

de Figueiredo, John M. 2001. "Litigating Regulation: Corporate Strategy in Telecommunications." MIT. Typescript.

Goldman, Sheldon. 1997. *Picking Federal Judges: Lower Court Selection from Roosevelt through Reagan.* New Haven: Yale University Press.

Grossman, Gene M., and Alan B. Krueger. 1995. "Economic Growth and the Environment." *Quarterly Journal of Economics* 110:353–77.

Howard, Robert M. 2001. "Wealth, Power, and the IRS: Changing IRS Audit Policy through Litigation." *Social Science Quarterly* 82:268–80.

Humphries, Martha Anne, and Donald R. Songer. 1999. "Law and Politics in Judicial Oversight of Federal Administrative Agencies." *Journal of Politics* 61:207–20.

Hunter, Susan, and Richard W. Waterman. 1996. *Enforcing the Law: The Case of the Clean Water Acts.* Armonk, N.Y.: M. E. Sharpe.

Kagan, Robert A. 1995. "Adversarial Legalism and American Government." In *The New Politics of Public Policy,* ed. Marc K. Landy and Martin A. Levin. Baltimore: Johns Hopkins University Press.

Kovacic, William E. 1991. "The Reagan Judiciary and Environmental Policy: The Impact of Appointments to the Federal Courts of Appeals." *Boston College Environmental Affairs Law Review* 18:669–713.

Krause, George A. 1996. "The Institutional Dynamics of Policy Administration: Bureaucratic Influence over Securities Regulation." *American Journal of Political Science* 40:1083–1121.

Martin, Andrew D., and Kevin M. Quinn. 2002. "Dynamic Ideal Point Estimation via Markov Chain Monte Carlo for the U.S. Supreme Court, 1953–1999." *Political Analysis* 10:134–53.

McCubbins, Mathew D., and Thomas Schwartz. 1984. "Congressional Oversight Overlooked: Police Patrols versus Fire Alarms." *American Journal of Political Science* 28:165–79.

Meier, Kenneth J. 1979. *Politics and the Bureaucracy: Policymaking in the 4th Branch of Government.* North Scituate, Mass.: Duxbury Press.

———. 1985. *Regulation, Politics, Bureaucracy, and Economics.* New York: St. Martin's Press.

Melnick, R. Shep. 1983. *Regulation and the Courts: The Case of the Clean Air Act.* Washington, D.C.: Brookings Institution Press.

Moe, Terry M. 1985. "Control and Feedback in Economic Regulation: The Case of the NLRB." *American Political Science Review* 79:1094–1116.

———. 1987. "An Assessment of the Positive Theory of 'Congressional Dominance.'" *Legislative Studies Quarterly* 12:475–520.

Ringquist, Evan J. 1995. "Political Control and Policy Impact in EPA's Office of Water Quality." *American Journal of Political Science* 39:336–63.

Ringquist, Evan J., and Craig E. Emmert. 1999. "Judicial Policymaking in Published and Unpublished Decisions: The Case of Environmental Civil Litigation." *Political Research Quarterly* 52:7–37.

Rowland, C. K., and Robert A. Carp. 1996. *Politics and Judgment in Federal District Courts.* Lawrence: University of Kansas Press.

Scholz, John T., Jim Twombly, and Barbara Headrick. 1991. "Street-Level Political Controls over Federal Bureaucracy." *American Political Science Review* 85: 829–50.

Scholz, John T., and B. Dan Wood. 1998. "Controlling the IRS: Principals, Principles, and Public Administration." *American Journal of Political Science* 42:141–62.

Selznick, Philip. 1949. *TVA and the Grass Roots.* Stanford: Stanford University Press.

Tate, C. Neal, and Roger Handberg. 1991. "Time Binding and Theory Building in Personal Attribute Models of Supreme Court Voting Behavior, 1916–88." *American Journal of Political Science* 35:460–80.

Tiller, Emerson H., and Pablo T. Spiller. 1999. "Strategic Instruments: Legal Structure and Political Games in Administrative Law." *Journal of Law, Economics, and Organization* 15:349–77.

Weingast, Barry R., and Mark J. Moran. 1983. "Bureaucratic Discretion or Congressional Control? Regulatory Policymaking by the Federal Trade Commission." *Journal of Political Economy* 91:765–800.

Wood, B. Dan, and James E. Anderson. 1993. "The Politics of U.S. Antitrust Regulation." *American Journal of Political Science* 37:1–39.

Wood, B. Dan, and Richard W. Waterman. 1993. "The Dynamics of Political-Bureaucratic Adaptation." *American Journal of Political Science* 37:497–528.

9

Legislative Bargaining and the Macroeconomy

E. Scott Adler and David Leblang

With only hours to spare before the U.S. government would default in June 2002, the House of Representatives passed legislation identical to the Senate's proposal to raise the national debt by $450 billion. The *New York Times* reported that the stock market had become skittish at the prospect of an executive-legislative standoff over the debt limit, potentially leading to a partial government shutdown as occurred in the winter of 1994–95 (Stevenson 2002). This eleventh-hour agreement between Congress and President Bush is just one of many instances where bargaining between Capitol Hill and the White House has important ramifications for the economy. In the first two years of the Bush administration, legislation such as the president's promised tax cut, fast-track authority on trade negotiations, and reform of corporate responsibility laws were a few more examples of the important role Congress plays in the nation's economic well-being. These, as well as numerous other statutes, and even some policy proposals that were not enacted into law, had important economic implications and required a delicate process of give-and-take between the executive and legislative branches before laws could be passed and policy enacted.

No doubt the casual observer would say that there is a close link between politics and economic performance in the United States. Yet if we survey the academic literature on the political factors that affect the U.S. economy, we would be hard pressed to find a sophisticated empirical study that takes political institutions as seriously as it takes economic modeling. It is not entirely clear why this is the case, but presumably scholars exploring questions of economic performance simply do not believe that policymakers, beyond the president, play a meaningful role in shaping the expectations of economic actors.

In this chapter we set out to not only highlight the importance of politics as a key determinant of economic performance, but also to challenge some of the existing work that does utilize political variables to model economic cycles. We argue that the dominant work in this field focuses solely on characteristics associated with the U.S. president and minimizes—or, more likely, ignores—the necessity of presidential-congressional bargaining. In the process of developing our argument, we also hope to illuminate a corner of the emerging field of research on the macropolitics of Congress that is significantly undertilled—the importance of executive-legislative interaction in managing the economy.

Exploring the relationship between political institutions and macroeconomic performance is no small task. Our goal, however, is more modest. We do not develop the behavioral microfoundations linking divided government, partisan politics, or governmental bargaining to economic outcomes. Formal models investigating these linkages have been developed—admirably we might add—by numerous scholars, notably Alberto Alesina and his coauthors (Alesina 1987; Alesina and Rosenthal 1995; Alesina, Roubini, and Cohen 1997). There is, to our knowledge, however, little work that empirically tests hypotheses relating divided government or governmental bargaining to trends in the economy; extant empirical papers focus solely on the partisanship of the president (see Herron 2002, for a notable exception). As such, our contribution is to examine how measures of divided government and governmental bargaining perform within the framework of political business cycle models. Our results, therefore, can be considered an initial attempt to identify the "stylized facts" pertaining to U.S. political institutions and the macroeconomy. In the conclusion we identify ways that these "facts" can lead to fruitful theory development.

We organize our arguments and evidence as follows. First we provide a brief review of the literature on political business cycles, highlighting partisan and divided government models and their implications for economic performance. The second section develops our indicators of legislative and institutional behavior. These variables are then used in the third section to help explain the variance in economic performance as measured by economic growth, unemployment, inflation, and interest rates using quarterly data from 1949 to 1999. The Final Section concludes and offers suggestions for future research.

POLITICS, POLICY OUTPUTS, AND THE MACROECONOMY

Political Business Cycles

Despite the growing number of achievements in the study of the macropolitics of Congress (many of which are highlighted in this volume), there have been surprisingly few advances in our understanding of how congressional organization and interbranch relations affect economic policy. This is particularly startling since the field of economics has such a well-developed literature on macroeconomic trends. Yet there has been little synergy in the two research traditions of economic fluctuations and the macropolitics of executive-legislative interaction.

Economic research into the relationship between "politics" and markets has a relatively long history (e.g., Block 1977; Lindblom 1977). Within this body of scholarship a significant vein examines the extent to which a policymaker's behavior—and thus policy—changes during the period surrounding elections. One strand of this literature, popularized by Nordhaus (1975), argues that policymakers behave opportunistically; that is, during the run-up to an election incumbents manipulate economic policy to create an economic boom and increase their likelihood of reelection (e.g., Nordhaus 1975; Tufte 1978; Hibbs 1987; Alesina and Roubini 1992).

A second strand of this literature, originally proffered by Hibbs (1977), examines partisan electoral cycles that arise *after* elections. The election of a liberal or an unemployment-adverse policymaker gives rise to expansionary policies resulting in an increase in economic growth, a decrease in unemployment, and a rise in inflation. Alesina's (1987) rational expectations take on this model produces predictions along the lines suggested by Hibbs but with a twist. The implication of rational expectations means economic expansions only occur as a result of policy (or political) surprises; thus, the real effects of expansions are only temporary.

Work by Alesina, Roubini, and Cohen (1997) represents the most complete test of partisan, rational, and opportunistic political business cycle models in the United States. The findings in this work generally support the proposition that there are rational partisan effects on the economy as a whole. Specifically, they find significant relationships between the party of the president and aggregate growth and unemployment and, to a lesser degree, inflation and interest rates. They find less support for the hypothesis that partisanship influences fiscal policy and no support for opportunistic (Nordhausian) political business cycle models.

Macropolitics and the Economy

Research on the macropolitics of Congress and interbranch relations is not as well developed as the literature on economic fluctuations, but its findings are still extremely important in guiding our analysis of how politics affects economic policy and economic outcomes. As can be seen in this volume, a good portion of the research on the policy consequences of interbranch bargaining focuses on divided government, gridlock, and their meaning for policymaking and policy production. Most often, these studies have focused on broad concepts of policy productivity.

In only a few instances have scholars of divided government touched on the subject of economic policy. For instance, Cox and McCubbins (1991) examine how different partisan configurations of government (unified Republican control, unified Democratic control, Republican president–Democratic Congress, etc.) result in various shifts in tax policy and the level of federal tax receipts. Moreover, they emphasize the importance of particular kinds of partisan control of the different branches of government as a means of effectively vetoing or forcing compromise in certain fiscal policy changes.

Herron's (2002) study of divided government, preference conflict, and interest rates is another good example of how scholars of American politics use theories of macropolitics to examine governmental effects for economic policy. Herron's focus, however, is on interest rates as an indicator of government gridlock. He finds that periods of divided government and periods where there is widespread conflict in preferences across legislative chambers and the presidency (often these two can overlap) are associated with low interest rates and thus, he deduces, policy gridlock.

Our concern with the economic effects of different configurations of government, while similar in some ways to Herron, does not profess to impart any particular political interpretation to fluctuations in economic indicators. Rather, our objective is to better understand macroeconomic fluctuations (interest rates, unemployment, growth, and inflation) by focusing on interbranch legislative bargaining in the United States. We assert that existing research on the economic impact of various governmental arrangements is greatly underspecified from a political perspective; this assertion guides our exploration to follow.

DEVELOPING MEASURES LINKING POLITICAL INSTITUTIONS TO MACROECONOMIC PERFORMANCE

Perhaps the most fundamental problem in testing the linkage between politics and economics is developing meaningful measures of governmental change that are useful in examining their effect on economic outcomes. How does one characterize the configuration of numerous governmental actors (the president, members of Congress, bureaucratic agencies, etc.) in a way that is logical and imparts meaning to our analysis of the relationship between politics and economics? In some respects this is one of the main obstacles confronted by all the work in the field of macropolitics—devising ways to understand how complex institutions like Congress and the president change over time and how those changes cause alterations in government output. As noted above, we are interested in not only understanding the effect of "government" on the economy, but gleaning whether or not it is specifically interbranch bargaining that has an impact on economic tides. Thus, we develop measures of divided government and governmental bargaining, described below, and use them in models of macroeconomic performance. We begin with very simple notions of U.S. political institutions and economic decision-making and gradually increases in complexity.

Before proceeding, however, we first consider the measures of economic performance and the expected behavior of relevant economic actors. Our notion of macroeconomic performance follows that used in most of the political business cycle literature and most notably in work by Alesina, Roubini, and Cohen (1997). Specifically we look at fluctuations in two sets of macroeconomic indicators: (1) economic growth and unemployment, and (2) interest and inflation rates.

Traditionally, studies of political business cycles focused on real effects in the macroeconomy—growth and unemployment—because it was felt that voters respond to fluctuation in these variables at election time. When the economy is good—high growth and low unemployment—voters favor incumbents and thus they are reelected. On the other hand, if economic growth is sluggish and unemployment rises, then politicians stand a greater chance of losing their elected offices. Heeding the admonition, "It's the economy, stupid," political business cycle models predict that policymakers will use all instruments at their disposal to increase growth and employment in the run-up to an election. Our use of these two dependent variables reflects this tradition.

In addition to providing a robustness check—growth and unemployment should move together, although in opposite directions—fluctuations in these variables reflect changes in a variety of macroeconomic policies. Economic actors—investors, unions, corporations, consumers, and so on—in anticipation of and in reaction to stimulative government policy engage in increased economic activity: contracts are signed, investments are made, workers are employed, technology is developed, and products are bought and sold. The consequence is that the economy grows and unemployment is reduced. However, when economic actors are uncertain about the future course of government policy or policy is expected to have contractionary effects, investment and consumption decisions are often put on hold; consequently labor contracts are not signed or extended, investments are put on hold, and so forth, and the economy as a whole slows.

Recently—with the rational expectation revolution—scholars studying political business cycles have begun to look for political effects on nominal variables. Because prices generally reflect the expectations of buyers and sellers, a more direct measure of expected policy change can be gleaned by examining movements in (nominal) interest rates and consumer prices. One need only recall the late 1970s to know that these two variables fluctuate together and move in the same direction. Interest rates—specifically the interest rate on 10-year treasury bills at auction—reflect expectations by buyers (whether they are institutional or individual investors) in the long-term performance of the economy. Holding constant the federal funds rate (as set by the Federal Reserve), fluctuations in interest and inflation rates generally reflect confidence (or lack thereof) in the economy as a whole. Market confidence, in turn, is a function of macroeconomic fundamentals and political expectations.

President as Economic Policymaker

We begin our examination of the effect of governmental influence on economic outcomes by exploring what most scholars have traditionally considered to be the key political actor in economic policymaking—the president. The view that the president is supreme in economic and fiscal policy is one that is widely held in both the political science and the economics literature. More often than not, research on economic policy refers to the policies of "president X," usually with only passing reference to the role of Congress in the development of that policy. As one scholar of the presidency bluntly put it, "the performance of the economy is presidential business" (Pious 1979, 293).

The first theory of executive dominance in economic policymaking is a fairly straightforward model of expectations regarding presidential influence. Hibbs (1977, 1987) constructed a retrospective expectations model of partisan control of the executive that posits Democrats are more concerned with GNP growth and unemployment than inflation, while Republicans maintain opposite priorities. Thus, presidential administrations will pursue economic and fiscal policies in accordance with the priorities of their party, and this should result in identifiable differences in the policies pursued between the two parties' control of the White House.

Tests of this theory can be easily captured through a dichotomous variable indicating the party of the president. In order to maximize comparability between our study and that of Alesina, Roubini, and Cohen (1997), we code this dichotomous variable positive 1 for Republican presidents and negative 1 for Democratic presidents. Descriptive statistics for these variables, as well as all others included in our analysis, are offered in table 9.1.

To test rational expectations versions of this partisan hypothesis—that is, to see if there is a structural break in the effect of partisanship on the economy—Alesina, Roubini, and Cohen (1997) modify their presidency variable to reflect the president's party for only the first four, six and eight quarters of a presidential term. We follow their lead and create a variable which is equal to the previous dichotomous variable for the first six quarters of a presidential term and zero for the remaining quarters.[1]

Our expectation, following that of the traditional scholarship on political business cycles, is that growth, employment, inflation, and interest rates will all increase under Democratic presidents and decrease under Republican presidents.

Unified and Divided Government

As we have argued, the almost exclusive focus on the president as the lone economic policy actor has neglected the effect of interbranch relations and

TABLE 9.1 Measures of Governmental Configurations for Purposes of Economic Policy Making

Variables	Measurement	Minimum	Maximum	Mean
President as policymaker				
President's Party	1 = Republican, −1 = Democrat	−1	1	0.037
President's Party (six quarters)	Same as above for first six quarters of term, 0 = otherwise	−1	1	0.028
Unified/divided government				
Divided Government I	0 = President's party same as both chambers in Congress, 1 = President's party different from *both* chambers in Congress	0	1	0.56
Divided Government II	0 = President's party same as both chambers in Congress, 1 = President's party different from *either* chamber in Congress	0	1	0.61
Divided Government (partisan varieties)				
Unified Democrat	1 = unified Democratic government, 0 = otherwise	0	1	0.36
Divided Government— Democratic President	1 = divided government with Democratic president, 0 = otherwise	0	1	0.13
Divided Government— Republican President	1 = Divided government with Republican president, 0 = otherwise	0	1	0.38

TABLE 9.1 (*continued*)

Variables	Measurement	Minimum	Maximum	Mean
Institutional conflict				
Gridlock Expansion/ Contraction	Krehbiel's measure using partisan change in seats in Congress and presidential turnover	−9.91	13.29	1.45
Size of Gridlock Interval	Using NOMINATE scale, the furthest distance between critical pivot actors	0.26	0.53	0.35
Vetoes	Cumulative vetoes within a congressional term (no pocket vetoes or private bills)	0	32.0	4.35
Institutional compromise				
Partisan compromise	Calculating the "midpoint" between the House and Senate using size of partisan majorities, then calculating the midpoint of that with president's party	−75.33	83.95	15.20
Ideological Compromise	Calculating the "midpoint" between the House and Senate using ideology scores, then calculating the midpoint of that with president's ideology	−0.30	0.23	0.001

bargaining as important factors in economic policy and outcomes. Governmental economic policy does not simply consist of unilateral executive action but includes statutory decisions such as ratification of trade agreements, new legislation to alleviate unemployment, changes in the tax code, consent on executive appointments, or, potentially, the lack of action on such matters. In this respect we redefine the term *government* as the *two* entities specified in the Constitution to be partners in the policymaking process—the executive *and* legislative branches.

At its most basic level, modern American government is generally characterized by conflict between the two major political parties. Thus, we utilize two different specifications of the relationship between the branches of government that underscores this partisan conflict. The first might be characterized as a classic divided government view of policymaking and economic control. The assertion is that there are fundamental differences in how government performs under unified versus divided government. A popular view is that divided government leads to policy gridlock—less legislation produced because of an inability of the Congress and the White House to agree on legislative changes, which stems from fundamental policy differences between the political parties. This conventional wisdom, however, is a matter of debate in the political science literature (Mayhew 1991; Kelly 1993; Fiorina 1996; Edwards, Barrett, and Peake 1997; Binder 1999; Howell et al. 2000).

The classic divided government variable has two variations: The first measures instances of divided government such that the president must be of a different party than *both* chambers of Congress. The second characterization of divided government includes those periods when one of the two chambers is simultaneously controlled by the party of the president.

A degree of partisan subtlety can be added to this blunt accounting of the consequences of divided government by simply distinguishing not only between periods that are unified and divided, but between those when unified or divided governments are of a particular partisan variety. As was noted above, the policy expectations of economic actors may vary when government (meaning the president) is Republican- versus Democratic-controlled. The same may be the case for instances where divided (or perhaps even unified) government is constituted by a presidency of one party versus the other. For instance, divided government with a Republican in the Oval Office may lead to certain expectations about economic controls and influence that are different from those where a Democrat presides over a divided government.[2] We therefore construct a model using three variables to account for the effects of economic influence by unified Democratic control of government, Democratic-led divided government, and Republican-led divided government, with Republican-controlled unified government serving as the baseline for comparison.

If the government is unified under Democratic (Republican) control, then our expectations follow those of classic rational partisan theory: growth and employment will be higher (lower) under unified Democratic (Republican) government. We also anticipate that interest rates and inflation will be higher under unified government, regardless of partisan stripe, than they will be when the government is divided. The logic is as follows: if divided governments produce less new policy, then they will also engage in less spending, will implement fewer tax hikes, and will be less likely to increase the federal deficit. Anticipating this, markets will not demand a premium in order to lend the government money in the form of treasury bills; hence interest rates (and inflation rates) will remain lower.

Institutional Conflict and Gridlock

In contrast to the previously described measures of divided government and gridlock, some authors have argued that the order of governmental business and institutional bargaining can serve as an indicator as to the *degree* of gridlock one is likely to see in policymaking. Here, the reliance is less on an a priori accounting of partisan control of each branch (or chamber) and more on what the preferences or actions of legislators might indicate about the potential for making profound legislative changes. It is not simple a matter of gridlock or no gridlock, but rather what markets expect about the capacity for policymakers to come to legislative agreements.

Pivotal Politics

The first of these theories relies on legislator ideal points as predictors of the potential for policy activity or inactivity. Similar to several efforts that employ ideology scores along with stylized models of the legislative process to understand and predict the capacity and direction for government output (including a number in this volume), we rely on Krehbiel's theory of pivotal politics (1987, 1996, 1998; see also Brady and Volden 1998). The pivotal politics model lends itself well to consideration of government capacity to influence economic policy. Like other theories of interbranch bargaining, this model describes the capability of Congress and the president to come to agreement on any number of policy matters. Constitutional mandates, rules of congressional deliberation, and the preferences of key political actors constrain the possibilities for public policy changes, according to Krehbiel. Specifically, he sees key veto and filibuster actors as the boundaries within which legislative change is very unlikely.

How does this work? Consider a situation in which a conservative Republican president is serving with a more liberal House and Senate (as measured by the preferences of the median legislator). It is likely that extant policies that are located around the median for the two legislative chambers will not be subject to change. The size of the "gridlock interval" on an ideological scale would be determined by the most conservative veto pivot of either chamber (two-thirds voter) and whichever actor of either the House median or Senate filibuster pivot (the three-fifths voter) is furthest away from the president. For instance, a status quo policy located precisely at the conservative veto pivot of the House is one that at least two-thirds of the chamber would not be satisfied with changing even further in the conservative direction—that is, toward the position of the president. The larger the distance between the critical pivot actors, the more status quo policies fall within the gridlock interval and the fewer policy changes occur.[3]

Gridlock expansion or contraction. To test the theory of government gridlock, we employ two specifications of Krehbiel's theory. The first is derived from a rough reading of expansion and contraction in the gridlock interval based on the status of the president and the swing in the proportion of seats controlled by the majority party in each chamber. First, Krehbiel computes the average in the proportion of change in seats after an election between the two chambers, where Democratic gains are positive and Republican gains are negative. This will determine the size of change in the gridlock interval.

Then, to determine if this swing results in an *expansion* or *contraction* of the gridlock interval, Krehbiel examines its relationship to the presidency. If the prior election results in a president maintaining his office (either during a midterm election or in a successful bid after the first term) and there is a loss of seats for the president's party, that results in an expansion of the gridlock interval. Of course, the opposite would be true in a gain of seats for the president's party; this would lead to a contraction of the interval. If the presidency changes parties, this is usually accompanied by a gain in seats for his party, and this is also considered a contraction. Finally, there were two specific instances in which the presidency changed parties, but concurrently there was a net loss of seats for his party (Kennedy in 1960 and Clinton in 1992). Krehbiel claims that the effect on the gridlock interval is unclear and thus leaves these two as indeterminate or a change of zero.[4]

The size of the gridlock interval. Alternatively, Herron (2002) applies Krehbiel's theory to the spatial locations of key actors on an ideological dimension (again, using NOMINATE scores), and determines the actual size of the gridlock interval in each congressional term. That is, using the ideology scores, he calculates the exact location of the chief filibuster and veto pivots and reports the distance in between as the size of the gridlock interval. Here, change is less a concern than the actual size of the interval at any given moment and its effect on the ability of government to alter policy.[5]

Following our earlier discussion we expect that governments with larger gridlock intervals will experience lower rates of both inflation and interest rates. The relationship between gridlock and economic growth and unemployment, however, is less clear. If gridlocked governments produce less legislation, then it is likely that growth- (or employment-) enhancing measures will not be enacted and gridlock will have a negative influence on these two variables. However, since gridlocked governments engage in less deficit financing, and markets know this, there is no need to delay investment decisions. As a result, we are relatively agnostic as to the relationship between gridlock and growth and employment.

Vetoes

Finally, as one further specification of the institutional gridlock perspective, we examine a more dynamic measure of interbranch hostility—vetoes. Rather than using *prospective* views of the probable capacity for policy change, one that does not alter during a congressional term, we look for actual indications of legislative-executive enmity through the use of the legislative veto. There are different ways to interpret the veto, not the least of which is a belief that the process of vetoes, amended legislation, and overrides is part of the practice of bargaining between Congress and the president (McCarty and Poole 1995; Cameron 2000). The interpretation employed here, however, assumes that fully informed congressional actors know *ex ante* whether or not a passed bill is something that is likely to be opposed at the presidential signature stage. Thus, when the legislature chooses not to work out a legislative-executive compromise beforehand and objectionable policy proposals are sent to the White House to receive vetoes, this is a public game of political chicken. By sending the bill back to the legislature the president is challenging Congress to either alter the proposal to something that is more acceptable or be forced to mobilize a two-thirds majority for override votes in both houses. Either way, a veto is a fairly clear signal of disagreement and turmoil in changing public policy.

Our belief is that the animosity between the president and Congress can build over time. As enmity increases, it fosters a belief that the two branches will not be legislatively productive. Legislative gridlock should affect all policy areas, including the economy. This measure of gridlock will have an effect on the economy similar to the previous two. We employ a quarterly measure of vetoes that is cumulative within a congressional term. That is, for every quarter we count the number of vetoes that occurred and add them to all the previous vetoes in that congressional term.[6] The slate is then wiped clean at the start of each new administration or congressional term.

Institutional Compromise

Expectations about the effects on the economy of different configurations of government may have a further refinement than the broad concepts of partisan preferences or even more subtle notions of gridlock. As has already been described, government output is not merely a product of Democratic and Republican presidential policy objectives, but also their ability to obtain, or more often compromise, those goals given the strengths and weaknesses of the political actors and the process of legislative bargaining. Outside economic actors, knowing that policy output is usually a result of negotiation between the legislative and executive branches, will generate expectations as to the likely location of policy outputs on an ideological continuum. The ideological location of policy is conditioned on the preference positions or partisan strengths of actors in the different branches. Hence, this approach does not assume that partisan or ideological divisions between the branches necessarily results in absolute or even partial gridlock. That is, observers are not presumed to think that government will be incapable of passing certain kinds of legislation because of partisan or ideological rifts between Congress and the president, but rather those divisions are seen as indicators of the likely *shift* in the ideological locations of new policies (how liberal or conservative) that are inevitably going to be produced.

The model is derived from Alesina and Rosenthal's "institutional balancing" discussion of policymaking (1995, 43–49). Legislative activity is seen as a two-stage process established by provisions in the Constitution (Article I, Section 7). In the first stage, policy proposals must be agreed upon by the two chambers in the legislature, and in the second stage that compromise must be reconciled with the position of the president. Given the structural demands for compromise, the simplest expectation of outsiders is a "split-the-difference" outcome. For instance, the likely product of bargaining between two chambers with differing preferences but equal powers is some midpoint position. This is often the case when House and Senate negotiators (frequently in the context of conference committees) are faced with the responsibility of merging the policy language of the two chambers' legislative proposals (Shepsle and Weingast 1987; Longley and Oleszek 1989).

Institutional Compromise: A Partisan Approach

We operationalize this variable in two different ways. The first examines the strength or size of majority parties in the two legislative chambers and the partisan control of the presidency. We start with a presumption of complete command of the executive branch by the party of president, and this is interacted with the percentage of each chamber controlled by its majority party. The assumptions underlying this partisan-proportions approach are (1) that members of the same party have similar economic and policy goals at a given moment,[7] and (2) that the size of the majority is meaningful for leverage with other actors in negotiating a split-the-difference midpoint. One can imagine several reasons why "size matters"; perhaps the most straightforward is that a larger majority in the chamber provides a wider cushion for defections.[8]

This measure is constructed by calculating the proportion of each chamber that is controlled by the majority party, and making that coefficient negative if it is Democratic and positive if it is Republican. In the first stage of this split-the-difference measure we find the midpoint (or average) of the House and Senate proportions. For the second stage we calculate the midpoint between the first-stage compromise and the president's position, where the president is scored either −1 if a Democrat or 1 if Republican. The trends in this variable are meant to track the expectation of the direction of policy outputs by outside observers. The trends should be extreme in one direction or the other under unified partisan control with large majorities in both chambers, slightly less extreme if those majorities are slimmer, even more moderate if the opposite party controls one chamber of legislature, and very close to the policy midpoint under completely divided government with large majorities in both chambers.

To a certain extent, this measure of institutional compromise derived from the size of partisan majorities is a more nuanced view of unified and divided government. Periods of unified government, such as the first two years of the Clinton administration, will have relatively extreme expectations about policy outcomes, while periods of divided government will have expected policies that tend toward the middle.

This variable is shown by the solid line in figure 9.1 where the expectation of liberal policies is on the negative side and conservative policies are on the positive side (using the left-side axis). This measure exhibits some fairly severe shifts when there are alterations in the partisan control of the different branches of government. The measure projects its most liberal expectations about policy during the periods of unified Democratic control—part of the Truman administration, the Kennedy and Johnson administrations, the Carter administration, and the first two years of the Clinton administration. Its most conservative years were the one term of unified Republican government during the first two years of the Eisenhower administration. Other than that we see many years of more moderate expected policy during divided government with various Republican presidents (Eisenhower, Nixon, Ford, Reagan, and Bush) and the remaining years of the Clinton presidency. The first six years of the Reagan presidency are slightly more conservative given Republican control of the Senate.

As becomes obvious from the construction of this institutional compromise measure, the influence of the three key actors (the House, Senate, and president) is not equal. In fact, because the order of moves, the president is afforded power that is equivalent to that of both legislative chambers combined. In light of the common perception that the president does have disproportionate influence over economic policy, this weighting of the components does not seem unreasonable. An alternative to this combination of variables would be to include each individually as well as interacted with each other to reveal their appropriate weights in influencing the economy. The problem with doing this is that we would lose their collective effect on expectations regarding government and economic policy.[9]

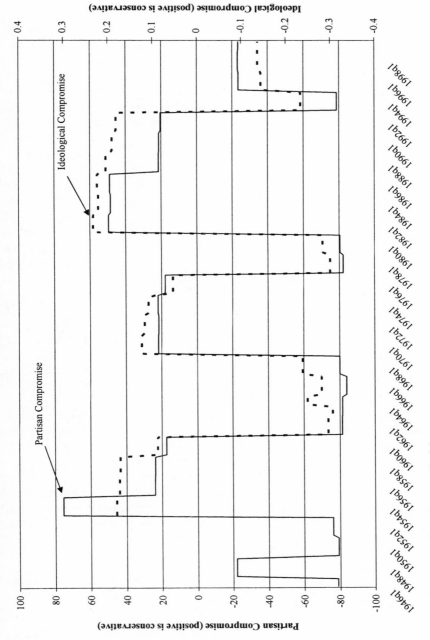

Figure 9.1: Institutional Compromise Measures

Institutional Compromise: An Ideological Approach

An alternative view of institutional compromise relies on policy preferences rather than partisanship. Following the perspective that party affiliation of legislators is less important than their individual ideologies and political proclivities (Krehbiel 1998), we create a similar measure of split-the-difference compromises using Poole and Rosenthal's common space NOMINATE scores. We, again, determine the policy position of each chamber's median in the same ideological space at different periods of time (Poole and Rosenthal 1997), as well as the ideological position of the president (McCarty and Poole 1995). We then employ these median positions to determine the expected equilibrium of interbranch policy compromises in a policy space. Thus, the first-stage compromise is the ideological midpoint between the House and Senate, and the expected second-stage bargain is the midpoint between the interchamber compromise and the president's ideal point.

The dashed line in figure 9.1 follows the trend of the institutional compromise variable as measured using ideology scores. As is clear in the figure, the institutional compromise variables measured either by partisan strength or by ideological position look very similar. Not unexpectedly, there is a very high correlation between these two variables (.97). The correspondence is largely driven by the disproportionate influence given to the president's position in both measures and, to a certain extent, the strong linkage between partisan strength of the two parties and the overall ideological composition of the chambers. There are some differences in the two measures. For instance, the loss of Senate control by the Republicans in 1987 has a much bigger effect on the partisan measure than it does on the ideological measure of expected policy position.

These measures of institutional compromise encapsulate some of the ideological and institutional components we have discussed earlier. We can make fairly reasonable predications about how they affect the macroeconomy. Institutional compromise leading to liberal policy outcomes should cause markets to anticipate policies that promote growth and stimulate employment while also releasing forces associated with inflation and higher interest rates (e.g., deficit spending). Compromise leading to conservative policy outcomes, on the other hand, should be associated with the opposite outcomes as markets anticipate less spending: lower growth and employment but also lower interest and inflation rates.

STATISTICAL MODELS AND RESULTS

We examine the relationship between political institutions and the macroeconomy using a time series of quarterly data from the first quarter of 1949 through the fourth quarter of 1999.[10] This sample encompasses and extends that used by Alesina, Roubini, and Cohen (hereafter ARC 1997). The 51-year period includes 10 different presidents (five Republican and five Democratic), and five "episodes" of divided government (all with Republican presidents, except the last with Clinton). All the instances of unified government are with Democratic presidents, except the first two years of the Eisenhower administration.

We examine the same economic variables as ARC: the growth rate of real gross domestic product, the civilian unemployment rate, the long-term interest rate, and the inflation rate.[11] The first two dependent variables provide alternative indicators of the economy's overall performance, while the second two variables measure monetary policy in general. All these variables are converted to annual growth rates based on quarterly data.[12]

Our specification of the baseline model for our macroeconomic variables follows ARC. The general model is[13]

$$y_t = \alpha + \beta_1 y_{t-1} + \beta_2 y_{t-2} + \beta_3 y_{t-3} + \beta_4 Politics_{t-1} + \varepsilon_t,$$

where y_t is one of the macroeconomic variables (economic growth rate, unemployment rate, inflation rate, or interest rate) and $Politics_{t-1}$ is a variable that captures the institutional variation described above. Three lags are used because that is the optimal lag length as determined via Akaike's Information Criteria; the political variables are lagged because it is argued that political influences take at a minimum one quarter to influence the behavior of markets. All the models reported passed standard tests for serial correlation, homoskedastic disturbances, omitted variable bias, and normality of residuals. To keep our exposition simple we do not report coefficients and standard errors for any lagged endogenous variables because we treat them as statistical controls and we are not interested in drawing inferences about them. We do note that the coefficients on the lagged endogenous variables for all four dependent variables are similar in sign, magnitude, and statistical significance to those reported by ARC.

We begin the discussion of our results by focusing on growth and unemployment before turning to the inflation and interest rate models. Columns 1 and 2 of table 9.2 add variables indicating the party affiliation of the president (1 = Republican; −1 = Democrat) to the baseline specification. Recall that the only difference between the variables in columns 1 and 2 is that this party variable is coded for the entire administration in column 1 and is coded as 0 after the sixth quarter in column 2. Again, these results are similar to those of ARC and provide support for the naive partisan and rational partisan hypotheses.

In column 3 we begin adding our variables of interest one at a time, beginning with the measures of unified or divided government. Consider first the coefficient on the Divided Government I variable. Recall that this variable is coded as "divided" (and hence as 1) if the party of the president does *not* control *both* chambers of Congress; otherwise it is considered a unified government.

TABLE 9.2 Economic Growth

	Model									
	1	2	3	4	5	6	7	8	9	10
President's Party	0.30* (0.09)									
President's Party (six quarters)		0.65* (0.15)								
Divided Government I			0.64* (0.20)							
Divided Government II				−0.59* (0.19)						
Unified Democrat					0.62* (0.28)					
Divided Government—Democratic President					0.15* (0.36)					
Divided Government—Republican President					−0.13 (0.27)					
Gridlock Expansion/ Contraction						0.00 (0.02)				
Size of Gridlock Interval							0.21 (1.38)			
Vetoes								−0.01 (0.02)		
Partisan Compromise									0.01 (0.00)	
Ideological Compromise										−1.28* (0.44)
Adjusted R^2	0.79	0.8	0.79	0.79	0.79	0.79	0.79	0.78	0.79	0.79
F-statistic	196.56	206.00	170.37	195.99	131.77	162.13	161.79	185.25	197.47	180.17
Prob. > F	0.00	0.00	0.00	0.00	0.00	0.00	0.00	0.00	0.00	0.00

Note: Cell entries are OLS estimates with standard errors in parentheses. The constant and three lags of the dependent variable are not reported.

*$p < .05$

The first six years of the Reagan administration are not included in this analysis because Republicans controlled the Senate. The coefficient is negative and statistically significant, indicating that the economy slows by a little more than one-half of 1 percent during periods of divided as compared to unified government.

In column 4 we broaden the definition of divided government and code that variable 1 for those cases when the president is of one party and *either* house of Congress is of the other party. In practice this adds the first six years of the Reagan presidency. This variable, Divided Government II, is statistically significant and also in the negative direction, providing additional support for the argument that unified government is more conducive to economic growth than divided government.

Finally, in column 5, we include three variables that provide a complete menu of unified and divided government possibilities by type of partisan control. These variables indicate whether the government is unified under a Democratic administration or divided with Democratic (Republican) presidents and Republican (Democratic) Congresses. A unified Republican administration is the omitted category. The results in column 5 support the partisan hypothesis but also provide evidence confirming the importance of divided government. Only the variable indicating a Democratic unified government is statistically significant at conventional levels. The coefficient is positive, suggesting not only that Democratic administrations are growth enhancing but that unified Democratic administrations grow faster than any of the three other alternatives.

Effects of governmental gridlock on economic growth are negligible at best. Columns 6, 7, and 8 contain our various indicators of gridlock and the measure of presidential vetoes. None of these variables approaches statistical significance, suggesting economic growth is neither helped nor hindered by institutional or policy disagreement. That is, expectations, as measured by the gridlock interval or even the reality of legislative discord—vetoes, do not significantly affect the behavior of market participants.

We get a better feel for this phenomenon in columns 9 and 10, where we include our measures of institutional compromise. At the negative (positive) extreme for the partisan indicator of institutional compromise we have sizable Democratic (Republican) majorities in both chambers and a Democratic (Republican) president. This increases the likelihood that policy compromises will better reflect the goals and objectives of a Democratic (Republican) agenda. The coefficient on this variable is negative and statistically significant, indicating that partisan compromise under Democratic majorities and presidents increases economic growth. As expectations of Democratic bargaining strength decline (Republicans gain control of either house and/or the presidency), economic growth declines as well. We get similar results using the ideology indicator of institutional compromise. This measure captures ideological rather than strictly partisan differences across legislative chambers and between the executive and legislative branches. Like the earlier measure, the ideological indicator is negative and statistically significant. Economic growth is significantly—in both a substantive and a statistical sense—greater under policy compromises that are expected to be more liberal.

In table 9.3 we conduct a similar analysis using the unemployment rate as the dependent variable. Since the growth and unemployment rates are correlated both theoretically and empirically,[14] we do not go through each set of independent variables separately but rather highlight interesting and anomalous findings. The only significant differences between the growth and unemployment regressions occur in the divided government models. While the results in table 9.2 indicate consistent support for the hypothesis that divided governments decrease growth, table 9.3 suggests that only when there is a unified Democratic government is there a reduction in the unemployment rate. All the other coefficients are similar and as expected: Democratic governments decrease economic uncertainty leading to unemployment. The institutional compromise variables tell the same story: anticipated liberal policy compromises reduce unemployment.

We examine the reaction of monetary indicators to various governmental configurations in tables 9.4 and 9.5. Here our expectations are different; extant theory (e.g., Alesina, Roubini, and Cohen 1997; Herron 2002) suggests less of a rational partisan effect than an institutional conflict influence on monetary policy. Beginning in table 9.4, we examine how these factors affect the interest rate on the 10-year treasury bill. Our findings indicate that the partisanship of the president does have a statistically significant influence on the interest rate, with rates being higher under Democratic administrations. This partisan difference only arises, however, when we use the variable measuring the president's party over his entire term (column 1), rather than the first six quarters (column 2). There is more consistent support for hypotheses concerning the relationship between divided government and interest rates. Interest rates are significantly (both substantively and statistically) higher under unified than under divided governments (column 3); again, however, this result is not robust to alternative notions of divided government (column 4). Column 5 confirms both partisan and institutional theories: interest rates are higher under unified Democratic administrations. In fact, this coefficient is larger in absolute value than that in column 1, suggesting the importance of combining partisan and institutional variables.

Gridlock has mixed consequences for interest rates depending upon the measure employed. The measure of governmental gridlock that simply examines expansion and contraction in the gridlock interval (Krehbiel's measures) does not seem to have any relationship to interest rates. However, Herron's measure of the actual size of the gridlock interval does have a relationship to the movements in interest rates. The coefficient on this measure is consistent

		Model								
	1	2	3	4	5	6	7	8	9	10
President's Party	2.12* (0.66)									
President's Party (six quarters)		4.15* (1.04)								
Divided Government I			2.47* (1.44)							
Divided Government II				2.13 (1.32)						
Unified Democrat					-3.93 (1.95)					
Divided Government— Democratic President					-3.69 (2.62)					
Divided Government— Republican President					0.50 (1.86)					
Gridlock Expansion/ Contraction						-0.09 (0.14)				
Size of Gridlock Interval							-5.23 (8.51)			
Vetoes								0.03 (0.12)		
Partisan Compromise									-0.04* (0.01)	
Ideological Compromise										7.72* (3.25)
Adjusted R^2	.88	.88	.87	.88	.87	.86	.87	.88	.87	.88
F-statistic	372.04	303.36	345.63	238.17	291.62	285.78	340.60	359.71	317.92	360.76
Prob. > F	0.00	0.00	0.00	0.00	0.00	0.00	0.00	0.00	0.00	0.00

Note: Cell entries are OLS estimates with standard errors in parentheses. The constant and three lags of the dependent variable are not reported.

*$p < .05$.

TABLE 9.4 Treasury Bills

	Model									
	1	*2*	*3*	*4*	*5*	*6*	*7*	*8*	*9*	*10*
President's Party	−0.12* (0.05)									
President's Party (six quarters)		−0.12 (0.08)								
Divided Government I			−0.26* (0.09)							
Divided Government II				−0.24* (0.12)						
Unified Democrat					0.47* (0.16)					
Divided Government— Democratic President					0.22 (0.20)					
Divided Government— Republican President					0.21 (0.15)					
Gridlock Expansion/ Contraction						0.01 (0.01)				
Size of Gridlock Interval							−2.07* (0.86)			
Vetoes								−0.02* (0.01)		
Partisan Compromise									0.00 (0.01)	
Ideological Compromise										−0.76* (0.26)
Adjusted R^2	0.95	0.94	0.94	0.95	0.95	0.94	0.93	0.95	0.95	0.94
F-statistic	883.38	865.53	761.49	882.10	595.69	618.48	584.99	878.68	896.71	684.71
Prob. > F	0.00	0.00	0.00	0.00	0.00	0.00	0.00	0.00	0.00	0.00

Note: Cell entries are OLS estimates with standard errors in parentheses. The constant and three lags of the dependent variable are not reported.

| | Model | | | | | | | | | |
	1	2	3	4	5	6	7	8	9	10
President's Party	0.01 (0.05)									
President's Party (six quarters)		0.01 (0.09)								
Divided Government I			−0.18 (0.11)							
Divided Government II				−0.18 (0.11)						
Unified Democrat					0.30* (0.16)					
Divided Government— Democratic President					−0.51* (0.20)					
Divided Government— Republican President					0.17 (0.15)					
Gridlock Expansion/ Contraction						0.00 (0.01)				
Size of Gridlock Interval							−2.68* (0.73)			
Vetoes								0.00 (0.01)		
Partisan Compromise									0.00 (0.00)	
Ideological Compromise										−0.23 (0.19)
Adjusted R^2	.95	.95	.95	.95	.95	.97	.97	.95	.95	.97
F-statistic	615.01	614.88	581.91	623.55	500.29	994.34	1068.55	614.89	619.22	1073.16
Prob. > F	0.00	0.00	0.00	0.00	0.00	0.00	0.00	0.00	0.00	0.00

Note: Cell entries are OLS estimates with standard errors in parentheses. The constant and three lags of the dependent variable are not reported.
*$p < .05$.

with Herron's findings: because the public expects little policy change from gridlocked governments, they are unlikely to demand a higher rate of return when lending money to the government. Finally, the coefficient on the vetoes measure is not significant related to changes in interest rates.

Both measures of institutional compromise have negative and statistically significant effects on interest rates. This result is again consistent with our priors. As economic actors anticipate policy compromises that tend to the liberal extreme—those that increase government spending, raise taxes, and potentially add to federal debt—they will demand a higher return on their investment before they purchase government securities. Policy compromises that are expected to be more conservative, on the other hand, tend to decrease this demand by the market and, consequently, are associated with lower interest rates.

Table 9.5 contains the results of our investigation into the political causes of inflation. In comparison with the results in previous tables, these findings are the least supportive of our position that institutional variables are an important source of information regarding macroeconomic policy. They do, however, demonstrate that—with the exception of the unified Democratic government variable—partisan politics do not play a role in generating inflation. Unified Democratic administrations have higher rates of inflation, and gridlocked (at least according to the Herron measure) governments experience lower rates of inflation. None of the other variables has a statistically significant influence on changes in consumer prices.

Robustness of the Results

Is there any evidence that the results reported above are spurious? For instance, are the findings of partisan influences on growth driven by the fact that Democratic administrations have lower rates of unemployment, and lower rates of unemployment drive an increase in economic growth? We examine the robustness of our findings using a vector autoregression (VAR) framework. In general, our VAR is written as follows:

$$y_t = \alpha + \sum_{j=1}^{J} \beta_j y_{t-j} + \sum_{j=1}^{J} \delta_j z_{t-j} + \lambda Politics_{t-1} + u_{1t}.$$

$$z_t = \alpha + \sum_{j=1}^{J} \theta_j y_{t-j} + \sum_{j=1}^{J} \phi_j z_{t-j} + \lambda' Politics_{t-1} + u_{2t}.$$

This setup allows one endogenous variable—growth, for instance—to be a function of past values of growth, unemployment, and political variables. In addition, unemployment is a function of past values of unemployment, growth, and political variables. Estimating these two equations simultaneously provides a safeguard against omitted variables biasing the coefficient on the political variables. In our models we include three lags of each endogenous variable; this lag structure was determined via the Akaike Information Criteria.

For ease of presentation we do not include the tables but simply report where the VAR results confirm or differ from our single equation models. The first models use growth and unemployment as the endogenous variables. The results from this VAR confirm those reported earlier. As a consequence we are more comfortable that the economic effects we have attributed to our political variables are not a result of omitted variable bias.

The results for the VAR using interest and inflation rates are a bit more interesting. While there still is no support for partisan influences on monetary policy, using the VAR setup we find increased support for theories of institutional conflict. The unified government and unified Democratic government variables have statistically significant and positive effects on both interest and inflation rates, while the other divided government measures have mixed effects. The gridlock interval derived from Herron's work is negative and statistically significant for both rates, but, unlike the findings in tables 9.3 and 9.4, neither of the institutional compromise variables is statistically significant. These findings indicate that for nominal economic indicators it is not simply the party of the president that matters—as might be suggested by previous scholarship—but rather the relationship between the president and Congress that influences market expectations.

CONCLUSION AND DISCUSSION

What is clear from the data and results presented in this chapter is that we have much to learn from disaggregating the "political" in political business cycles models. In part our findings can be seen as a confirmation of the influential work of ARC; however, we go a step further. Not only do markets respond to the partisanship and electoral behavioral of the individual occupying the White House, but they respond to the composition of the legislative bodies located further down Pennsylvania Avenue. The economy performs better—in terms of increased growth and decreased unemployment—when there is a Democrat in the Oval Office and when there is the likelihood of partisan compromise along more "liberal" lines between the president and Congress. This composition of institutions, however, is the proverbial double-edged sword: economic stimulation carries with it higher interest and inflation rates.

This chapter represents what we hope will be the beginning of a sustained interest in the macropolitics of Congress and the macroeconomy. There are at least two avenues for future research that are worth exploring. First, the arguments advanced in this chapter suggest that market participants engage in political speculation about the composition and productivity of the executive and legislative branches. It would be fruitful to investigate whether private asset markets in general (e.g., stock and bond markets) respond to these expectations. If markets have rational expectations and can predict the extent of partisan or institutional compromise, then they should be able to hedge their investments in private equity markets.

A second avenue for examination concerns the relationship between divided government, the macroeconomy, and congressional elections. While Alesina and Rosenthal have examined—at least theoretically—the relationship between presidential elections and the macroeconomy, there is little evidence that similar dynamics are at work during congressional elections.

NOTES

1. We also created the equivalent variable for four and eight quarters, but did not find significant deviations from the results we report below. This is the same finding reported by Alesina, Roubini, and Cohen (1997).

2. We include in this variable the exceptional case of Reagan's first six years, when he faced a Democratic-controlled House but a Republican-controlled Senate.

3. For a more complete description of the pivotal politics model, see Krehbiel 1996.

4. Krehbiel footnotes the possibility of contraction codings (1998, 61).

5. Herron's interpretation of the gridlock effect on economic factors is slightly different from the one we employ. He assumes that a wider gridlock interval will result in less new policy enacted, but that this is likely to have a positive effect on the economy (in his study, it will push down interest rates) because there is less uncertainty about the influence of government through new public policy.

6. We only count those nonpocket vetoes that were clearly for public, rather than private, bills.

7. Literature examining conditional party government (CPG) shows that the acceptability of this assumption waxes and wanes over time (Rohde 1991; Cox and McCubbins 1993; Aldrich and Rohde 1998).

8. One possible refinement of the "size matters" approach is to note party majorities under divided government that are veto-proof (larger than two-thirds) and thus able to override presidential opposition, or under unified government when the Senate is filibuster-proof (enough votes to invoke cloture) and thus able to prevent bills from being killed in the Senate. Such instances are much more the exception than the rule in Congress.

9. We prefer our formulation as opposed to developing a fully interactive model for two reasons: (1) our specification is more parsimonious (one variable versus six variables), and (2) in a theoretical sense we believe the weighted index should be combined in an additive rather than multiplicative manner.

10. The exception is when we use the ideological compromise measure; that data series begins with quarter 1 of 1953.

11. All data was obtained from the St. Louis Federal Reserve Bank's website, http://research.stlouisfed.org/fred/

12. Growth rates are calculated as $y_t = ((x_t - x_{t-4})/x_t)*100$ where y is the rate in question and x is the level of GDP or unemployment.

13. The only exception is when the dependent variable is the inflation rate. Following Alesina, Roubini, and Cohen (1997), we include a dummy variable for the years following the end of the Bretton Woods international monetary system (post-1973) and a variable measuring the quarterly price of oil as economic controls in all models.

14. Unemployment and growth have a bivariate correlation of $-.80$.

REFERENCES

Aldrich, John, and David Rohde. 1998. "Measuring Conditional Party Government." Paper presented at the Annual Meeting of the Midwest Political Science Association; Chicago.

Alesina, Alberto. 1987. "Macroeconomic Policy in a Two-Party System as a Repeated Game." *Quarterly Journal of Economics* 102:651–78.

Alesina, Alberto, and Howard Rosenthal. 1995. *Partisan Politics, Divided Government, and the Economy.* New York: Cambridge University Press.

Alesina, Alberto, and Nouriel Roubini. 1992. "Political Cycles in OECD Economies." *Review of Economic Studies* 59:663–88.

Alesina, Alberto, and Nouriel Roubini, with Gerald Cohen 1997. *Political Cycles and the Macroeconomy.* Cambridge: MIT Press.

Binder, Sarah. 1999. "The Dynamics of Legislative Gridlock, 1947–96." *American Political Science Review* 93:519–33.

Block, Frank. 1977. "The Ruling Class Does Not Rule: Notes on the Marxist Theory of the State." *Socialist Revolution* 7 (3):6–28.

Brady, David, and Craig Volden. 1998. *Revolving Gridlock: Politics and Policy from Carter to Clinton.* Boulder, Colo: Westview Press.

Cameron, Charles M. 2000. *Veto Bargaining: Presidents and the Politics of Negative Power.* New York: Cambridge University Press.

Cox, Gary, and Mathew McCubbins. 1991. "Divided Control of Fiscal Policy." In *The Politics of Divided Government,* ed. Gary Cox and Samuel Kernell. Boulder, Colo: Westview Press.

———. 1993. *Legislative Leviathan: Party Government in the House.* Berkeley and Los Angeles: University of California Press.

Edwards, George, Andrew Barrett, and Jeffrey Peake 1997. "The Legislative Impact of Divided Government." *American Journal of Political Science* 41:545–63.

Fiorina, Morris. 1996. *Divided Government.* Boston: Allyn and Bacon.

Herron, Michael. 2002. "Divided Government, Preference Conflict, and Gridlock." Northwestern University. Typescript.

Hibbs, Douglas A., Jr. 1977. "Political Parties and Macroeconomic Policy." *American Political Science Review* 71:1467–87.

———1987. *The American Political Economy.* Cambridge: Harvard University Press.

Howell, William, E. Scott Adler, Charles M. Cameron, and Charles Riemann 2000. "Divided Government and the Legislative Productivity of Congress, 1945–94." *Legislative Studies Quarterly* 25:285–312.

Kelly, Sean. 1993. "Divided We Govern: A Reassessment." *Polity* 25:475–84.

Krehbiel, Keith. 1996. "Institutional and Partisan Sources of Gridlock: A Theory of Divided and Unified Government." *Journal of Theoretical Politics* 8:7–40.

―――. 1998. *Pivotal Politics: A Theory of U.S. Lawmaking*. Chicago: University of Chicago Press.

Krehbiel, Keith, Kenneth Shepsle, and Barry Weingast 1987. "Why Are Congressional Committees Powerful?" *American Political Science Review* 81:929–45.

Lindblom, Charles. 1977. *Politics and Markets: The World's Political-Economic Systems*. New York: Basic Books.

Longley, Lawrence, and Walter Oleszek. 1989. *Bicameral Politics: Conference Committees in Congress*. New Haven: Yale University Press.

Mayhew, David R. 1991. *Divided We Govern: Party Control, Lawmaking, and Investigations 1946–1990*. New Haven: Yale University Press.

McCarty, Nolan, and Keith Poole. 1995. "Veto Power and Legislation: An Empirical Analysis of Executive-Legislative Bargaining from 1961–1986." *Journal of Law, Economics, and Organization* 11:282–312.

Nordhaus, William. 1975. "The Political Business Cycle." *Review of Economic Studies* 42: 169–90.

Pious, Richard. 1979. *The American Presidency*. New York: Basic Books.

Poole, Keith, and Howard Rosenthal. 1997. *Congress: A Political-Economic History of Roll Call Voting*. New York: Oxford University Press.

Rohde, David. 1991. *Parties and Leaders in the Postreform House*. Chicago: University of Chicago Press.

Shepsle, Kenneth, and Barry Weingast. 1987. "The Institutional Foundations of Committee Power." *American Political Science Review* 81:85–104.

Stevenson, Richard. 2002. "House Raises Debt Ceiling and Avoids a Default." *New York Times*. June 28, 2002, A16.

Tufte, Edward. 1978. *Political Control of the Economy*. Princeton: Princeton University Press.

PART V: *Understanding the Macropolitics of Congress*

10

Lawmaking and History

David R. Mayhew

The "macropolitics" of Congress has become a success story. That would seem to be the main lesson to draw from the uniformly fine chapters of this volume. They are a heterogeneous lot. It would be gratuitous to try to summarize them one by one, probably unhelpful to reach for overarching generalizations (I cannot think of any) or in the cases of several chapters pointless, given my own background, even to comment.

Instead I would like to discuss a few of the chapters, or rather to address questions raised for me by a few of them. All my comments bear on the relation between databases and their accompanying theories, on the one hand, and actual legislative history as I see it on the other.

AGENDA SIZE

Charles R. Shipan asks in chapter 6: Does divided government increase the size of the legislative agenda? Yes it does, and significantly so, he plausibly demonstrates in his analysis of congressional lawmaking, both achieved and attempted, from 1947 through 1992. This is a welcome answer to a first-rate question. It casts light on whether policy change taken by itself (numerator indexing, let us call it) or, alternatively, policy change as a proportion of proposed policy change (ratio indexing, let us call it) should serve as a preferred measure of government production or productivity. If, in the context of divided versus unified government, legislative agenda sizes are appreciably endogenous, they are, to put it another way, artifactual. That realization advances the idea of relying on numerator indexing rather than ratio indexing as a gauge of government production.

I speculated about this subject, although I did not address it squarely, in writing my own work *Divided We Govern* in 1991. My judgment back then was that actual policy change is what observers of the American regime should be chiefly interested in. All the rest can be a kind of vapor that surrounds real legislative action without being very real itself. Politicians are always proposing things. Parties are always proposing things. That is what politicians and parties are expected to do. But such offerings are often vague, shifting, untested, infeasible, or otherwise insubstantial. In general, a sensible public will discount all of them at a very high rate. Actual government production is the news chiefly worth paying attention to. To be sure, legislative enactments themselves can be vaporous achievements: Implementation is yet to come. But enactments ordinarily possess a certain solidity.

In addition, however, I did suspect back then that agendas are in certain interfering ways artifactual. That could be because, as in Shipan's account, both parties are in a good position to contribute to them under conditions of divided party control and thus render them on average larger. Another concern I had was personal idiosyncrasy, which might or might not iron out over time. This implicates particularly the presidency, where one person rather than a party has a chance to promote an agenda on Capitol Hill. Presidents can aim for large agendas or small ones. At opposite extremes, consider two historical instances. In 1913, incoming president Woodrow Wilson, fresh from the example of his acclaimed governorship in New Jersey, is said to have aimed for exactly three legislative achievements: banking reform, tariff reduction, and corporate regulation. That was all. He got them. That is a shrewd route to a perfect record. At the other extreme, President Harry S. Truman during the election season of 1948 asked the Republican 80th Congress to enact a lengthy laundry list of bills, assuming that they would not. They did not. That was a shrewd way to inject a large denominator into the system and then blame a "do nothing" Congress for its weak performance. In recent years, there is the instance of Newt Gingrich on the congressional side. Whatever else the Contract with America may have achieved in 1995, it brought into play a large congressional agenda. One result, in the circumstances of 1995–96, although I have not made any calculations, might have been a lowered ratio of accomplishment for that Congress.

To be sure, there is a political reality to the agendas of Wilson, Truman, Gingrich, and others. They are not nothing. On this subject, ratio studies are accordingly one good way to proceed.[1] But the taint of artifactuality that attaches to agendas, combined with their relatively high vapor content, argues for keying on actual changes from status quo policy to index government production or productivity.

POLICY REPRESENTATION

From my vantage point as an analyst of lawmaking, the work by Robert S. Erikson and his coauthors (see chapter 3) is a major achievement. It reaches across several subareas of political science, it is inventively grounded in both theory and data, and it embeds policymaking in public opinion in a way no one had succeeded in doing previously. The authors' coding of congressional enactments since 1952 into liberal-tilting or conservative-tilting ones, as well as a large residual category tilting neither way, seems to be nicely done. It relies on judgments by expert contemporary observers (Erikson, MacKuen, and Stimson 2002, chap. 9). The result is a convincing dynamic of "policy representation" geared to the left-right dimension.

An unsettling by-product of the analysis, however, is the authors' documentation that liberal-tilting laws have outnumbered conservative-tilting ones by nine to one! At the per-Congress level: "On average, the net change (Laws) is between five and six major laws in the liberal direction, each Congress." What are we to make of this remarkable half-century march to the left? Is it believable? Has American public policy really been cumulating that way?

One answer is yes, the trend as measured is believable, at least to a considerable degree. Notwithstanding the Reagan revolution, the Gingrich revolution, and other conservative expressions, the argument would go, the actual role of U.S. conservatives is to prevent liberals from enacting more programs, not to reverse ones that have already been enacted. In general, rollback moves are not attempted or else they fail. That answer captures the history of, for example, entitlements programs quite well.

But another answer is that measurement error of a sort may be entering in. (It would be largely my own error in *Divided We Govern*.) Perhaps many liberal-tilting enactments are later undermined, chipped away at, or otherwise negated through processes, for example appropriations processes, that are not as flashily public as the initial enactments of the laws. Such instances of attrition might not make it onto "important laws" lists. Possibly this line of thinking has some truth in it too. For example, many high-reaching housing programs created through statute after statute from the 1940s through the 1960s seem to have withered away rather than been repealed. The higher the incidence of trajectories of this latter sort, the more clouded is the idea of a nine-to-one liberal edge in laws.

Yet I believe there is a third answer. Consider the following list of congressional enactments. All of them were selected from the list of important post-1946 laws included in *Divided We Govern* (1991) or else, since 1991, from updates I have posted through 2002 at http://pantheon.yale.edu/~dmayhew/.

1954   Authorization of the St. Lawrence Seaway
1954   Atomic Energy Act (laying the basis for a private atomic energy industry)
1955   Reciprocal Trade Act extended (with reformulated presidential authority)
1956   Federal Highway Act (authorizing the interstates)
1956   Upper Colorado River Project (big dams, irrigation)
1958   Creation of the National Aeronautics and Space Administration (NASA)
1962   Trade Expansion Act (promoted by President Kennedy)

1962   Communications Satellite Act (creating a private corporation to run it)

1968   Central Arizona Project (more big dams, irrigation)

1970   Rail Passenger Service Act (establishing Amtrak)

1973   Authorization of the trans-Alaska pipeline

1973   Regional Rail Reorganization Act (establishing Conrail)

1973   Structuring of Health Maintenance Organizations (HMOs)

1974   Foreign Trade Act (new "fast-track" authority to the White House)

1976   Copyright law revision (to cover photocopying, cable-TV royalties, etc.)

1978   Airline deregulation

1979   Foreign Trade Act extension (the Tokyo Round to reduce barriers)

1979   Chrysler Corporation bailout

1980   Trucking deregulation

1980   Depository Institutions and Monetary Control Act (deregulation of S&Ls)

1982   Garn–St. Germain Depository Institutions Act (more S&L deregulation)

1984   Cable Communications Policy Act (remake of cable-TV regulation)

1989   Bailout of failed savings and loans

1992   Deregulation of electric utilities

1993   Approval of North American Free Trade Agreement (NAFTA)

1994   Approval of General Agreement on Tariffs and Trade (GATT)

1996   Deregulation of telecommunications

1999   Deregulation of banking

1999   Y2K planning act (to ward off computer problems on January 1, 2000)

2000   Approval of Permanent Normal Trading Relations with China (PNTR)

2001   Bailout of airlines after September 11, 2001

2002   Federal terrorism insurance (an aid to construction industry)

In the language of Ira Katznelson and John Lapinski (see chapter 4), all 32 of these statutes are probably classifiable as "domestic: planning and resources" or "domestic: political economy." To put it another way, all of these statutes have either shaped the infrastructure within which the country's instruments of production have operated, or else they have directly shaped the structure of those instruments of production. For the years since World War II, it would be hard to come up with any other list of enactments as vital to the American business community.

Here is the point: Of the 27 of these laws enacted through 1996—the most recent year reached by the Erikson et al. coding scheme—*not one* scores as either liberal-tilting or conservative-tilting in that coding scheme (and again, nothing seems to be wrong with the coding scheme). They were not seen by expert observers as liberal or conservative victories. All are plausibly rated "neutral." It is a good bet that the five laws listed above that were enacted during 1999–2002 would be rated "neutral," too, if they were comparably judged. The lesson seems to be: To a remarkable degree, elements of the U.S. business community have gotten what they needed from Congress during recent generations through statues that have been, so to speak, "off cleavage." Granted, the needs or wants of the business community do not exactly equate to "conservatism." Still, the promotion and upkeep of private capitalism does somehow seem to be a fundamental interest of conservatism. Indeed, in the American brand of conservatism, is anything else as fundamental? The volume and importance of the items listed above seem to add a prominent qualifying asterisk to the evident nine-to-one liberal advantage among statutes that were enacted *on* cleavage.

Is this off-cleavage pattern involving the business sector any surprise? If it is placed in the full context of 216 years of U.S. national history, it does seem to be. Questions of foreign trade, banking and currency, "internal improvements" (to use the nineteenth-century term), and more generally issues of economic structure and infrastructure used to be exactly *on* cleavage. For generation after generation, from Alexander Hamilton through Herbert Hoover on one side and Thomas Jefferson through Cordell Hull on the other, nothing seems to have defined the American parties and their ideologies more cleanly than tariff policy, unless it was banking and currency policy. Consider Hamilton's credit and banking initiatives, the Jay Treaty in 1795–96, the banking controversy under Jackson and Van Buren, the Republican tariff hikes in 1861, 1890, 1897, 1922, and 1930, the Democratic tariff cuts in 1894, 1913, and 1934, and the controversy between Bryan and McKinley over silver versus gold. Internal improvements—questions of roads, railroads, rivers and harbors—also tended to divide the parties of the nineteenth century, with Whigs and then Republicans on the pro side and Democrats on the anti side.

It may not be wise to discern a "left-right" or a "liberal-conservative" cleavage in American history before, say, 1900 or so. Before that time these terms may be anachronistic. Yet any analyst sifting through congressional enactments back then, looking for major ones that tilted one way or another on the decisive ideological cleavages of those times, would no doubt have identified such statutes as Hamilton's banking plan, the Jay Treaty, the Walker Tariff of 1846, the Pacific Railway Act of 1862, and the McKinley Tariff of 1890. Proceeding into the early decades of the twentieth century, such a list might include the Aldrich-Vreeland Currency Act of 1908, the Underwood-Simmons Tariff of 1913, the Smoot-Hawley Tariff of 1930, the Glass-Steagall Banking Act of 1933, the Reciprocal Trade Agreements Act of 1934, and the Public Utilities Holding Company Act of 1935 (restructuring the utilities industry). Instruments like these would very likely have been rated as *on* cleavage.

Why the contrast between then and now? What seems to have happened is
that the relation between capitalism and American electoral politics underwent
a basic shift in the mid–twentieth century, perhaps as a joint result of the New
Deal and World War II (see Gerring 1998, chap. 7). A range of issues that once
made the ideological juices flow ceased to do that. "Anti-monopoly," as Alan
Brinkley has written (1995), went out of fashion as an ideological litmus test.
The country seems to have settled into an acceptance of private capitalism and
the need to sustain it.

This does not mean that parties and ideological activists have had nothing to
fight about since World War II. Liberal or conservative policy victories remained available or became so, as witnesses the Erikson list, in the areas of
welfare state provision, taxation levels, regulation of labor markets, environmental protection, consumer protection, civil rights, and (this is outside the
Erikson data set) hawk versus dove stances on foreign policy. But old standbys
such as trade and banking went off cleavage, and new questions having to do
with the structure or infrastructure of production arose without making it on
cleavage. Consider the following contrasts: The enactment of the Public Utilities Holding Company Act of 1935 featured one of the twentieth century's
great high-wire showdowns between "antimonopoly" forces and private capitalism, whereas the comprehensive deregulation of electric utilities six decades
later in 1992 was technocratic and unexciting—a page-19 event. The Federal
Reserve Act of 1913 remains one the Democratic Party's proudest accomplish-
ments, whereas the highly important deregulation of the banking and related industries in 1999 was a cross-party, hard-to-understand, backroom deal.

Am I implying that the 32 statutes listed above were not, or could not have
been, achievements that deserve the name "policy representation"? That is not
my aim. Exhibited in the Erikson study is *one kind* of policy representation—
that is, a kind associated with neatly liberal-tilting or conservative-tilting victories. Yet all of the 32 statutes listed above generated new policies, many of
them emerged from spirited public controversy (consider NAFTA), and in all
cases the records would probably show that dense representation was somehow going on. Lacking, for what it is worth, was the clear left-right victory
motif.

THE 107TH CONGRESS OF 2001–2

The recent Congress of 2001–2 was unusually productive, and the content of
its policy enactments was, to say the least, unusual.[2] How does that Congress
fit into contemporary analytic tendencies, including those of this volume? Below are 16 enactments that seemed to emerge as important.[3] (As it happens, 15
of them, all but the Bush tax cut, were enacted under conditions of divided

party control after the defection of Senator James Jeffords in early 2001 gave control of the Senate to the Democrats. The Republicans controlled all three elected branches in early 2001 when the Bush tax cut passed.)

Enactments during calendar 2001:

Bush tax cut. $1.35 trillion over 11 years (provisional) repeal of the estate tax, cuts in top rates, doubling of child credit, relief from the marriage penalty, some immediate tax rebates. Largest tax reduction in 20 years.

Education reform. To redirect aid to poorest schools, mandate annual testing of student performance, hold schools accountable, hike federal spending. Bipartisan measure maneuvered by the White House and Senator Edward Kennedy. First major overhaul of the Elementary and Secondary Education Act since its enactment in 1965.

The following five enactments during 2001 ensued from the terrorist attacks of September 11:

Use-of-force resolution. Authorized president to use force against nations, organizations, or individuals involved in acts of terrorism or its harborers, including in Afghanistan.

USA Patriot Act. Sweeping new government powers to track and detain suspected terrorists and combat related money-laundering.

$40 billion emergency spending. For defense, domestic security, recovery of New York.

Airline bailout. $15 billion to airlines for grounding of flights, passenger drop-off, victim benefits.

Airport security. New government program to hire 30,000 airport screeners and inspect all baggage.

Enactments during calendar 2002:

Campaign finance reform. To ban soft money contributions to parties and curb attack ads just before elections. McCain-Feingold bill in Senate version, Shays-Meehan bill in House version. First major overhaul of campaign finance regulation since 1974.

Agriculture subsidies. $180 billion over 10 years including a $40 billion hike in grain and cotton subsidies; new environmental and conservation efforts. A rollback from free-market-oriented agriculture act of 1996.

Corporate responsibility act. Broad new regulation of businesses and their auditors, stiffer penalties for fraud, new oversight board for accountants. Sarbanes-Oxley Act. After Enron scandal. Toughest new restrictions since the 1930s.

Fast-track trade authority. Broad new presidential authority to negotiate trade deals with other countries subject to unamendable up-or-down congressional votes. Old authority had lapsed in 1994. New adjustment assistance and health insurance aid for workers unemployed due to foreign competition.

Election reform. $3.86 billion to the states to upgrade voting equipment and election administration. "Provisional ballots" and "second chance voting" to be allowed, computerized voter lists linked to driver's licenses to be required.

Iraq resolution. Authorized president to use armed forces "as he determines to be necessary and appropriate" to defend against "the continuing threat posed by Iraq" and to enforce all relevant UN Security Council resolutions on Iraq.

New Homeland Security Department. To fold 170,000 federal employees from 22 agencies into a new cabinet-level department charged with defending against terrorism. Broad presidential authority to hire, fire, and reassign employees. Largest government reorganization since 1947. Proposal hatched by Senator Joseph Lieberman, embraced by the White House.

Terrorism insurance. Government to reimburse insurance industry up to $100 billion a year for claims resulting from future terrorist attacks. An aid to construction industry.

Commission created to investigate September 11 attacks. To probe government's failure to anticipate the attack. Ten members, five from each party. To report in 18 months. This was the commission that came to be cochaired by Thomas Kean and Lee Hamilton.

Obviously, the dominant theme in this mix is the government's response to the September 11 attack. Eight of the 16 enactments—9 if the White House's logic on Iraq is accepted—were reactions to that attack. What does that say about the 107th Congress? One answer might be: Well, all this post–September 11 action should not really count. It is off the charts. Political science can take a holiday until Congress reverts to its familiar, more agreeable agendas like taxes and the welfare state on which most academic analysis dwells. I believe that that answer would be a mistake. Reacting to emergencies is as enduring a theme of congressional lawmaking as anything else. In lawmaking terms, the best analogues of the Congress of 2001–2 are probably those of 1861–63 during the Civil War, 1917–18 during World War I, and 1941–42 and 1943–44 during World War II. Issuing from those Congresses were enactments providing for immense spending, taxing, and delegation, even if the U.S. Code was not greatly altered (see Heitshusen and Young, chap. 5). Some of those moves proved to be long-lasting. As a consequential revenue enactment, probably nothing in American history tops the shift, by statute, to income tax withholding during World War II via the Current Tax Payment Act of 1943 (Murphy 1996). Another candidate for a good analogue is the Congress of 1933–34, particularly its "hundred days" phase of early 1933. Although the New Deal is ordinarily discussed under "party programs," it is well to remember that, in general, "the significant enactments of the Roosevelt One Hundred Days of 1933 [were] driven by the exigencies of the Great Depression, crisis economic conditions that were uniquely traumatic to the nation" (Frendreis, Tatalovich, and Schaff 2001, 868). The economy was collapsing.

There seem to be two implications here for political science analysis. First, a shift of status quo policy outside the congressional "gridlock interval" can be spectacularly caused by events other than elections. This is not a trivial point. Even in relatively normal times, interelection events can be necessary and very close to sufficient causes of major lawmaking (although of course the exact contours of the enactments are up for grabs). Consider the Marshall Plan in 1948, the McCarran Internal Security Act of 1950 (enacted at the peak of McCarthyism during the Korean War), the National Aeronautics and Space Act of 1958 (just after *Sputnik*), pharmaceutical drug regulation in 1962 (after the thalidomide scare), the Civil Rights Act of 1964 (after the Birmingham police dogs), the Economic Stabilization Act of 1971 (giving wage-price control authority to Nixon), the Emergency Petroleum Allocation Act of 1973, the bailout of New York City in 1975, an economic aid package for the former Soviet republics in 1992, and the Corporate Responsibility Act of 2002 (after the collapse of Enron). In the emergency contexts of 1861, 1917, 1933 (the U.S. banking system was collapsing in the late Hoover months *after* the election of November 1932), 1941, and 2001, it was searing interelection events brought on legislative drives that absorbed entire sessions of Congress.

The second implication involves level of conflict. Emergency contexts tend to press Congress toward unanimity, or at least toward lopsided results. This puts a strain on dimensional interpretations of congressional performance: How can one tell whether a roll call fits onto a general left-right (or something like that) dimension if every member votes yes? Political scientists have a habit of cold-shouldering unanimous, or nearly unanimous, congressional roll calls on the ground that they are unimportant. They are "hurrah" votes as in honoring national nasturtium week. Leaving out such votes is a great aid to statistical analysis. But there is a cost. Roll call analysis becomes motored by a theory of conflict rather than by a theory of lawmaking or policymaking. By what defensible standard, for example, can it be said that the congressional declaration of war against Japan in 1941, which drew one nay vote in the House and none in the Senate, and the use-of-force resolution in 2001, which brought the same pattern, were unimportant?

NOTES

1. As in Binder 2003. Binder has her own plausible coding scheme for arriving at biennial ratio-type indexes.

2. The succeeding Congress of 2003–4 was not particularly interesting or productive.

3. Two of the entries are joint resolutions rather than regular statutes: the use-of-force resolution following September 11, 2001, and the Iraq resolution of November 2002. In the list of laws in *Divided We Govern* and my biennial website updates to it through 2002 I did not include joint resolutions (see Mayhew 1991, 41). Yet it is hard to do justice to the legislative harvest of 2001–2 without including these two resolutions. In hindsight, I think I made a mistake not to include major joint resolutions previously. Certainly they can be important, and they emerge from the same process as ordinary laws—enactment by majorities in both congressional houses with the option of a presidential veto and a two-thirds override. Recently, I have checked back through 1947 to see which joint resolutions I should have included earlier. There are not very many. The plausible increments, all granting authority to presidents in topical foreign policy areas, are the Formosa resolution of 1955, the Middle East resolution of 1957, the Tonkin Gulf resolution of 1964, and the Persian Gulf resolution of 1991. For a discussion, see the currently posted material on my website that covers 1991–2002, as well as the 2005 edition of *Divided We Govern*.

REFERENCES

Binder, Sarah A. 2003. *Stalemate: Causes and Consequences of Legislative Gridlock*, Washington, D.C.: Brookings Institution Press.

Brinkley, Alan. 1995. *The End of Reform: New Deal Liberalism in Recession and War*. New York: Knopf.

Erikson, Robert S., Michael B. MacKuen, and James A. Stimson. 2002. *The Macro Polity*. New York: Cambridge University Press.

Frendreis, John, Raymond Tatalovich, and Jon Schaff. 2001. "Predicting Legislative Output in the First One-Hundred Days, 1897–1995." *Political Research Quarterly* 54:853–70.

Gerring, John. 1998. *Party Ideologies in America, 1828–1996*. New York: Cambridge University Press.

Mayhew, David R. 1991. *Divided We Govern: Party Control, Lawmaking, and Investigations, 1946–1990*. New Haven: Yale University Press.

———. 2005. *Divided We Govern: Party Control, Lawmaking, and Investigations, 1946–2002*. 2nd ed. New Haven: Yale University Press.

Murphy, Kevin. 1996. "Child of War: The Federal Income Tax." *Mid-America* 78(2): 203–29.

11

Rational Choice, History, and the
Dynamics of Congress

David Brady

The study of the dynamics of American politics has held the interest of a large portion of those in our profession who study the American system of government. For over two decades realignment theory dominated the study of the dynamics of American politics. The work of V. O. Key (1955, 1959) and Walter D. Burnham (Burnham 1965; Burnham and Sprague 1970) provided those who examine American politics with a periodizing mechanism, which neatly delineated American history into matching electoral and policy periods. With the ebb of realignment theory the study of the dynamic aspects of American politics came under the purview of two contending schools of thought—those who either align themselves with the rational choice approach to American politics or those who align themselves with the American political development camp. Rational choice scholars, despite the brilliant foray by Kramer (1971), were latecomers to dynamic studies. In large part this was due to the considerable amount of time they spent trying to account for why the chaos theorem did not seem to exist in the policy world. Gordon Tullock's now famous question, "Why so much stability?" was answered when Shepsle (1979) showed that institutional arrangements could lead to policy equilibrium. Once it had been shown that through committees, structurally induced policy equilibrium could exist, scholars of the rational choice persuasion slowly began to turn to studies of Congress. The resulting and essentially distributional model of both the inputs and the outputs of Congress dominated rational choice scholarship for about a decade.

This distributional model was challenged by a series of informational models, which disputed the nature of congressional decision-making, and the policy results engendered. Gilligan and Krehbiel (1989, 1990) and Krehbiel (1993, 1999) viewed Congress as organized such that the median member of the body maximized information flows, and thus policy was in fact majoritarian (median member) and not distributional through a series of political deals. Over the last decade rational choice scholars have begun to do historical analysis in part because extending the time series increases the variance in key variables, allowing them better tests of competing theories.

The other major approach to the study of American politics has been American political development, where studies of movements, institutions, and their effect on policy have been seminal. Skowronek (1982), Bensel (2000), and Skocpol (1992, 1995), among others, have produced major works where the overview of American political development is seen as in part the result of previous arrangements of institutions. This view of institutions is more sociological than the economics-based rational choice view and ultimately sees institutions as more complex than does the straightforward rational choice view (see Powell and DiMaggio 1991). The focus in the development area is on how institutions and policy came to be formed and how we might learn from that past about the present (see Skocpol 1992 for a classic example). The nature of the institutional arrangement is often seen as the result of social pressure movements and the institution's past history. Understanding the history of how the institution came to its present condition is crucial for understanding the development of the American system of government.

In short, the rational choice school and its adherents studied individual actors and asked how the pieces fit together to impede, shape, or make public policy. The other school, American political development, studied institutions, periods, and policy from a much broader, less individualistic methodology. The American development school has often used history to show how change occurred and to explain why certain policies persist or were passed over. Rational choice scholars also use history, but their approach is more likely to be quantitative, and involve analysis that employs time series, econometrics, or comparative statistics.

These two modes of analysis have for quite some time in our profession been moving on separate tracks. One mode has been oriented toward time-series analysis, rational choice theory, and quantification. Scholars for about a decade—roughly the 1980s—combined with quantitative historians like Joel Silbey and Alan Bogue to make inroads into both American history and political science as disciplines. However, as historians have turned away from political history, the field has been left to political scientists. The second mode of analysis made inroads in both political science and sociology (see McAdam, Tarrow, and Tilly 2001). This mode has been largely anti–rational choice and relies on sociological theories of institutions. While sometimes this field is quantitative, it is often driven, by the nature of the question, to be more qualitative.

This book, in an interesting way, bridges the gaps between these two approaches to the study of American politics. It does so in two ways. The first is to use the institution of Congress as an independent or dependent variable on its own. The second is the use of history as a laboratory for testing theories. "History as a laboratory" combines the obvious practice of using time series to increase variance in the variables used and also the less obvious notion that history is a tough test for theories to overcome. It is in the nonobvious use of history that I see the two schools of thought having room to challenge each other, debate issues and policy, and on occasion come to an agreement or at least a better understanding of where the disagreements lie. The chapters herein contain work that builds on micro theory by combining institutions, thus offering both predictions and explanations for major shifts in either institutional arrangements or public policy. In these very good chapters the variables accounting for governmental activity or policy include public opinion, preferences, actors' ideologies, elections, divided government, political parties, supermajority institutions, bureaucrats, incentives, and medians in various places. These chapters measure broad policy changes à la Mayhew, measure governmental activity and direction of policy, and offer new coding schemes. In addition to the broad change variables there are specific policy areas such as permit decisions concerning telecommunications and the number of policies on the national agenda.

With both sets of variables there are, in addition to the normal issues of measurement and specification, special problems regarding macropolitics. Specifically, measurement of policy change over time and the measurement and meaning of the right-hand variables such as public opinion are problematic in macropolitical analysis. The question of specification of models over time especially in terms of which institutions are included and the role of voters and elections at different time periods is also crucial in the study of macropolitics.

All of these problems are to be expected given that the goals of macropolitics are at a minimum to be able to (1) say when government activity will increase and the direction the activity will take; (2) specify how the various parts of government—elected, appointed, and permanent—work together or against each other to either limit or enhance government activity; and (3) say how mood or public opinion interacts with elections and government actors to yield policy activity levels. Or to put it another way, macropolitics seeks to understand the nature of the equilibrium between mood, elections, institutions, and policy and to explain how an equilibrium shifts.

This is obviously a full agenda for those interested in macropolitical issues, and there is little guidance from other disciplines. In economics, macroeconomics went in two directions: first, let models take us where they may (which subsequently resulted in two schools—fresh and salt water) and second, empirical studies based on reduced form techniques. While the results have not been earth shattering, progress has been made in understanding macroeconomics. Given the work in this volume, we have every reason to believe that progress will be made in our field. These chapters all explain or help us to understand what happens in the political world, and their techniques and methods are heterogeneous.

Using a baseline of governmental inactivity allows us to study change, and here Krehbiel's chapter on pivotal politics tells us a great deal about why status quo policies are hard to change. The theory holds that elections are the mechanism of change. Progress is made on the issue of checking and validating macropolitical and policy variables. Additionally, there is useful information on specific policy areas over time, and in my opinion fusing specific policy area analysis with the broad macro picture is one of the better ways to validate patterns over time. Do the specific policy areas track together and in composite do they add up to the broad policy area, or are they separate and not aggregate? Such cross-mapping surely enhances our understanding of macropolitics.

Some chapters in this volume use broad-ranging variables like divided government to show how agendas and policy shift. Others go to great length to measure policy and institutional shifts. Rather than discuss the chapters individually, I wish to praise them broadly by claiming that they are all attempts to use history in interesting ways that will enhance the dialogue across approaches to the study of American politics. What scholars in this volume have in common is a desire to understand both institutions and policy over time.

There are some very important themes and ideas contained within the volume that deserve further attention. Understanding the dynamics of American politics over time means we hold that at any one point in time public opinion (mood), elections, institutions, and policy are roughly in equilibrium. While these words appear to be more in the rational choice camp, I believe they are compatible with the American political development camp. It is true that the different schools would weigh these variables differently, but each holds that there is a pattern to these interactions and that any given state of the system has an explanation for why it is as it is. Skocpol's work on welfare policy has an explanation for both the nature of the policy and its origins. Moreover, understanding such policy in the past is a sine qua non for understanding contemporary policy.

What are some of the major differences between the approaches? First and foremost is that rational choice scholars and their adherents put a great deal of emphasis on elections as the driving force in American politics. Congress as an institution is often seen as organized to enhance members' reelection bids, and policy is the result of what is necessary in order to be reelected. Election and reelection is in some rough sense the equivalent of price in economic theory. Just as price drives demand and supply, so too do elections drive individuals to choose institutions and policy. American political development scholars do not emphasize elections to this extent. Second, for rational choice scholars public preferences, viewed à la Stimson's (1991) moods or as in Erikson, MacKuen, and Stimson in this volume, are crucial to explaining electoral results, institutional design, and public policy. My read of American political development literature is that preferences matter but not to the extent they do in the rational choice field. Ideology as tied to or formed by socioeconomic status groups is emphasized in the development literature much more than it is in the choice school. Third, American political development literature seeks to understand history as a way to grasp development. Bensel's (2000) work on the industrialization phase of U.S. history is an excellent example of this mode of analysis. Choice scholars have used history as a laboratory for testing their theories; thus, in some sense the strategy is not to get the history wrong, since that could lead to a bad or invalid test of the theory. In contrast, development scholars want to get the history right.

In spite of these differences in priorities and approach there is agreement on what things we need to know to resolve these issues. (It should be clear that they will not be resolved any time soon.) On the input side the configuration of opinions and interest groups over periods of time is crucial. An additional question is how such opinions and interests interact to affect election results, and the answers should vary over time. Of further importance is how Congress interacts with both interest groups and other branches of government to make its policy choices. Finally, at the heart of the enterprise is how to understand which policies are chosen, why they are chosen, and how both the policies and the causes of the policy choices change over time.

Well covered in this volume are the institutional features of Congress, especially relations with other branches and policy outputs. Krehbiel's chapter shows how political institutions interact as interdependent variables to produce political results. Likewise Canes-Wrone, and Adler and Leblang, use multiple institutions to account for public decisions. Both chapters clearly show that separation of powers can account for policy outputs. Shipan's chapter also fits into this pattern in that he shows that divided government significantly increases the size of the political agenda. Again the work demonstrates that the interaction of separate institutions affects policy decision-making.

The chapter by Erikson, MacKuen, and Stimson is part of a larger project where the authors show how public preferences can in fact be quite predictive and determinative of governmental outputs. The authors use the general liberal or conservative mood of the electorate to show that as mood shifts, so to does the policy output of the government. The interesting feature of this work is that "black boxing" the legislative process does not seem to affect policy direction. This is the only chapter herein that specifically deals with public preferences or moods and is of course limited to the time period where surveys are known.

Chapters by Freedman and Cameron, Heitshusen and Young, and Katznelson and Lapinski all use history in a crucial way. Katznelson and Lapinski argue that policy is not unidimensional and that the multiple dimensions can and have had different representational patterns over time. Heitshusen and Young use changes in the U.S. Code to assess significant legislation and ultimately the forces that affect such change. Freedman and Cameron use a slice of historical time to demonstrate that the U.S. Congress and an administrative agency have patterned relationships such that they can ascertain the conditions that stimulate changes in policy. The use of time segments to develop and test theories is nicely utilized in this chapter. More work like this that deals with specific policy areas and institutions could help cross-validate longer time series.

Ostensibly the Huber and McCarty chapter is the least historically grounded. However, the authors build historical moments into their game-theoretic model in such a fashion that it can predict when changes in institutions will affect performance. Moreover, the model takes into account different moments of congressional history.

Thus it is clear that all the chapters in this work either use history in the body of their work or they build the potential for use over time into their work. The components of the equilibrium analysis I developed above are undoubtedly present, as everything from public moods to policy outputs is covered. No clear picture leaps from the pages as to the story of the dynamics of American politics, but wisdom and insight are present.

David Mayhew's interesting comments point to a problem of interpreting past events in terms of the present meaning of the liberal-conservative continuum, and I would like to elaborate on this point. This is certainly a concern, but the problem is exacerbated as we go back in time. The work of Stimson (1991) and others on mood has greatly enhanced our understanding of contemporary post–World War II politics and policy. However how shall we measure such "moods" when surveys of American opinion are not available? If we are to test and develop theories that explain change over time or dynamics, we must have measures that are comparable over time. Democratic systems are sensitive to public opinion, as Erikson et al, have shown, but surely the extent of concern with public moods and governments' response to it varies over time, and the pattern of variation can tell us much about American political development. Measures of American opinion "mood," had there been survey research, certainly would have discerned Manifest Destiny and the reaction against it. Discovering substitute measures for such moods would enhance our ability to understand how leaders are able to shape and change moods and movements to their own ends. The rise of abolition sentiment in the antebellum period and the gradual transformation of abolitionism to free men, free soil, free labor, and the rise of the Republican Party and Lincoln was surely more significant than how Ronald Reagan converted antitax sentiment into his presidential victories. Yet both events are clear instances of the interaction among the public opinion, political leaders, institutions, and policy shifts, all of which are the sine qua non for the dynamic study of politics.

Given the importance of the mood or opinion variable in theorizing about the dynamics of American politics and policy over time, the search for nonpublic opinion measures is crucial if we want to generalize about the period before the 1940s. Again I take the connecting thread to be that at any given point in time there is a rough equilibrium between mood and election results or institution and pubic policy. Change in any component will bring about change in the others. Institutional change and policy change, while difficult to measure, are easier to measure than mood. Indeed a number of the chapters in this volume deal with institutional and policy change over time, yet no opinion study is pre–World War II. My suggestion for this problem would be the use of presidential voting in congressional districts or counties. Erikson and Wright (2000), Canes-Wrone, Brady, and Cogan (2002), and others have shown how presidential vote in the district is the best measure of district preferences, and in an excellent study, Ansolabehere and Snyder (2002) have extended the use of this variable through the World War II era. Clever uses of votes for third-party candidates in counties and districts can aid in the process of ascertaining preference shifts. Solid analysis of voting over the 1840 to 1860 period could show the evolution of opinion on slavery from isolated abolitionism to free men, free soil, and free labor—a winning issue. Indeed, in *The Partisan Imperative* Joel Silbey (1985) produced an interesting record for New York State showing that until the Republicans added registration laws, the Know-Nothing Party left the Democrats competitive. When the Republican Party agreed to a registration law, there were strategic Know-Nothing Party withdrawals, and the Republicans became the majority of the delegation from New York and the permanent majority in the House of Representatives. Analysis such as Silbey's done from a political science perspective could shed light on the connection between issue preferences and election results. Work on the dynamics of institutions and policy will proceed at a faster pace since those concepts have multiple public records associated with them. Of course, this is not to say that such work will be easy. Rather it is to say that to have a full picture of the dynamics of American politics we will have to work harder to ascertain the public mood. This is a valuable effort because without measures of the public mood or preferences the dynamics of Congress will be incomplete. Perhaps even more importantly, without such measures we shall not be able to ascertain the extent to which elections drive American politics, an area where American political development and rational choice scholars disagree.

These comments are not intended to be critical of this volume nor the macropolitical theory that builds on micro theory. Macropolitical approaches see institutions themselves as variables, which can be used to both predict and explain major shifts in either institutional arrangements or public policies. Many chapters herein use broad-ranging variables like divided government and public moods to explain how agendas and policies shift. Other chapters go to extraordinary lengths to measure public policy, public opinion, and institutional shifts. These studies vary in approach, method, and question, yet in a strong sense all either use history in an interesting way to address the dynamics of the American system, or the argument made, or the model used takes history seriously. On the whole these studies individually and collectively enhance our understanding of congressional dynamics.

REFERENCE

Ansolabehere, Stephen, and James M. Snyder. 2002. "The Incumbency Advantage in U.S. Elections: An Analysis of State and Federal Offices, 1942–2000." MIT, typescript.

Bensel, Richard Franklin. 2000. *The Political Economy of American Industrialization, 1877–1900*. New York: Cambridge University Press.

Canes-Wrone, Brandice, David Brady, and John Cogan. 2002. "Out of Step, Out of Office: Electoral Accountability and House Members' Voting." *American Political Science Review* 96:127–40.

Burnham, Walter Dean. 1965. "The Changing Shape of the American Political Universe." *American Political Science Review* 59:7–28.

Burnham, Walter Dean, and John Sprague. 1970. "Additive and Multiplicative Models of the Voting Universe: The Case of Pennsylvania: 1960–1968." *American Political Science Review* 64:471–90.

Erikson, Robert S., and Gerald C. Wright. 2000. "Representation of Constituency Ideology in Congress." In *Continuity and Change in House Elections*, ed. David Brady, John Cogan, and Morris Fiorina. Palo Alto: Stanford University Press.

Gilligan, Thomas W., and Keith Krehbiel. 1989. "Asymmetric Information and Legislative Rules with a Heterogeneous Legislature." *American Journal of Political Science* 33:459–90.

———. 1990. "Organization of Informative Committees by a Rational Legislature." *American Journal of Political Science* 34:531–64.

Key, V. O., Jr. 1955. "A Theory of Critical Elections." *Journal of Politics* 17:3–18.

———. 1959. "Secular Realignment and the Party System." *Journal of Politics* 21:198–210.

Kramer, Gerald H. 1971. "Short-Term Fluctuations in U.S. Voting Behavior, 1896–1964." *American Political Science Review* 65:131–43.

Krehbiel, Keith. 1993. "Where's the Party?" *British Journal of Political Science*, 23: 235–66.

———. 1999. "The Party Effect from A to Z and Beyond." *Journal of Politics* 61: 832–40.

McAdam, Douglas, Sidney Tarrow, and Charles Tilly. 2001. *Dynamics of Contention.* New York: Cambridge University Press.

Powell, Walter W., and Paul J. DiMaggio, eds. 1991. *The New Institutionalism in Organizational Analysis.* Chicago: University of Chicago Press.

Shepsle, Kenneth A. 1979. "Institutional Arrangements and Equilibrium in Multidimensional Voting Models." *American Journal of Political Science* 23:27–59.

Silbey, Joel H. 1985. *The Partisan Imperative: The Dynamics of American Politics before the Civil War.* New York: Oxford University Press.

Skocpol, Theda. 1992. *Protecting Soldiers and Mothers: The Political Origins of Social Policy in the United States.* Cambridge: Harvard University Press.

———. 1995. *Social Policy in the United States: Future Possibilities in Historical Perspective.* Princeton: Princeton University Press.

Skowronek, Stephen. 1982. *Building a New American State: The Expansion of National Administrative Capacities, 1877–1920.* New York: Cambridge University Press.

Stimson, James A. 1991. *Public Opinion in America: Moods, Cycles, and Swings.* Boulder, Colo.: Westview Press.

Index